Street-Level Sovereignty

Street-Level Sovereignty

The Intersection of Space and Law

Edited by
Sarah Marusek
John Brigham

LEXINGTON BOOKS
Lanham • Boulder • New York • London

Published by Lexington Books
An imprint of The Rowman & Littlefield Publishing Group, Inc.
4501 Forbes Boulevard, Suite 200, Lanham, Maryland 20706
www.rowman.com

Unit A, Whitacre Mews, 26-34 Stannary Street, London SE11 4AB

British Library Cataloguing in Publication Information Available

Library of Congress Cataloging-in-Publication Data Available

LCCN 2017946998 | ISBN 9781498535038 (hardback : alk. paper) |
ISBN 9781498535045 (electronic)

♾™ The paper used in this publication meets the minimum requirements of American National Standard for Information Sciences—Permanence of Paper for Printed Library Materials, ANSI/NISO Z39.48-1992.

Printed in the United States of America

Contents

Figures

Acknowledgments

From Sarah:

As a graduate student at the University of Massachusetts Amherst, I was somewhat dismayed by the titles of available course offerings in my department until I saw a course with the name *Street Level Sovereignty*. As fast as I could, I signed up. What an interesting title! With "street" and "sovereignty" both in the name, this was sure to be an accessible and captivating study of everyday life! I was right. This course, taught by John Brigham, an innovative and creative scholar in the field of Public Law and "a guy from California," was exactly what I had been hoping for. Since then, I've continued to learn from John and have been fortunate to have him as my dissertation chair, my mentor, my friend, and now, my colleague. I would like to dedicate this book to him on the eve of his much deserved retirement.

From John:

Sarah has embraced the idea of law at the street level as she embraces life. She describes an intuitive connection to this kind of work. This seems right because it is at the level of intuition or practice that law operates in the sense covered by this volume. Law at the street level operates quietly and intuitively. Sarah has contributed significantly to understanding law in this way. Street-level law, like our professional practices, express, and constrain, who we are. Sarah's professional work is an expression of her practices as a scholar. She is thoughtful, industrious, kind, and generous. It is with all those attributes that she has organized this collection.

Introduction

Law Happens

John Brigham and Sarah Marusek

Law happens in the everyday places where we live, but it doesn't just happen; it is lived. In living the law, we enact its norms and its sovereignties. When we stop at a stop sign, whether out of fear of uniformed enforcement or more of normative ordering, we may accept the sign as authority and tacitly accept the authority of those who placed the sign.

When we, or our kids, take a selfie of that first party with alcohol or, perhaps with the same camera and maybe even the same blurred intensions, we take a video of an arrest (for whatever reason), a simple record may become a matter of law. It might be evidence in court or in a family confrontation or it might be a start as a record of the sovereign authority of uniformed enforcers and then become the basis for challenging that authority itself, as has been the norm with the videos that fuel the Black Lives Matter movement.

And when, as is rarely the case, we raise a gloved fist or sit down for the national anthem in protest, we are living with the sovereignty of the law. The law will be a factor in the reaction, albeit probably awkwardly, and the reactions to the reaction.

We find the living life of law often reported but generally understudied. Too often the law that is "alive" is the law of the police, or lawyers or courts. We have said for half a century that the American constitution "lives" but that often simply meant that the justices adjusted the rules to fit the time. And Justice Holmes famously said the life of the law is experience but often that experience has been taken to mean the experience of judges. Even the "Wise Latina" sobriquet that has been associated with Sonia Sotomayor is a matter of hierarchy (2009).

THE STREET

The lived law that we examine here is most often far removed from the Supreme Court but it is a source of meaning and, in its place, of authority. When we look down from the Supreme Court through the cases they take, we see law on the street but when we look from the street we rarely see the Supreme Court. This makes sense. The Supreme Court is rarely there. It can be, but usually it is not. On the other hand, some of what happens in the street can be authoritative both as to what a society understands to be acceptable and sometimes what the Supreme Court comes to accept as the living law. The stop and frisk in New York City that Mayor Michael Bloomberg and his police chief touted as crime control was, near the end of his administration and into the next declared unconstitutional, at least at the level of the street.

The "street" in our framework draws inspiration from Michael Lipsky's *Street-Level Bureaucracy* (1969) to which we have returned from time to time. Lipsky's framework was the more literal and storefront existence of bureaucratic processes and we have ventured into more abstract terrain with the issue of sovereignty. The chapters that follow, focus on contests that challenge the law and the authority behind it. But the sense that these challenges are at the level where people live is the same.

Our street is thus a broader concept than Lipsky's. It contains storefronts and precinct houses but also buses and police cars, invasive amphibians and standup comedians, the Secret Service and the Transportation Security Administrations, moms on the playground, and service members in uniform. The variety is a challenge but incorporating variety in the whole is one of law's characteristics.

But, though we aspire to offer something broader, we are indebted to the nuance of Lipsky's framework and others who have come before. Lipsky's work confronts the sense that hierarchy and authority are higher on some structure of authority and probably farther away. But a little later, in the 1970s, Boaventura de Sousa Santos illuminated law in the favela's of Rio where few then and even now expect it (Santos, 1977). These foundations are incorporated into the contemporary formulation by Mariana Valverde in a number of places but most explicitly in "Laws of the Street," which she published in 2009. In that piece, she explores "uses of law" and advocates systematic study to document how "spaces and activities are organized" (163). She also speculates as to why studies of cities, where the legal aspects of social life are at their most intense, tend to avoid discussion of law. Some of the failure is the marginalization of law in Marxism and some of it is the formalism in professional legal circles that can't help but make legal practices seem marginal. A shift to "law in action" is heralded by Valverde as a move in the right direction.

The relationship between societal norms and legal rules reveals a tension involving the material operationalization of justice. In these spaces and places, the framework of the public good is contrasted with the privatization of interest and is manifested in quotidian responses to rules and authority. In this way, governance and power are constituted in the banalities of our daily activities in contexts that characterize aspects of legality that are often overlooked for their informality. These places generate understandings about law through a variety of legal symbols that represent law and our constitutive response to how law works in society.

SOVEREIGNTY

Lipsky's "street-level bureaucracy" formulation came out about the same time that Mario Savio, a student at the University of California, Berkeley, spoke of putting bodies in the cogs of the machine. Savio's 1964 image was Chaplinesque in its reference to getting caught in the machine, but his inspiration was not particularly cinematic. Like ours, it called attention to the aspect of street-level law that encompasses sovereignty and struggles over it.

For some of our encounters with the law at the level of the street we may not be aware of where authority resides. This might be the case when we are awakened by a loud motorcycle or told to stay out of land with no obvious inhabitation. Even if we were to make a guess about where the authority comes from for particular prohibition, as when we are barred from entry by an anonymous "No Trespassing" sign we can't always be sure. We don't have survey material but we can hazard a guess that most people are not aware of where the authority for enforcement of signage like that in supermarket parking lots that limits access to fuel efficient vehicles, carpools, or pregnant women.

And, many of the most interesting matters of street-level sovereignty operate when at least one party involved is unaware of the authority behind a norm or even of the norm itself. In the United States, people who will enforce signs without any particular authority, like a nonsmoking sign, can be found. They may or may not be ready to be challenged. Much of the humor of Lenny Bruce drew crowds to his shows at the same time that local police often chose to close them down. And in one of our examples in this collection, a bounty on coqui frogs in Hawaii, which had been planned for school children, was soon abandoned when animal cruelty issues arose.

Sovereignty is to law as parent is to family, sometimes. It relates to law as belief does to religion. Sovereignty is to law as connoisseurship is to an auction house. Or maybe it is as an auction house is to an auction. The sovereign is a source of authority.

Thomas Hobbes gave us a vivid statement of authority and even a suggestion of what the sovereign looked like. This was "the Leviathan," a giant metaphorically, or perhaps mythologically, holding it all together.

Americans mostly think of the sovereign in terms of monarchies and sometimes we extrapolate from that to more democratic institutions. But when the people are sovereign the reality on the street can range from confused to highly contested. The bicentennial of the American Constitution in 1987 fostered a celebration of the Constitution managed by a former Chief Justice of the Supreme Court for a system that strongly suggests the Supreme Court is sovereign when it comes to constitutional law. But in many respects the conventional wisdom or "official story" of the justices determining the meaning of the fundamental text is only partially true. From abortion and equal marriage to gun control and police misconduct there are many instances where the people in the United States are out ahead of the US Supreme Court.

In fact, in some important respects justices like Sandra Day O'Connor, Ruth Ginsburg, Antonin Scalia, Clarence Thomas, and Sonia Sotomayor have gained considerable authority in their roles as justices from their personal experiences in the community or, in the sense in which we are using the term, on the street. Sotomayor's biography, which has very little to say about the law and a great deal about to say about growing up in The Bronx, contributes to her public presence and Ruth Ginsburg has become a somewhat surprising cultural diva as "the notorious RBG." Both personas, with more connections to the street than to jurisprudence, have enhanced the stature of these justices.

The classic political science text, *The Semi Sovereign People*, by E. E. Schattschneider, emphasized the desire of public authorities to contain the scope of contests over authority. Sovereignty is strongest when it is assumed rather than contested and Schattschneider was concerned, in 1960, that active political contests took too much effort.

Street-Level Sovereignty is a collection of scholarship that considers the mutuality of law that is subject to social interpretation for its meaning and importance within which the constitutive legal framework involving race, deviance, property, and the communal investiture in health and happiness are sustained and challenged. This book evaluates the dynamic of law's social enforcement. In this dynamic, enforcement is informal and self-determined with the presence of law existing in the background. Here, the background means that law is not visibly present, but is clearly determinant in the consciousness of those acting out the law as well as responding to law's transgressions. The book also examines the intersection of spatiality and law. Through the construction of place, law is materially framed. In these places, law can be overtly present, yet hidden from view, through changing definitions of authority and reaches of power. Law is manifested in ways that, on their face, do not generally resemble formal legal persona or legal places.

Lastly, the book articulates the ways in which language, culture, and materiality reflect the positioning of law. Hearing, reading, or conversing about law brings its lingual and semiotic immediacy to the forefront of our discussion of everyday instances of law's constitutive presence.

Through the legal crafting of culture, the purpose of this book is to illuminate a jurisprudence of visual representation, image, and cultural meaning that develops everyday aspects of how law works with regard to place and representation. Contributing authors will draw from cultural, social, economic, and political contexts and their artifacts to examine legal forms of materiality, spatiality, and representation that convey understandings of embodiment, power, and authority. Through these contributions, this book makes a vital contribution to the expanding field of constitutive legal theory, legal geography, and legal semiotics as the emerging realm of jurisprudential analysis examines the accessibility of legality and its myriad applications. The approach taken by the authors empowers undergraduate students in political science, legal studies, the sociology of law, and cultural anthropology.

There are various ways to draw connections among the chapters in this volume. Some of these have been suggested in the preceding paragraphs. Some are drawn from the discussion of each chapter that follows.

We put Jan Broekman's chapter first because he provides a framework for understanding the aspects of contests over law that are contests over sovereignty. Jan is a professor of law, philosophy, and legal theory and has started our discussion of the street "as theory" through the concept of the self. The self as pedestrian and likewise, the pedestrian's self, are frameworks to consider the meaning of sovereignty on the street. Sovereignty becomes a lens through which the commonality of experiences characterizes the emergence of the self as a sign of an evolving society.

As society, evolves, so does law. And so does the street. In the second chapter, Andrea Pavoni, a postdoctoral fellow in Lisbon specializing in urban studies, law, and spatiality, expands the meaning of the street as law happens in the shared spaces of the urban streetscape. For Andrea, urbanity is the melding of spaces previously distinct from one another. In traffic spaces and in traffic politics, the spatiolegal negotiation of shared space involves bodies, cars, and roads in urban settings. Sovereignty, in this sense, may be understood as the tethering of individual space to the vehicularization of being.

The relationship of cars to people invites a reconsideration of the street as being just for cars. Instead, the street becomes a site of motion, not only for those who drive, but for those who sit. Not all streets are thruways for cars, as Richard Mohr and Nadirsyah Hosen assert. Instead, streets are regionally specific locales of culture. Rick and Nadir, Australian legal scholars, consider the spatial terrain of the street through layers of cultural standards and accompanying expectations of regionally specific behaviors. The spatial proximity of the streets to buildings on the street that may include cafés, restaurants, and other food stores compels a particular understanding of law. Here, law is informally tethered to—as well as juxtaposed with—formal law in ways that invite territorially defined standards of ways of being on the street.

For Margaret Mott, political theorist from Vermont, territoriality involves the body. In her chapter, Prof. Mott considers the neoliberal manipulation of consent in sexual assault cases as the rhetoric of consent has been framed on American college campuses through Title IX as a discourse of market-driven sexuality. When seen through market metrics, sexual autonomy is dichotomized between freedom and violence. However, such a dichotomy invites an ever-watchful state apparatus to reductively blame victims for not being autonomous, or effectively sovereign, enough.

Violence that has neoliberal foundations is also the focus of Andrés Fabián Henao Castro. Andrés, political theorist from Boston, considers the biopolitics of police violence according to the intersectionality of race and gender. In his work, biopolitics and sovereignty are sources of necropolitics which produces what Andrés refers to as asphyxia, or the use of police violence to suffocate and make breathing impossible for racial minorities in the United States. Sovereignty, in this chapter, is the ever-diminishing ability simply to live.

Living takes on new meaning when seen through a military context. Allen Linken, political scientist from Alabama, examines the role of law in the controlled setting of the US military. Authority, hierarchy, and tradition become sources of law that govern the lives of those serving in the military versus those living civilian lives. Codes of chivalry are transformed into structures and positions that serve as the basis for morality and justification for dominance in a military-based culture. Here, sovereignty is limited and compartmentalized within a militarized context of living, even to the extent of getting a haircut.

From the banal to the even more banal, street-level law operates in ways that structure our daily lives. For political scientist John Brigham, law operates as gatekeeper through body scanners in airports and arenas. Such scanners challenge an understanding of sovereignty through the manipulation of law's ability to perceive threat. This threat is linked to the possibility of terrorism and operates through our passing through these scanners to become more safe. This compliance of what is dangerous, and how to minimize that risk, is the transference of gatekeeping from the presence of the scanner to its ubiquitous acceptance as unquestioned law.

Maybe, order is the structure of law. Maybe sovereignty is freedom from that ordering. Or maybe that freedom invites a new sense of ordering. Laughter may be the release from order, as laughter when politicized, serves as social commentary. Comedy, and the ability to laugh, is a source of resistance to racialized injustice. Sovereignty for Aaron Lorenz, political scientist from New Jersey, is the destabilization of a racialized subconscious through humor. Humor is a tool of sovereignty that serves as catharsis for the seriousness of a racialized necropolitics.

However, death is not always seen in the same light by either law or by culture. For example, the death of small creatures at the hands of an angry neighborhood does not seem as serious as the situations described by either Andrés or Aaron. Yet, law appears consistently as a source of control in both scenarios. Small, but deafening, coqui frogs invade the peace and quiet of the Hawaiian rainforest and frame a segmented and socialized understanding of belonging in the chapter by sociologist Marilyn Brown and legal geographer Sarah Marusek. In this way, the coqui, an invasive species to the Hawaiian Islands is subject to eradication efforts taken on by impacted residents in response to failed efforts by the state to control this audible nuisance. In this way, sovereignty returns to the streets in which coqui are sought and killed by those who seek to quell the noise of the noisy frogs.

Perhaps as noisy as frogs, but perhaps much more appreciated, the noise of children playing on a playground invites a closer look at the playground as a place to see where law happens. Patrícia Branco, legal researcher from Portugal, studies this site of child's play as a site of conflicting layers of sovereignty. Law happens on the swings, in the sandbox, and through the stages of growth. This growth happens when children grow into teenagers, who grow into adults. This growth also happens for law as legal presence is asserted, grows rusty, and then disappears as informal laws set in. Formal law grows old in the face of energized youth and reclaimed structures for resistance.

REFERENCES

Chaplin, Charlie. *Modern Times,* United Artists, 1936.

Ewick, Patricia and Susan Silbey. *The Common Place of Law: Stories from Everyday Life,* Chicago: University of Chicago Press, 1998.

Lipsky, Michael. *Street Level Bureaucracy,* Madison: Institute for Research on Poverty, 1969.

Santos, Boaventura de Sosa. "The Law of the Oppressed: The Construction and Reconstruction of Legality in Pasargarda," *Law and Society Review* 12: 5–126, 1977.

Savio, Mario. "Speech before the FSM Sit-in," December 3, 1964, Berkeley, California.

Schattschneider, E. E. *The Semi Sovereign People,* Holt, Rinehart, and Winston,1960.

Sotomayor, Sonia. *My Beloved World,* New York: Vintage Books, 2013.

———. "Wise Latina," Senate Confirmation Hearings, 2009.

Valverde, Mariana. "Laws of the Street," *City and Society*, Dec. 2009: 163–181.

Chapter 1

"Street" as Theory

Jan M. Broekman

Streets, squares, and avenues are not what they were before. Their changes parallel the ever-changing meaning of their names. A fascinating aspect is that one *experiences* life as it unfolds "on the street" but does not fully *reflect* upon it. In other words, practice and immediacy of everyday life may fit to the street concept, but reflection and reconsideration most often not. The tendency to not accept a separation of experience and reflection illustrates a new tendency in meaning when considering the "street" concept. One feels the forceful cohesion between what is *experienced* and what is *achieved by reflection* all around streets and squares. On them, in the midst of all occurrences of everyday life, one faces what it means that reflections reflect upon experiences. They open up to other experiences, in particular to self-reflection and self-understanding. But neither does unfold beyond a powerful culturally determined pattern of constraints in the form of values or norms.

One particular element of such a pattern is often heard on the street—it says: law and its fixated procedures are the reliable concepts we need. But they are in reality a continuously challenging change in which society's theory and practice participate. That opens wider perspectives on how law and legal discourse are reality in the sign pools of life. The basic question is here, whether what is thought and experienced on the streets, fits to legal and political discourses. Does the language of law fit to the language of everyday? Are the words lawyers and judges think or say in conformity with citizenship awareness and its sociopolitical thoughts? The "street level," which now indicates a new space of experience and reflection of modern citizenship, implies the need to expand the notion of "street" also in law, politics or social sciences.

That has already been exposed in initial semiotic explorations of law and legal discourse during the first decade of the 20th century. At first, it was presented as a *linguistic* topic: people in the street did literally not understand the functionaries in courts and law offices. That lacking congruency of two language levels (everyday and legal language) was understood as a *sign* of deep structures of language. All this required reflection associated with social experience! The same is the case when we consider law, values, and norms on the street. The abyss between legal and everyday language will confront new forms of self- consciousness and meaning in law with life unfolding on the "street." Before exploring further dimensions of the "street" concept, we should in particular engage with the so-called "legal consciousness" on the "street." It will make us recognize that the *self* of all who walk the street is concerned when the "street" is at issue.

LEGAL CONSCIOUSNESS

A legal consciousness seems to be an important component of a citizen's self-understanding. That consciousness keeps an exclusively *legal* opinion alive, in which legal meanings are appreciated as a reliable and ultimate truth in human existence. Law's language has therefore to focus on the subject and its unique creative power with a glorious standing in time and society. However, experiences on the street show limits as soon as subjects indicate that they are no longer at home in the legal denomination as the bearer of rights and duties. The basic prejudice of the subject's legal qualification is its individualism. On the "street," a subject becomes aware that there is never a subject without an object and the latter a world beyond subject–object partitions. Subject and object are only *temporary* positions engraved in our consciousness to envisage our self and our world. That view was often accessed on the street.[1]

The idea of a "legal consciousness" is important here. Its existence is supposed to build a bridge between theory and practice, especially in legal discourse. But, does this bridge ever exist, and if so, how? Two important studies, written with nearly a century between them, illustrate the importance of this concept: the Dutch lawyer, politician, poet, and author Jacob I. De Haan's inaugural lecture at the Amsterdam University in 1916 (a first on legal semiotics/significs in the world) and Butler/Grier's 2012 studies on the Russian legal philosopher Ivan Ilyin, which expose the close ties between Russian and a German philosophy of law.

Different Languages

The discussion on legal consciousness provides a clear insight in the differences between speaking about law *as a citizen* and speaking about law *as a lawyer.* The gap between law and citizenship at the level of those two different discourses is clearly detectable. The danger of misunderstanding the language of law inspired De Haan to explore significs/semiotics in law. He expected that this approach, with its intense study of meaning and sign, would help to bridge the gap between the two levels. He located where that bridge would be most useful and socially effective: in a legal consciousness of each individual in Occidental civilization. That would create commonly apprehended discourses with a mutual comprehension of lawyer and citizen—a socially desirable and philosophically precious outcome. All this became even clearer when Husserl reformulated his basic idea: the difference between a *naïve natural* (citizen, layman) and a *non-naïve natural* language/attitude (lawyer, lawmaker) would be surmounted. Discussions at the beginning of the 20th century, as for instance among members of the Amsterdam Significs Circle, or between Victoria Lady Welby in the UK and Charles Sanders Peirce in the US, unfold semiotic approaches by means of a deeper understanding of those two types of natural attitude. De Haan as well as Ilyin illustrated the fact that components of legal consciousness dealt with truly semiotic issues.[2]

Legal Significs and Origins of Semiotics

Semiotics of law has never been a simple application of meaning and sign. Semiotics in the sense of the lawyer and other legal professionals unfold in considerations about the quality of a citizen's awareness of law. De Haan articulates in 1916:

> signific research about the many words peoples use for what we call "law" would be important for our knowledge of psychology and for a philosophy of law.[3] Take the word "legislation." This seems a simple word: the legislator gives laws to the people and the people accept those laws and with them the Law. But what is a law?—an ensemble of determinations. However, modern States print laws. A law became a book. Here, the materialization began. We, as we saw before, abandoned our soul and replaced it with an external world, which is independent from us. In the same way we made the law, which is part of our psychic life, into a booklet of that external world and in which we read what a lawmaker wanted—often living decades ago, dying in an external world.[4] We transformed the law into a booklet and the legislator into a person. We thus speak of "the will of the legislator" and the "intention of the legislator" which the judge has to find in the course of his judgments. Only by exception it is noticed that these words are dangerous linguistic images and many of us are misled by these crafty expressions.[5]

The structure and the inherent ambiguities of the expression "legal consciousness" are difficult to describe. That conclusion is fully comprehensible. Legal consciousness is not strictly individual and thus at home in psychology, but it is also not a completely sociopolitical issue and thus perhaps at home on the street. Those difficulties do not solely arise from a categorical ordering: there are deeper issues to consider. The deepest and most difficult is the naïve presupposition that the expression "legal consciousness" has a *meaning* which is always *social* because it comprises a form of *sharing*—no matter when and where, no matter in what language and among whom. De Haan had already explained to his students that a word or a specific expression has never the absolute same meaning for diverse individuals. That touches the basis of *sharing,* as it is even true for speakers and hearers in the same conversation or in the speech line of one and the same performer. "'The' meaning of a word cannot exist; it 'is' united with an infinite number of meanings by something that cannot be perceived and that composes a word from an infinite number of meanings. Our thinking separates the words in their numerous meanings as it unites those meanings to a word. Thinking cannot split or unite the continuous and the discrete, but it can only separate and unite *at the same time.* The word also splits in numerous meanings and unites these again in that one word." So one asks: what is at stake in a "legal consciousness"—a solely linguistic issue, a particular experience, or the result of a general materialization in culture? Mauthner was quoted in this Amsterdam inaugural lesson. He argued in his 1913 "Sprache und Grammatik" [Language and Grammar] that all linguistic categories (name, verb, past or present time, conjugations, etc.) are solely the result of a spiritual activity, which creates a false, in reality not–existing series of sensual impressions.[6] That does also happen in our materialization of law and in the general formation of legal knowledge. Laws became texts and books, legislators became persons with intentions, and so became our consciousness a legal consciousness! But the gap between the two levels of language, the level of the lawyers and that of the citizen or ordinary, everyday individual, is not bridged. De Haan concludes: "The expression 'legal consciousness' on its own is misleading. Whose consciousness is at stake? Legal consciousness is a sense or feeling only within a community. But each individual of that community develops this awareness as an individual, that is: in distinction from others."[7]

Contemporary experiences with the "street" challenge *and* confirm this observation. Has that any sense for us? Today we live in times of "class action" and have a different opinion on the position of the subject in law—particularly in the world of Civil Law. A community would be able to develop an awareness of the common, a sense of consciousness beyond stringent subject positions of individuality. Does the concept of legal consciousness not show in what ways society creates what we thought to be individual? Are there not alternative forms of consciousness, with a non-individualistic, *social* character—some perhaps rightly called "ideology?" Is that question not crucial in times of a global IT communication?

Individualism and Materialization

Today's interest pertains to the positioning of *individuals* in political society and *the selves they unfold*. De Haan called individuality the dominant feature of consciousness. The above thoughts are relevant "for the motivation of each individual who acts in accordance with his or her legal consciousness—a consciousness purely personal." "Personal" means for De Haan: "individual"; in his days one could hardly think otherwise. He formulates that "there are limits: legal consciousness seems imbued with diverse interests. The actor or the individual who profits from the act will first of all experience the legitimacy of that act. The illegitimacy will on the other hand be first and strongly perceived by those who are the victims of that act. The relation between legal consciousness and interest is complex and difficult."[8] Materialization seems to be one of the most powerful forces that profile our consciousness once we become confronted with the law. Traces of that process can be read in the words we use to express that consciousness. The legislator becomes a person with will and intention; the laws are written and become books and texts, and all these changes in expressiveness influence our idea of legal consciousness—a consciousness of lawyers as well as citizens.

There exists a great diversity of levels as well as a multiplicity of structures in each text, especially the lawyer has to cope with that complexity. Consider in addition, that Law does not speak but only lawyers, politicians, and ordinary citizens. Profiles of a legal consciousness become visible in the gradual understanding of the materialization, which takes place in law and in the general culture of the Occident. Only a limited number of professional speakers are institutionally allowed to speak law: "the legal significian has to unfold its views . . . not in . . . the language of the law issued as law. Those words do not need to be spoken and they can in essence not be spoken in the language we actually use. *Law as law is not spoken, but speaks to us in the dynamics of our legal consciousness* (my italics, *jmb*). But as soon as law became transformed into the major force for maintaining social order, the law had to be spoken/articulated by the legislator as well as the judge. The task of the legal significian is to research the essence of the various types and categories of words and to compare the numerous meanings of words of legal language with that essence . . . I add that the theories of Freud about the power of the unconscious on linguistics are an important theme, in particular when he highlights his analysis of words with contrasting meanings."[9]

Signs and Meaning

The observation that "Law as law is not spoken, but speaks to us in the dynamics of our legal consciousness" was formulated on the basis of an *individualistic* approach of law in legal semiotics.[10] But the activity of a (legal) consciousness expressing itself in speech does not lead to purely individualistic occurrences. Consciousness may be of central importance in the "law-language" relationship, but it can never be understood as a solitary event. Speaking cannot be a solipsistic act—that is a crucial observation in the context of meaning and sign. Charles S. Peirce stated that a sign alone is not a sign. Semiotics remains confronted with infinite strings of signs. Their string character abolishes an understanding of reality in strictly individualistic terms—any person is a sign, Peirce noted, and any human consciousness has sign character. An individual exists only in so far as it is a part of that infinite string.[11] A consciousness called "legal" can because of this string/sign character only be treated in social terms. But, *can the "street" practice this insight?* It could very well be! Semiotics illustrates the complexity of the labyrinth of human culture. One should keep in mind that there is (as Eco once concluded) no human culture without a fundamental *sharing* of norms or values in the many ways signs are practiced. This process of sharing is not possible without accepting that a culture is itself an infinite network of interpretants (not only interpreters)—a conclusion closely neighbored to "streets" which are available on Google, Facebook, and other IT communications.

Legal Consciousness

Here is the issue again: does a legal consciousness comprise law *at all levels of society*? How does the "street" appreciate a consciousness of law? Is it a factor that contributes to appreciate law and legal discourse positively or is it a cause of rebellion or even anarchism? There is no straight and direct answer to formulate. Legal meanings are represented in all theories dealing with legal consciousness, from positivism to natural law, from Marxism to structuralism. Each of them contains an awareness of the abyss between the lawyer's word and what is spoken on the street while appealing to a legal consciousness. But that abyss is not their first concern, as Butler & Grier illustrate. The majority of legal theorists, they conclude, wrote about legal consciousness in terms of law as an institution and consequently about the "legal consciousness" of a legal professional. In particular German jurisprudence, heavily influencing Russian legal scholarship in the first decade of the 20th century, discussed the issue. It focused only in exceptional cases on the legal consciousness of the layman, the citizen or the street![12] We also learn, that the legal sociologist Eugen Ehrlich[13] attempted to categorize legal consciousness while including a fuller understanding of society, but he never paid attention to the "street" or any such form of citizenship. Ehrlich is quoted: "At the present as well as at any other time, the center of gravity of legal development lies not in legislation, nor in juristic science, nor in judicial decision, but in society itself." These words do not solve the issue. When society and law are at opposite sides of an abyss in meaning and expressiveness, legal consciousness cannot be a perspective on the "street" as a component of law in modern life.

Grier's research and his great translations of Il'yin's work confirmed that his essay *On the Essence of Legal Consciousness* stayed within the boundaries of the German historical school of jurisprudence. It understands the social dimensions of law and legal discourse primarily in a legal sense. Law can for him only be effective in an "established supremacy of law and the legitimate authority of the State"—central concerns of traditional jurisprudence. These are, as Grier explained, marked by the counter-revolutionary opinion of Von Savigny that any deduction of legal norms from abstract and universal propositions cannot be tolerated.[14] What characterizes the link between "legal consciousness" and the gap in understanding law by the "street" does not open new possibilities for understanding the "street" as a possible *locus* for law and its procedures as long as this specific intolerance dominates.

Streets, corners, plazas, and parks of our big cities as well as the lofty avenues of wealthy neighborhoods are often confronted with various forms of legal consciousness of the citizenship. However, the latter seems to exist solely within the boundaries of law and legal discourse as determined by legal professionals who formulate "the law"—even on the street. Indeed, the meaning of the term "legal consciousness" is in the first place important for persons who possess, determine and expand that consciousness on the one hand (the professionals) and for those who just take part in one of the multiple forms of legal consciousness on the other (the citizens). But it is clear: legal functionaries are in a different mode of consciousness than citizens. Not only legal language and everyday language differ, but legal meanings maintained by lawyers also differ from those of citizens. Lawyers practice seldom on the streets (although today, some try to be there, perhaps learning their lesson from Solon) because their ties to the institution appear to be decisive for their task.

Introducing the "street" creates difficult questions: who bears what meaning in a legal consciousness? What means: the legal determination of a human consciousness? Legal consciousness concerns everyone in a culture, state, or region. An initial conclusion is the power to determine the meaning of a legal consciousness is predominantly anchored in its institutional context. *Legal consciousness is in principle plural.* This plural character withstands a "correct" legal definition and the presupposition about a well-functioning law and legal system as Von Savigny maintained. What the "street" often hesitatingly calls legal consciousness fits neither to the individualism of the legal subject nor to the defining power and institutional entitlement of the legal professional.

THE STREET

The title "Street-Level Sovereignty" suggests more than the introduction of the "street" as a dimension of social power and legal consciousness. The "street" is the perhaps most important *sign* at issue because a mainly non-professionally determined meaning of law (a not *legally* acknowledged component of law) characterizes the consciousness of citizens on the street.

The "Street" Concept

It means that a "street"–consciousness is probably based on a non-individualistic self-understanding of the citizen. The "street" functions as a major reminder of the fact that an immense variety of *otherness* (legal as well as non-legal, individual and non-individual) characterizes life. The "street" embraces social forms, which did hitherto not play a significant role in politics, semiotics, or social sciences. The latter may surprise: we cherish some insights in how social life of the Ancient Greeks was linked to the "street," what happened on the "street" in their cities when they worshipped their Gods—a worship that was often a specific "street"-connected event. And we remember Walter Benjamin's widely appreciated and discussed *Passagen-Werk* [The Arcades Project] with equally important, often even tradition-breaking background analyses of some principal features of our 20th century. The two, the Ancient Greek as well as Benjamin's features had experienced the power of a legal consciousness inspired by political experiences. Others, like Habermas, had completed those views by means of their research on changes of meaning in the concept "public." All these views may be a first attempt to broaden and surpass law's boundaries when the "street" is at issue. So, we ask again: what is implied in the "street" being a manifestation of "otherness?" The question should, first of all, *not* be understood as a call for an alternative *dialogic* understanding of the "street"—based on the implicit presence of otherness—but rather as a call for a *semiotic* approach. Sign and meaning surpass any appeal to dialogue, semiotic dimensions make it possible to assess intersubjective relations as meaningful. The "street" thus fulfills the task of being a *sign* in this evaluative possibility. The *sign* illustrates that meaning making *as well as* meaning managing *should be viewed as an important political act.*

Three major components characterize the "street" concept: (1) *philosophy*, bringing together a legal consciousness and the concepts of person, citizen, and reality; (2) *social sciences* which highlights the "street" concept as a component of an open society and emphasizes the ideas of the commons, of representative and direct democracy as well as community; and (3) *semiotics* with spatial features that characterize the "street" concept.

Philosophy: Person, Citizen, Reality

De Haan and Ilyin focused, not unlike Hobbes, on the *person* as the most evident subject/owner of a consciousness. Thomas Hobbes' famous definition of "a person" in Chapter 16 of his *Leviathan* suggests "A person is he whose words or actions are considered, either as his own, or as representing the words or actions of another man, or of any other thing to whom they are attributed, whether truly or by fiction. When they are considered as his own, then is he called a natural person: and when they are considered as representing the words and actions of another, then is he a feigned or artificial person." The "street" changed this description and awakened a forceful awareness about dissimilarities between individuals, which understand themselves as citizens. Some of them are relevant for the "street." It opened our eyes for the plural and institution-bound character of our consciousness. Linguistic activity meets law in this view. But that is not all: word and representation are already for Hobbes tied to *otherness*, as his expressions "considered" and "representing" illustrate. But he still described the naturalness of a person in terms of ownership, that is: in terms of law. "On the street" is the otherness of the other essential for the person in social practice.

A key issue is that the self-identification of a person relates to his or her belonging to a community, and law formatted that community. When and under what circumstances and conditions is a citizen brought to think of him/herself as a sociopolitical subject? In essence is the role of *others* the key to that question and the basis for any possible type of self-realization of the political subject as a citizen. To interpret one's self in the context of deep layers of legal meanings presupposes that the "street" could be understood as a determination of identity performed by *others*.

That policy of subjectivity is a major dimension of any politics of citizenship. A self-identification of citizens on the "street" differs from the classical and highly traditional idea that each subject represents (a form of) social order in the first place. The inner conflict in that classical opinion is that a social order represents (too often just "sub-*jects*") first and foremost its citizen/subject—and particularly the latter concerns the first outcry one can hear on the "street" today. In other words, the question "who am I, and how I can express my identity" depends on my understanding of my own (legal) subjectivity—a strongly debated issue on the "street."

How can his be understood? Forms of subjectivity are axes of meaning in society. They are in no way given by nature but powerful constructs of a legal and/or political discourse and therefore *an artifice* as Kelsen already noticed. That artificiality is embedded in a process of *enculturation*, which is a process of creating, mastering, and adapting basic values and norms. Enculturation shapes the close ties between a physical person and institutional structures, as Hobbes' *Leviathan* illustrated. While doing so, he made his important observations regarding the subjectivity of the citizen in political discourse. Politicians, not unlike jurists, conceal and silence the importance of subjectivity and do seldom explicitly refer to the legal subject as a major constituent of citizenship in states or other political settings. We conclude therefore with emphasis (what is particularly difficult to accept for a Common Law lawyer): the "street" is a milieu in which artificiality and enculturation integrate while profiling a citizen's self-understanding, which most often contrasts institutionalized legal and political practices.

The "street" is a modern achievement on the basis of a particular view on reality; it is in that regard a theme with rich semiotic relevance. Signs are exchanged everywhere as meanings multiply. These semiotic components confirm a fundamental difference with the "street" concept in the 20th and 19th centuries. "Street" is today no longer a subject of philosophical, cultural, or aesthetic reflections but a harsh reality *in se*. It is a complex issue because of its multiple references: "street" is a reference to other (cultural, aesthetic, political) realities and a reality itself, therefore dissolving traditional references of any kind. One experiences especially in art and politics that strict borderlines between domains are dissipating. Museums open up and become even a "street" phenomenon (Rome's museum of urban art, the "MURo"), parliaments open up and go viral while watched on the street via social media. It illustrates how the "street" does no longer represent one specific domain of reality, but refers to an impressive simultaneity of domains in multilayered representations.

Social Sciences

Any togetherness of idea and word conceals an enigmatic power: *the power of derangement* or, in other words, of disruption. Without the latter exists no philosophy. Is the "street" symbolized by that power? The "open society" and "community" are considered here.

Open Society

An innovative form of living is in this light characterized by a doing what *cannot* be done; which is a challenging component of an *open* democracy. The "street" enables the life of disrupted institutions: on it unfolds power of innovation. We encounter roots of social change and a concept of democracy, of which the "street" is one of the major components. That suggestion supports Karl Popper's work *The Open Society and its Enemies*. Is a democratic society "open" because of disruption and innovation coming together in the attempt to evaluate the "street" as a valid concept in semiotics and society?

Popper coined the concept of an *open society* (in a contrast to a closed or tribal society), which "sets free the critical powers of man." The "street" could in this context been associated with an unfolding of critical powers—an association which is often proved to be true! It fascinates to read already in his 1943/45 text how "an open society may become, by degrees, what I should like to term an "*abstract society*." It may, to a considerable extent, lose the character of a concrete or real group of men, or of a system of such real groups . . . We could conceive of a society in which men practically never meet face to face—in which all business is conducted by individuals in isolation who communicate by typed letters or by telegrams, and who go about in closed motor-cars. . . . Such a fictitious society might be called an abstract society. Although we do not always drive alone in closed motor cars (but meet face to face thousands of men walking past in the street) the result is very nearly the same as if we did—we do not establish as a rule any personal relation with our fellow-pedestrians."[15] The "street" *can* be an abstract concept in an abstract society, and *is* very real at the same time—both attitudes populate the mind of citizens. This repeating hallmark "abstract" will be met in various contexts to come.

Notice, that the "open" society today will not be understood as a society on an individualistic basis. The "street" is a concept that deeply reflects this issue: is any pursued autonomy a property of the citizen in the "street?" Many would accept today a definition of the "street" if it were a concept that realizes such an individual autonomy! But "individual" is today a very different feature from what it was in the days of Benjamin, not to mention Hobbes. In other words: the "street" should accomplish what more traditional organic institutions in society could not achieve. Charles Taylor suggested in this context: "What is truly important is that one be able to exercise autonomy in the basic issues of life, in one's most important commitments. Now, it is very dubious whether the developed capacity for this kind of autonomy can rise simply within the family. . . . What it is to be an autonomous agent, to have one's own way of feeling, of acting, of expression, is an identity, a way of understanding oneself, which men are not born with." This is a clear reference to citizenship as an accomplished way of self-reflection and self-understanding, both resulting from complex processes of enculturation. This is also in Taylor's words: "a way of understanding oneself, which men are not born with." He continues: "They have to acquire it . . . Thus we live in a world in which there is such a thing as public debate about moral and political questions and other basic issues. We constantly forget how remarkable that is, how it did not have to be so, and may one day no longer be so."[16]

These words prepare for the "street" as a new place for debate and for political as well as ethical considerations—a place very different from the traditional family context. A first effort to meet upfront is in one of the many buzzwords of actual social and political philosophy: the citizen in an open society. John Rawls tried to develop the concept as a link between a "self" and a "(legal) subject." Our interest in the "street" shows new ways to complete individualism and liberalism: individual rights are always embedded in community bonds. Those bonds are above all most important steps in the development of social dimensions, which are vital for the emergence of an actual *Self.* They can, however, be destructed when deception, protest and negativity reign. Many dimensions of the welfare state did so in the course of its history. They brought indifference and apathy in institutional settings and on the streets. Politics as well as active participation in environmental issue became the victim. Their complete opposite: violent nationalism and extreme radicalism seemed equally dangerous. All those positions are at a new location: the "street." On the "street" became clear, that an understanding of justice beyond law and legal discourse would not automatically lead to a functional democracy! The latter depends upon qualities and attitudes of its citizenship, which reach far beyond a balanced functionality of law and the legal system.

The openness of society can be interpreted as an important instrument to forward a responsible and active citizenship. Roots of that type of citizenship are, however, in forms of togetherness, which are not found in the citizen's relation with the powerful national and international institutions nor with the dominant corporations or their lobbyists driving around in the political landscape in "closed motor cars" (Popper). Neither governmental or cultural institutions, nor internationally oriented corporations are able to perform what was evident in traditional family life: *education.* Initiatives of citizens to build relations with public institutions do not flourish by nature—they are the result of education, and thus of an appropriate conversation. Without honoring that background, citizens may accomplish what is legally required but will fail to unfold a social life publicly. That may be an important dimension of the "street": a new locus where education through conversation takes place. It does so at many levels, in many languages, in great varieties of opinion and perhaps in the shadow of a notion of justice, which is not exclusively defined by legal specialists or democratically elected lawmakers. The "openness" of modern society includes foundational aspects of the "street." An exclusively moral judgment about the latter seems misplaced. Meaningful social activities find their roots in those aspects, but (as one experiences in these days) also in extremisms, as recent radicalization shows. Terrorists are not educated in schools, family circles or Mosques, but on the "street." The latter limitation contributes to the formation of an attitude in which the "street" becomes loaded with negative connotations: a place for incivility, for anti-politics, for a decline of cultural values and standards, for anarchism and even terrorism. Today the "street" is even viewed as an antipode of all bourgeois values, an absolute opposite of what states, state-unions, corporations, and other international organizations wish to achieve in the name of human rights and democracy. Such positive and negative connotations belong to the multiple aspects, which prepare for a clear insight: *the "open" society gave the "street" importance via the citizen and its sustained capacity of conversation and education.*

Commons and Community

The latter have one feature in common: the "street" is a social form to fight any *exclusion* of the individual. That is visible in the many modes of commonness, which citizens as well as radicalizing youngsters strive to experience via the "street." Exclusion is the opposite of what the "street" wants to realize. All forms of inclusion fight the evil of a not belonging. But during that fight, the difference between commonness and not belonging is often lost. It forceful social dynamics includes a mastership of meanings and signs under all circumstances. The street knows a continuous renewal of social values, changes of social order and unfolding views on a future—not to mention a diminishing of the restrictive and binding powers of institutions. "Street" words are embedded in discourses of social media but also in words, texts and films of terrorists and jihadists. A combination of a forceful belonging with an equally forceful desire to be freed from institutions seems to determine the "street" experience. The terms "common" and "community" are often a decisive mark in texts and discourses that want to support this "street" experience.

Two different value systems are effective within one social structure. The "street" fights the exclusion of the individual. But it stresses the positioning, that is: the perfect fit of subject, individual and citizen in a society with that action. "Street" action should halt that dangerous perfection, because it threatens the freedom of the citizen! This ambiguity is one of the critical points when the acceptance of the "street" concept is debated. It leads to the consideration whether it is possible that *the "street" accomplishes what the state fails to put into practice*? "Nation State" versus "street" as a "common": forms of community forcefully filled with ambiguities. And: does the "street" perform *directly* where the "state" can only deliver an *indirect* democracy with institutions and other representational activities? There seem to be at least four specific issues concealed in those questions. They are (a) citizen identity, (b) individualism in social life (c) "local vs. (inter)national," and (d) institution power.

Citizen Identity

A general observation is, that an "open" society needs participants with a strong self-profiled consciousness. The continuous plurality of features in an "open" society, such as mother tongues, levels of education, horizons of interest, political, religious or cultural views, causes that such a profile is necessary for everyone. That clarity is not at issue where only suppressive forms of government and administration are developed. Clarity results from the requirements of openness of society. But that is not simple: transparency and openness are based on feelings of belonging. That has consequences for politics, political philosophy or law, which are a valuable contribution to the acknowledgment of the "street" as a concept in its own right.

Individualism

Once the concept of "street" becomes accepted as a constitutive element, the citizen's task is understood as *representation*. That task is not simple to fulfill, because *representation* is no longer the exquisite privilege of a nation-state citizen. An example is the changing status of citizens of EU Member States.[17] It is remarkable how representation practices in a national and a Union context (such as the equality of citizens, their fundamental liberty, their freedom and respect for Human Rights and the rule of law) reinforce *individual* properties, mostly activated by professionals, which are members of institutions or lobbyists of corporations. The citizen cannot fulfill its task as a creator of rules in public life because of this individualism: he or she has to take passively part in them and live through *indirect* lines of representation. A point of serious criticism is that a citizen of the nation-state can only enjoy *rights created by others* and represent the individualistic features of others (persons as well as institutions), which limit them in living a full social life. That is also a roadblock in the "street!"

Local vs. (inter)national

Citizen profiles unfold in significantly smaller dimensions of geographical and legal nature than in the traditional notion of a national state or any state union. In times of displaced persons, mass refugees and terrorists, national states do not play the prominent role they fulfilled in earlier days. Their contractual relations are sometimes the only way out of an impasse. One of the causes for a nation-state impasse is in their internal struggles for an identity formation and the limited role those identities play worldwide. Global tendencies override national decisions. Decision-making in economy, law, and politics seems a matter of specialists, which have an identity that transgresses national features. Knowledge and language of decisions made, are globalized and most often the result of electronic data, analyses and communications.

National interests are perhaps the sole domains of a specific political rhetoric—where else are they appreciated? If the concept of a nation-state is encapsulated in an argumentation, the state rhetoric refers to interest groups, which have no or only limited relations with the citizens of that nation. The "street" registers this, and refers to other anchors of awareness: to regions, local authorities and municipalities. *Regions are identities with greater chances for a global future.* Their municipalities became centers of multiple interests, which are accessible for citizens, and centers of direct representation and power near citizens. New types of solidarity were propagated in times before our modern excesses of "social media." What does this mean?

Institution Power

The established powers of social and state institutions already challenged Walter Benjamin's scribbles while walking as a *flaneur* in the *Passages* of Paris. He noticed that the institution-bound architecture represented another form of democratic social life than the *Passages*. The latter evoked a hitherto in the languages of institutions unaccepted mode of life, which he called *improvisational*. That expression contained a wealth of affections and challenges to limit or even change the power of the state and its institutions. A *renewed opening* of the "open society" should lead to a free and direct access of the citizens to governance and sovereignty and a reduction of administrative powers as well as an appeal to plurality. Every idea, Benjamin suggested, contains an image of the world. Citizens should be free to express themselves in plurals because they have different views based on different images that inspired them to shape social life. The *Passages* and their dissolution of spiritual and architectonic barriers between *internal* and *external* were meant to be a powerful sign.

That observation has many consequences. The "street" is a sign of the spirit of a new perception, liberated from limiting powers that flourish under the heading of "democracy." Watching people, architectures, and merchandises while walking in the streets and seeing how life evolves, challenges the consideration what images fitted to what feelings. None of them can be linked to the power of a representative or a direct democracy. A social ambiguity became visible on the pavements and shop windows of the streets. "Belonging" is the keyword; it can only be realized in an open society with smaller dimensions and lower levels of hierarchy. *The "open society" needs* local *communities and* smaller scales *of life in order to truly be "open."*

Semiotics

Considering a semiotics of the "street" embraces the idea or image of a *community* and the experience of *togetherness*. Is this a call to revive the ideals of the 1871 French Revolution *Commune*? European history is indeed not without often-forceful transformations of the national state into local and regional administrations and authorities. The strength of region or "street" is not that they provide alternative organizational forms of governance, but that they create forms of governance as an effect of a citizen-directed human quality: of *togetherness.* In other words: the "street" wants first of all to realize *togetherness* and that brings a diversity of forms of *governance* to the fore. A discussion about admitting the "street" as a concept should be fully aware of this implication. One should not discuss the "street" as a political form but as an epistemological achievement: the "street" is a *sign* of the world as a *common image*, and only as such can it be the subject of political discussion. That *commonness* must be concrete in all "street" actions and remain at distance to any romanticizing interpretation.

The *common* is on the "street" the most organic feature that semiotics, law and politics can bring to the fore. The *common* reminds us of the *Magnus Homo*, a *body-figure*, which Hobbes portrayed on the title page of his famous *Leviathan* 1651 publication. A huge human figure portrays the state and all individuals are at walk to that figure to become incorporated in it while leaving churches, houses and streets behind, emptied and without any humane meaning and sense. Their common wish is to become *one body*—a metaphor for those operating today on the "street." That wish would automatically lead to new forms of direct democracy—an immediacy, which was translated by Hobbes in words of the social contract. One should not forget, that in his days the legal term "contract" fulfilled the role as a concept for near-absolute freedom. That culturally and psychologically determined determination of freedom interpreted a *bond* between humans as the highest value in life and created awareness about the fact that there is no hegemony or sovereignty possible without such a *bond.* With the same words one concludes today: *the "street" is the sign of a deep desire,*[18] enforced by the experience that the nation-state is not able to provide any bond among its citizens other than by legally determined articulations of life. A conclusion could be, that the suggested *bond* does not suffice to understand the social impact and features of the "street" concept.

The latter has influenced nearly all reflections on life and social provisions in our Occidental culture and shaped many centuries of its civilization. Body, organism, togetherness, contract, freedom and rights have been understood in the meaning of the State, which in its turn was understood as a "super-bond." How did the latter shape our thoughts, and patterns of philosophy, science, and psychology? We cannot abolish its influence and oftentimes feel the necessity to conceptualize the "street" as an exquisite organism to accomplish what the State could not complete. The word *Commune* seems in this context an expression filled with desire and frustration because it remembers the citizen on the "street" that clashing political realities cause social and political disasters; the latter are loudly audible around the world.

But there is more to say: meanings and their signs that live a state-determined life are as such not the cause of those disasters—they stem from a grandiose defect and an equally broad and deep ambiguity: it appears de facto impossible to think the common, the social enclosure of humans or new forms of togetherness. It is an onerous thought, that neither of those concepts can be fully employed within the boundaries of a state-determined view on reality. The discovery of that limitation goes hand in hand with the semiotic question in how far the "street" is acceptable as a foundational meaning. No wonder, that meaning making as well as meaning managing must be qualified as first-order political acts.

Public Spaces, White Spaces

The "street" is a spatial concept.[19] Its character of being a public space might cause problems because the implicit meanings of the word "public" are the result of state-determined views on reality. Accepting the meaning of "public" as a component of the expression "public space" for a life in the "street" implies restrictions in maintaining meanings. This indicates in its turn a more fundamental issue. Law would describe the spatial character of the "street" as the *locus* within which a legal subject is allowed and stimulated to act. The spatial character is, understood in those words, an index for legally determined behavioral patterns. A legal space indicates a subject's freedom *and* limits to act legally. But is such a legally determined freedom also meaningful in a human existence in its totality?

Human existence in the *modus* of belonging or togetherness inspires each citizen to profile its authentic *self*. This profiling must take place in a determinable space. It is true: a *self* was lost in state-enforced meanings, social roles, and plurals in need to claim togetherness. That claim is not determined by means of prescribed forms of sharing, by instrumental requirements or partitioned individual situations. Even a social situation, in which "I" and "You" share, requires an interpretation of the self as an authentic *self*. The existential reality of a human individual embraces the *plural* of a *self*, which leaves no room for an individualistic self-determination. The "street" concept refers to this transcendence of individuality by means of expanding support for unfolding one's self. As a consequence, one should perceive the spatiality of the "street" in an *existential* manner and not as a *geographical* or abstract-*scientific* feature.

The latter will leave white spaces in "street" experiences. A legal or political consciousness is generally regarded as abstract, diverse and mostly a matter of professionals. Social scientists or psychologists are not surprised to encounter white spaces everywhere. They understand a legal or political consciousness as the product of a subject in abstraction and artificial (legal) terms. That view disregards vital specificities: a person has always habits, colors, traits, a voice, a way of walking or of hearing and listening.

Law and the "Street"

The "street" concept is not built of stone or bitumen but formulates a common confrontation with the world. Its desire to achieve new forms of governance will not be satisfied by a change of power levels. That experience motivates a semiotic "street" policy: *the inclusion of the citizen completes or even replaces important fields of law, legal regulations and procedures.* Is that a Utopia?

Issues like *people being together,* or *citizen responsibility* should not be romanticized. It is easy to understand them in that way, but it will never contribute to an unfolding of the "street" as a truly epistemological question, which broadens our knowledge of the concept. The "street" is a reality *and* a concept—one should not forget that abstractions also belong to reality. Each social aspect in dealing with the "street" pertains to *interactivity*. Moreover, considering the "street" always pertains to the *quality* of relations on the street—not solely their structures, forms or dynamics. That suggestion leads to a more encompassing reflection: how will law appear when it is made fit for a democracy that includes the "street?" With what words should law be narrated on the "street?" Is the above-mentioned appeal to a "legal consciousness" sufficient, or is it in this context no longer conceivable? With what words should the story of the "street" be narrated?

Preliminary Conclusions

We investigated the crucial issues one needs for acknowledging the "street" as a fully acceptable concept in social sciences, semiotics, and philosophy. The following appear to be decisive and thus need further semiotic and social science research:

Otherness is a most important *sign* for dealing with the "street" concept;

The "street" is a sign of a deep *desire* to bond and to think the "common." It is, however, conceivable that the reality of a *bond* is not enough to answer the desire;

Meaning-making and meaning-managing is a *political act* anchored in institutional "street" contexts;

Meanings on the "street" originate from citizen capacities to withdraw from individualism and to *educate*;The *spatial* features of the "street" regard not architectonic or geographic but communicative qualities of citizens;

The *open society* needs local communication and small scales of life to be truly "open";

The "street" is expected to offer an opportunity to replace and overcome malfunctioning state-determined laws, regulations and procedures through appropriate *inclusion* of citizens.

THEORY

The concept "theory" related to "street" and "street–levels" implies various viewpoints. It focuses in the first place on the complex processes of the street's *reception* of meanings, ideas and experiences. But the concept focuses also on the street's *formation* of opinions, meanings and experiences articulated by citizens, social institutions and free minds in a society at large. And the richest, most encompassing, probably also most collimating, component might be its implicit but continuous *reference* to its Ancient Greek roots. As was repeatedly said before: awareness of that reference could lead to a deeper understanding of the "street" concept that articulates specific social structures and situations. In simple words: "street" is not only a matter of *passively receiving*, but also of *actively creating* values and meanings—as was already illustrated on Athenian streets during the 5th and 4th century BC. While exposing the latter, we discover (1) that Greek citizens were brought to experience their "being on the street" as an *act in community*, sustaining individual health as well as social order; (2) that the *numbers* of individuals on the Greek streets mirrored the complex structures of their political culture, and (3) that the concept of "theory" in its specific connection with "street" made the word *theoria* a key issue in philosophical and political considerations.

On Athenian Streets—Community

"Theory" and "street" are expressions for intertwined practices in Ancient Greece. How can we understand the "street" as a practice or as an act of any importance? A noteworthy aspect of studies on the Athenian democracy is its lacking oversight of explicit mentions of the "street."[20] "Theory" relates to the name of a specific fund in its various forms and functions during the 5th age BC called the "*theoric fund.*" The profile of Athenian pedestrians in that century recovers some meanings of "theory." Ties between the fund and the profile of citizens on the street should, however, not be underestimated. The fund shaped the mind of pedestrians in Ancient Athens.

Greek streets were bordered by private houses, commercial or even governmental buildings, temples, toilets and bath—all creating a specific togetherness. The latter is a key for our understanding of the Athenian *theoria.* A "Main Street" or any other street name is never mentioned, but inscriptions related to the street are not only linked to dust, stones, rocks, bumpy roads and steep slopes of streets but also to water systems that were vital in urban layouts. No road was without water and water systems that support social behaviors. Research on Roman archeo-biology illustrates the relation between the street and what we nowadays call "hygiene."[21] Streets were in Greek city planning guided by the desire to construct an urban environment, which expressed and nurtured the ideals of its inhabitants. They were occasionally straight, broad, intersecting, and retaining wide central areas for marketplaces and agoras.[22] But they never met modern standards of cleanliness; Greek latrines always bordered streets (like the Roman would do later) and a public eye was continuously present (often from a Goddess: Tyche in Greek, Fortuna in Roman days). Seats with stone slabs sticking out of the walls connected to water provisions possessed public dimensions. Men were primary users, but women, slaves and freedmen as well as citizens rich and poor had equal access to the latrines. The situation brought a rude confrontation with the unpleasant aspects of human life. Water was the sole means to soften it: Tyche's connection to water was meaningful also here and water politics appeared to be an integral part of the "street"–codes in Ancient Greek societies.[23] The public toilets or latrines bordering the street illustrate that the street must be understood as an act embedded in and sustained by a theoria as well as a milieu of city, state, individual personhood and togetherness.[24]

On Athenian Streets—Numbers

Numbers sustaining our insights can be given by approximation only. Contemporary authors studying Ancient Greek life and culture proposed such estimations regularly. Their numbers differ according to their references. We consider three prominent scholars, the first emphasizing law and legal institutions (Starr), the second viewing the general social structure of Athens (Jones) and the third the citizenship, its professionals, aliens, and slaves (Hansen).[25]

Starr refers to a legal-political criterion: the number of voters in the Athenian Assembly. He estimates the population in Athens just before the Peloponnesian War begins, at 172,000 citizens and 30,000 slaves so that the total population in Athens during the 5th and 4th century BC was below 200,000 individuals. Appreciating Jones' taxations of Athenian population's wheat consumption, ownership of land and money, soldiers, slaves and children, the final number comes to 124,000 free persons, children included, and 20,000 slaves—a total of 144,000 individuals. Although "The Athenians themselves would not have been able to answer . . . with exactitude" the number of inhabitants of city and state, Hansen brings a number of 150,000 Athenians.[26]

Many individuals would not walk the streets of the city frequently. We do not possess a sociological investigation of any street population—not in Ancient times or the European Middle Ages, nor in our days. It is, however, clear that men were in the majority on the streets, in the public toilets or the public spaces around these as well as the agoras or the theatre scenes. Women and children were supposed to live in and around the houses, in particular where agrarian surroundings were near the city centers. *Metics* (registered aliens) and slaves would also not frequently be seen on the street, although several of them were famously rich. Citizens as well as *metics* and slaves performed all sorts of agrarian work, which kept them away from streets. An agrarian mentality dominates, as we can read in Plato's *Laws*, and that spirit is also not intensely street-directed. The suggestion is that many were together on the streets, but that important streets were never overcrowded and that smaller and less important streets were more frequently used, because citizens and other individuals did not connect to anything comparable our contemporary "big town" mentality.

Some characteristics of the Athenian citizenship on the streets are thus reconstructed. Citizens were at a relatively low number compared to the totality of the population. Legal citizenship was not always easy to obtain, and in certain periods very restricted, as in times of Pericles. Their main privilege was political rights, and that has many consequences. Every adult male citizen had the right to attend the Assembly, to be a magistrate or a legislator or a juror, he owned further the right to financial and land property, to explore the minerals of the land and the rights to hold concessions.[27] They were the prominent pedestrians—even while in low numbers and by no means always wealthy. So the streets showed a mixed population with a male dominance, without an important racial mixture but certainly with a mixture of those who were bearer of political rights and those who were not.

It is clear that the *features of spatiality were not based on distinctions we are used to explore*. Differences between small and large, long and short, high-bordered or low-bordered streets are not found and did not cause a specific mentality. Streets were a component of a totality—houses, buildings, toilets, agoras and theatre stages—but apparently not an issue in itself. Their Goddesses or Gods did, however, mark the image of the streets. Large and little stone pillars imaging the God Hermes were placed before the houses that bordered the streets. This has not drawn much attention to those who studied Ancient Greek cultures, but it illustrates a deeper layer of public life being anchored in religious motives. It was not only the liturgies and the Festivals, but it was also daily life on the streets that reminded the citizenship of its religious anchors. Hermes was the preferred God to keep those reminiscences alive. The Greek word "*hermaion*" meant piles or even pillars of stones positioned on hills in the countryside and in the city streets as marks belonging to the houses. Hermes lived in those stones to guide the walkers and wanderers. The messenger of the Gods protected travelers as well as merchants, and thus heralded the Roman *pater familias*. It fascinates: *no Greek street is without Hermes!*

On Athenian Streets—Theory

But if Hermes stayed in piles of stones erected in front of the houses, did he thus protect the family and the owners? Pay attention to an inversion: his face was *not* directed to owners—but to the street, to the public and to those who were without house, without protection and often without any asset. All who were on the street perceived Hermes' home in the stone piles, and that is a unique semiotic phenomenon. *A messenger of God is a God himself*: the sign is itself what it signs (or signals). Is Hermes a sign on its own? Can that be, can a sign be a sign on its own? We'll discuss this later. Hermes doubles, intensifies, creates a plurality in life, and at the same time he de-doubles, singles out and enforces a single identity of which the citizen is a witness while carrying its legally fortified citizenship. Stones are signs of a justification; Hermes' homes protect the homeless. Owners do not worship Hermes for themselves, but for others. Is this Greek inversion of worship the basis for their democracy and a socially effective altruism?

People on the street could inverse such a high-pitched opinion. Streets were open spaces for debate, discussion, and argument: speech was in those days not primarily for an exchange of information. The openness of the *polis* was demonstrated in the sounds one could hear on the street: "Greek culture took form by opening to an ever widening circle—and finally to the entire *demos* (community)—access to the spiritual world reserved initially for an aristocracy of priests and warriors," Vernant concludes.[28] Athenian streets were to a great extent filled with those who strictly exercised their citizen rights, and that could only be done at the expense of slaves, women or aliens. The latter did not have rights and could not participate in the political life of the city. But to enjoy your rights you need sufficient leisure! It is understandable that only a fraction of the total population had the possibility to take part in the directness of the Athenian democracy: a "have–not" may have been watched by the Gods but he received occasionally a small sum of money from one of the branches of the "*theoric* fund."

That fund paid citizens (and *metics*) for instance to participate in the *liturgies* which took place hundred times a year and thus created for the streets each year more than 100 liturgical and festive days. In Demosthenes' days were even 400 liturgies mentioned, religious and naval together.[29] These liturgies profiled the street population accordingly; their organization was a duty for the wealthiest citizens nearly every two years but reached out to ordinary citizens. The preparation for a religious Festival or a naval Liturgy took a year. Numbers of citizens involved were high, and costs considerable—the latter were in the first place an issue for the well to do because their provision was forcefully understood as a "public service for the state."

The influence of the "*theoric* fund" on public life, and thus on life on the street, was immense. The fund, like all funds in all ages, was a turning point in the flow from state wealth to private (dis)-comfort. It impresses how strongly the Festivals of Athens influenced a possible reverse of a psychological, philosophical or a financial situation. Many of the citizens, *metics*, and (perhaps sometimes) women participating, even those voting the prizes drama and tragedy authors, were paid by the fund. The word *theorika* was on everybody's lips; it indicated a generally approved institution, in its most active and appreciated form during the years of Pericles. *Theoroi* were those who saw, had seen, experienced, attended and voted during the Festivals for or against an author, in particular during the Athenian Greater Dionysia. "Street" and "theory" do intertwine meanings; their togetherness is a key to understand our citizens walking modern streets.

On Parisian Streets

Who is invited to think of walking *Athenian* streets in the 5th century BC might think of Aeschylus, Euripides or any other winner of a Dionysian Festival or of dramatic, even comic texts from that period. Who thinks of *Parisian* streets at the end of the 19th Occidental century, can only think of Walter Benjamin and his *Arcades Project*. The indicative function of the title embraces much more than a title alone. The two words refer to the impressive English language publication issued almost half a century after the philosopher's death[30] as well as the formula Benjamin and his friends used for the totality of his work: books, essays, letters, and other texts had the Arcades continuously in mind, and with that project the issue of "street."

We mentioned already that a differentiation between interiority and exteriority seems untenable for Benjamin's project: facts and situations, events and circumstances, speech and context show always two faces of the same. A window mirror projects the outer world in the interiority of the living room and the room is a room because it is filled with reflections of the exterior, Adorno once remarked.[31] A moment of the past thus becomes owner of the momentary and its future. The dissolution of spiritual and architectonic barriers between *internal* and *external* became a powerful sign. The "street" assigns the spirit of a new perception. The historical always intrudes the actuality of the intimate. Our perception is the product of such an intrusion. Arcades illustrated the variability of such intrusions, so that *the architectonical conditions for the unfolding of a new life on the streets* came with new actualities. While covering, indeed roofing the street, they form a veiled and concealed situation in which any dissimilarity of interior and exterior could be abolished. They constituted abstract communication lines between abstract individuals, and provided the necessary conditions for an equally abstract system of commodity exchange, as Popper foresaw. Indeed: the imagery of a new economy and philosophy of state emerge in the citizen's mind as powerfully as possible. The pedestrian enters a scene that changed continuously and provides a sequence of associations like in an ever-lasting dream or phantasm. *Architecture did what speech did in an equal rhythm*, Hannah Arendt could have noticed; every step of the pedestrian concluded with "amen" to embrace "reality" and exchange commodities *ad libitum.*

It is not a surprise, that in line with his earlier essays on a philosophy of language Benjamin focused on the *names* of streets in Paris—their history, their changes, their sign character and their inner expressivity. Those names are in many respects a counterexample of the numbered streets. The latter express a greater distance to history and more efficiency so that those streets became an entity without identity. It reinforces Benjamin's view when we notice that numbers can also become a name: In New York, *Fifth Avenue* is definitively *not* a numbered street! But in all cases, streets are no longer an element of the internal space of a town or village—they became spaces, fields of anonymity, plazas of phantasmagoria filled with anonymous communication. The observations in the *Arcades* project appear to be at the border of the street as a communication issue. Benjamin underlines, that there are still "little squares that are suddenly there, and to which no name attaches. They have not been the object of careful planning . . . and do not enjoy the patronage of world history; but owe their existence to houses that have slowly, sleepily, belatedly assembled in response to the summons of the century. In such squares, the trees hold sway; even the smallest afford thick shade."[32]

Street names, embedded in the development of a century, are interesting for their implications of a philosophy of language and of Occidental culture. A "theory of street names" was quoted in the *Arcades* text, which formulated an axial insight and quoted Leo Spitzer's 1928 *Stilstudien*: "Proper names, too, have an effect that is conceptually unburdened and purely acoustic . . . proper names are "bare formulas" which Proust can fill up with feelings because they have not yet been rationalized by language." Benjamin refers to numerous aspects of a street's name; he writes on "the magic of street names" and contrasts a "street" with the older expression "way": "the way brings with it the terrors of wandering . . . there is even today, for the solitary wanderer, a detectable trace of the power of ancient directives over wandering hordes. But the person who travels a street, it would seem, has no need of any guiding hand. It is not in wandering that someone takes the street, but rather in submitting to the monotonous, fascinating, constantly unrolling band of asphalt."[33] The fascination of the street name seems to exist since the French Revolution. The mirrors erected all around crossings of *arcades* at the end of the 19th century, the new light sources, their unknown quality effect the citizen's mind as well as the unexpected panoramas created by the new architecture. They built a bridge to the "street" concept of our days. The phantasmagoria of communication becomes more and more general in the "street"-notion's political practice, and appears surprisingly intertwined with the Ancient Greek concept of *theoria.*

Theoria

Theoria played an important role on Athenian streets—an issue often neglected in studies on the Ancient Greek as well as modern social theory. The ancient and the modern street displays perhaps technical but no principal differences. We are all watched on the street, perhaps not by Gods but by cameras constructed on the basis of the same Greek principles: support for individual well-being combined with rights and duties formulated by the state. Do streets offer a position to balance the two? Some want to, pretend to, might even be successful in just doing that. But none is beyond the more fundamental meaning of the word *theoria.* What is concealed in one of the most important roots of Occidental culture?

Each individual seems in the course of life to renounce a naïve-natural position. That practice embraces language, morality, society, and above all, otherness—but all components remain enclosed in an evolving, often troublesome harmony within the "self." So there is no doubt about what the "street" illustrates: a human individual is continuously in reconciliation with its self while recognizing itself through others and otherness and even discovering otherness as a source of dynamics deeply inside it's self. That process is more than any "internal conversation" within the self because it definitively transcends "I-" and "You-" positions: it is a socializing practice. The "street" is the *locus* of that practice and enlarges and deepens that recognition, we learn. The unfolding of a self occurs (among other paces) on the "street." The Greek *theoria* as an *unfolding a human self* brings something new and uncalled-for to the front. It leads beyond what is directly present and perceivable into the realm of social, political and humane essentialities of life in the *polis*, which develop a human self: the Greek *theoria* is a *sign* to grasp the implicit meanings of our awareness and self-unfolding with the "street" as its milieu. Although connecting persons to persons (and in particular citizens to citizens), "street"-meanings are not a part of fixated sign patterns, as are for instance "I-" and "You-" patterns. Awareness of the "street" is far more holistic and not a system of precisely defined concepts.

"*Theoria*" colors a path to individuality and citizenship in political contexts. A renouncement of any naïve-natural attitude (including a renewed interest in language with its roots in regions or nations and a reformulation of cultural values) is altogether a *theoric* feature of the "street," often exercised with vehemence. The citizen is like an author of a successful novel: embedded in a social context, expressing values and norms, positioning in/against traditional institutions, at distance from individual resourcefulness and geniality, unfolding appropriate thought patterns. In this regard is "street": *theory*—and *theory* is here much more than an incidental metaphor. One of the important aspects of the ties between "street" and "theory" is the emphasis on *participation,* a specific ability of the subject/citizen. In other words, "street" is a direct expression for the various spatial, cultural, moral or political coordinates of participation in the sense of a "being there," whereas "theory" expresses the unity and almost holistic character of the presence of the individual and its participation. This is what the *theoric fund* wanted to effectuate in Ancient Greece—it is, however, hardly different from what contemporary philosophers, social scientists and politicians envisage today. The fund brought a genuine philosophical insight about the essence of a human being into practice. Its payments (long before the concept of commodity entered social relations) were meant to profile the citizen's mind by means of a specific alienation that expresses itself in actions on the street.

It is of essence to understand the dimensions of this alienation. Plato explained in his *Phaidros* that a citizen's presence at the Liturgies was a participation which had to be neither subjective nor objective, neither practical nor theoretical, neither financial nor spiritual, but a full and un-divided and not partitioned act to be described only as a being there.[34] The structures of the human mind that were leading to this presence are therefore a key to understand "*Theoria.*" They included *a form of alienation* for the subject to become a *self* that was provoked by a most radical otherness (the otherness being money), a "*positive ecstasy.*" The Greek provision for a deep involvement in the drama's and tragedies created togetherness. The involvement, resulting from *theoric activity,* was fed by money and thus provoked the *self* by an alienating power. Modern citizens may walk their street and yet experience such an ecstasy—be it with different attitudes or views. What does this observation imply for the *theore*tical dimensions one encounters in contemporary philosophy and social sciences?

Sovereignty and the Riddle of "Theoria"

"*Theoria*" concerns *exteriorization* as a most powerful component of a human consciousness. It is a force that forms the basis for a unique completeness and wholeness of all participation on the "street." The completeness does not result from a subject's continuing "inner dialogue" as continental philosophers of the 20th century wanted to profile. On the contrary: the completeness of "street" participation expresses *that the ties between "street" and "theoria"* are at its origin—a fact that will be fully perceivable once the "street" becomes accepted in philosophy and social sciences. Participants on the "street" behave by integrating external *and* internal powers of body and mind, as the Ancient Greek fund already wanted to achieve. Their activities aimed at opening the so-called *inner* dimensions of "the subject's mind"—a new occurrence in psychology and philosophy and perhaps not yet fully integrated in modern politics.

For political thinking, it is important that understanding the "street" inspired by the powers of a "*theoria*" brings the problem of *sovereignty* to the fore: the word expresses in its conventional meaning the desire "to calm down (or even oppress) all sorts of social change and rebellion that are hard to understand or accept but should under given circumstances be tolerated." It is about the full right and power to govern (from state to street) *without accepting interference* from external bodies, institutions, opinions or meanings. That *exteriority* named "sovereignty" also plays a role *in* the dynamics of the human mind itself. In other words: *in the self are forces like exteriority at work*—they provide insight in the *self* during the unfolding of any self-awareness of the citizen and/or pedestrian.[35] That is exactly what the ancient *theoria*-concept wanted to stand for. It justifies us to redefine the "street" as the place where rebellion occurs against *"totality inflicting from an outside/exteriority"* in the name of the "*totality called the holon.*"

That seems a truly challenging tension, and a different, more than incidental political rebellion so often associated with the "street." One thus concludes: "street" is the place for a fight of the *self* against determinations originating in a form of sovereignty and exteriority on commodity-concepts. A consequence is clear: *the ultimate goal of accepting the "street" is an evocation of a holistic self-awareness in foro publico*. So, what happens *outside* also happens *inside*: "the differentiation annihilated"—a new slogan emerges for the rapper as well as psychologist related to the culture of the "street." Benjamin's "phantasmagoria" linked to the Arcades were in an *inside*. Now we see its practices also on the street, that is: on the *outside*—a move that absolutely abrogates the difference between the two. Should we say that the street has no longer an inside and an outside?—"The street perhaps never had," an Ancient Greek observer would suggest! Streets obliterate a disharmony between internal attitudes and external forces in the minds of citizens, and while doing so create a new challenge in understanding citizenship and the necessary re-deployment of cultural roots in a democracy. That understanding of the "street" is in essence an understanding of a *shared* experience, which became defined by a territorial notion (called "street"). But the "sharing" is not enough!

Accepting the "street" as a contemporary concept implies new types of *self-management of the human mind in public settings.* It tells us in what ways modern pedestrians are sign-bearers of a consciousness that copes with the dominancy of an alienating commodity, which is continuously manifested on and around the street. Those signs are embedded in a renewed view on self-awareness and a fuller but never completed self-understanding of the subject on the street. The "street" concept is in that regard of immense importance for a modern subject/citizen, and its ever-changing milieu that always refers anew to man and society in an ever-changing relevance of modernity. A final consideration may underline that view before we formulate a conclusion.

Street as Theory

One could understand the "street" as an ultimate indication for the overall and deeply entrenched process of commodification, and the latter as a major character of modern society. Semiotics highlights that this commodification brings the desire to the fore of each pedestrian to become a "sign alone." How can this be? Did not Peirce tell us, that a "sign is never a sign alone?" Yes, but he did not tell Hermes, who practiced the same intention. Hermes' home in the stone piles created a semiotic phenomenon: the messenger of God a God himself: a sign alone is itself a sign. Is Hermes' sign a sign on its own? Do not forget, that any such observation remains the result of a specific understanding of the Self and its sociability. But the modern citizen's desire expresses a desire beyond sign-signs. That desire pertains to *identity* and *freedom in social context.* Although that desire cannot be completely fulfilled in sign theory, it strives for a realization in social contexts. This is exemplified in almost all literature on the "street," from its social history and political ideas up to its practices striving for a direct democracy and to anarchist ideas. Literature referring to the French Revolution underlines the new horizons and political practices while remembering the Commune. "What constitutes the commune is the mutual oath sworn by the inhabitants of a city, a town, or a rural area *to stand together as a body.* . . . A commune was a pact to face the world together. It meant relying on one's own shared powers as the source of one's freedom. What was aimed for was not an entity; *it was a qualitative bond, and a way of being in the world.* . . . It was this long lost, original, medieval meaning of the commune that was somehow rediscovered by the federalist faction of the Paris Commune in 1871," the *Invisible Committee* writes 2014. "And it's the same meaning that reemerges periodically since that time."[36] In the light of the considerations of the *Committee,* the "street" can be defined as a *territorially expressed whole of shared experiences.* In the *sharing* is the riddle of the *social*. The *sharing* withstands any glorification of the Commune and its underlying social structures, and awakens the desire to be "a sign alone." Such a desire challenges our social theories—a position that was already fortified in the Greek *theoria*.

What is at issue? No more and no less than that a one-sided understanding of "the social" dominates all of our social sciences and their political philosophy: *the idea that "the social" always relates to a form of "belonging."*[37] And the "street" is unique in that it does not embrace this one-sidedness: exactly that feature is most powerful in the expression "street level." Are social relations and is "the social" possible without any defined belonging? The answer is: yes, it is—and that is exactly the case where the desire of the pedestrian was characterized as *the desire to be a sign alone*. On the "street," the walking citizen is socialized even when she is not belonging. The rapper, the walker and the smart phone with its tiny screen replacing the many mirrors of the Arcades illustrate how you are abstract (as Popper foresaw) and with no identity beyond a phone number or an e-mail address. The phantasm of identity reflects in the *selfie* on the street: a romantic view about the Commune becoming an IT issue. Always and everywhere being contactable is the street's phantasm on communication, thanks to its displacement into the virtual. In other words, the pedestrian can interpret herself as a liberated *Self* only because sociability reaches *beyond* belonging.[38] The latter insight abolishes sovereignty's power as a feature of exteriority for each individual.

That insight, which unmasks the political phantasm creating subject/citizens possessing rights while unfolding life, opens new dimensions of the Self. The spirit of semiotics invigorates the question: when, and under what circumstances, is a meaning a sign? When does a meaning lead us to a sign that is "a sign on its own," as Hermes' position was characterized? The formula "the Self as a Sign on its Own" is a post-Peircean positioning of components of the Self, which does *not* place any sovereignty in an *exteriority* of that Self. The riddle of the "social" is that the "I" does not accept any delimitation between interiority and exteriority of itself. Social theory and political philosophy focus on structures of emergence, which an unfolding Self makes visible.[39]

STREET, SELF, SIGN: A CONCLUSION

To *walk the "street*" thus embraces a new meaning: while walking, the walker/pedestrian explores a wealth of possibilities of the Self, including the virtual dimensions of which a "*selfie*" is a sign. The latter is, at least, a sign pertaining to the fact that the "street" cannot be understood without a notion of a multiple-dimensioned "Self" and its constitutive powers. That notion has become more urgent, where a "street-level sovereignty" moves away from any nation-state sovereignty. The latter emphasized "common" and "communal" features—but these are no longer appropriate for the "street." Sovereignty justifies the ideal of commonness, which hypostasis forces based on the social articulation of powers internal and external to the Self. That observation illustrates the intimate proximity of semiotics, law and society. But any acceptance of the "street" reinforces the *street credibility* of the Self beyond any type of sovereignty. No one knows what Self will emerge once that credibility is established in a future "street," and no one knows what social, philosophical or political changes will be relevant for the Self that became a Sign Alone. The "Self/Sign" and the "street" challenge us. Indeed, streets, squares and avenues are not what they were before or what we think they will become. Their changes occur in relation to the ever-changing meaning of the pedestrian's Self.

NOTES

1. F. Stjernfelt: *Natural Propositions. The Actuality of Peirce's Doctrine of Dicisigns.* Boston, 2014, concludes on p. 307: "As soon as you take the starting point as being hard divisions like those between inner and outer, body and soul, mind and matter, perception and cognition, images and logic, you will be sure to spend the rest of your conceptual life by trying, in vain, to bridge those dualisms."

2. See Jan M. Broekman: "On the Origins of Legal Semiotics" in: *The Journal of Comparative Law,* London, Vol. VII, Issue One, 2012, p. 26ff; W. E. Butler & P. T. Grier: "Legal Consciousness and the Legacy of I. A. Ilyin," in: *-Idem-* p. 40 ff.; Jan M. Broekman & Larry Catà Backer: *Signs in Law-A Source Book. The Semiotics of Law in Legal Education III*, Springer 2015: "Jacob Israel de Haan, the First Legal Semiotician," pp. 51–55, and: J. I. de Haan: "Essence and Task of Legal Significs," pp. 55–73.

3. On the word "law," see: Hermann Weck: *Die Sprache im deutschen Recht*, Berlin, 1913.

4. On the phenomenon of materialization, see: Michel Bréal: *Essai de sémantique*, [Essay on Semantics] Paris 1897, Chap. XIII: "Des mots abstraits et de l'appaississement du sens." This is the way the word "mark" has become materialized. Originally it referred to a sign on an object. Later it referred to an object that has was made for this mark. Art. 3. of the "Patent and Trademark Law" is vague and dangerous to use. Compare the materialization of the mark and the stamp. A fiscal advocate for the Marines and the Army went very deeply into that process of materialization —see: *Algemeen Handelsblad* Sept. 17, 1916— and remarked: "Here, one is a slave of the law." I would say: "Here is one slave of one's spiritual life!"

5. See De Haan's text in: Jan M. Broekman & Larry Catà Backer: *Signs in Law-A Source Book. Op. Cit.* p. 60.

6. Fritz Mauthner: *Beiträge zu einer Kritik der Spache*, Stuttgart 1901, Vol. III, p. 241.

7. De Haan: *Op. Cit.,* p. 67.

8. De Haan: *Idem,* p. 67/68 (today we no longer mention "significian" but "semiotician"; see note 9).

9. De Haan: *Idem,* p. 70f.

10. It is an interesting problem in its own right to mention that here is perhaps an important difference between *semiotics* and *significs* as conceived in the first decade of the 20th century. See the Works of Ch. S. Peirce, Victoria Lady Welby and others. See Broekman: "On the Origins of Legal Semiotics," *Op. Cit.* p. 35f.

11. Joseph Brent's biography of Peirce: *Charles Sanders Peirce; A Life*, Indiana UP, 1993, reproduces on page 309 a fascinating Peircean drawing of *the labyrinth of signs*, to be viewed at the Harvard University Archives.

12. See Butler & Grier, *Op. Cit.,* p. 42 f, p. 49 f.

13. *Idem,* p. 52 ff; see: E. Ehrlich: *Grundlegung der Soziologie des Rechts* 1913, [Fundamentals of the Sociology of Law, W. Moll, Tr. 1936]

14. See Butler & Grier, *Op. Cit.,* p. 55 (incl. note 45).

15. K. Popper: *The Open Society and its Enemies, (1945),* 5th Ed 9 1966, p. 177.; see also H. Bergson: *Les deux sources de la moralité et de la religion,* 1932. [Engl. Ed.: Two Sources of Morality and Religion, 1935, 1977]

16. Charles Taylor: "Atomism" in: Shl. Averini & A. De-Shalit (Eds): *Communitarianism and Individualism,* Oxford UP, 1992, p. 43 ff.

17. See further details in Jan M. Broekman: *A Philosophy of European Union Law.* Leuven, 1999, p. 332 f.

18. The literature on Hobbes' *Leviathan* never noticed that the emptiness of the streets, homes and buildings/churches was meant to be a *sign* of the unfulfilling character of the State. That *desire,* which is a strong desire for fulfillment (like today one encounters often on the street) made all citizens walk towards the *Other*: the *Magnus Homo.*

19. The Invisible Committee: *To Our Friends.* (Tr. R. Hurley) Semiotext(e), Intervention Series No. 18, Cambridge, MIT Press, 2015, p. 197 ff. See also Ruth Padel: "Making Space Speak" in J. J. Winkler & F. I. Zeitlin (Eds): *Nothing to Do with Dionysos?* Princeton UP, 1990, p. 336 f., and: –Id.–: *In and out of the mind: Greek images of the tragic self.* Princeton UP 1992; the theme of the *spatial* character of the "street" relates to an important theme of mainly European philosophy in the fifties of the last century. Diverse thinkers as Arendt, Habermas, Heidegger and Gadamer focused on the interpretation of the *public* character of space in terms of the strong relations between *praxis* and *action* on the one hand and *language* on the other. See: Hannah Arendt: *The Human Condition,* Chicago UP, 1958, p. 179: "No other human performance requires speech to the same extent as action."

20. Sir Arthur Pickard-Cambridge: *The Dramatic Festivals of Athens.* (J. Could & D. M. Lewis, (Ed. 2nd Ed.) Oxford UP, 1988; Chester G. Starr: *The Birth of Athenian Democracy,* Oxford UP, 1990; H. W. Parke: *Festivals of the* Athenians, London 1977; M. H. Hansen: *The Athenian Democracy in the Age of Demosthenes,* Oxford/Cambridge Mass., 1991; M. M. Austin & P. Vidal–Naquet: *Economic & Social History of Ancient Greece,* California UP, 1977.

21. Günter E. Thüry: *Müll und Marmorsäulen. Siedlungshygiene in der römischen Antike.* Mainz, Zabern 2001.

22. Hansen, *Op. Cit.,* p. 322 mentions Hippodamus and offers a map of an Athenian Agora, constructed by the American School of Studies in Athens, which indicates streets connecting buildings and designed places.

23. On Tyche, toilets and water provisions, see: Ann Olga Kokosi-Ostrov: "Dura-Europos: Water, Baths, Latrines, and the Goddess Fortuna in a Desert City" in Lisa R. Brody & Gail. L. Hoffmann (Eds): *Dura Europos. Crossroads of Antiquity.* McMullen Museum of Art, Boston College, 2011, p. 251 ff. See also Jan M. Broekman: "A Goddess for semiotics of law and legal discourse" in *DADA-Rivista di Antropologia post-globale,* A. Palmisano (Ed.) Trieste 2011, pp. 7–24.

24. That act, in Graeco-Roman days protected by a Goddess and many Gods, is nowadays founded on a Constitution—that is: founded in Law. If an Ancient Greek "street" concept would have existed at all, then the concept would have included the act of inclusion and certainly not of any protected intimate privacy, which tends to exclude whatever form of otherness. The "street" would thus have embraced an altruism that shaped the social value of street walking as a matter of togetherness and not an efficient traveling, as is the case in our days.

25. Starr, *Op. Cit.* Ch. III; A. H. M. Jones: *Athenian Democracy.* Baltimore, 1957; Hansen, *Op. Cit.* Ch. V, p. 86 ff. Those three publications based their provision almost exclusively on the estimation of numbers of registered citizens. For instance the *metics* ware left out, because registered aliens did not possess any rights comparable to those of the citizens. This does, however, not mean that citizens and *metics* on the street did not exchange opinions or sentiments. Pedestrians are not numbered, and the mentality, spirit or mind on the street and its social level differs from any number of participants.

26. Hansen, *Op. Cit.,* pp. 90–95.

27. See: R. K. Sinclair: *Democracy and Participation in Athens,* Cambridge UP, 1988, p. 196 f.

28. J.-P. Vernant: *Les origines de la pensée grecque,* Paris, 1962 [Engl. Ed.: *The Origins of Greek Thought* Cornell UP 1982, p. 51].

29. See Hansen, *Op. Cit.,* p. 110 ff. See also: –Id.–: "Demographic Reflections on the Number of Athenian Citizens," in: *American Journal of Ancient History,* Vol. VII, p. 172 ff.

30. Walter Benjamin: *The Arcades Project,* (H. Eiland & K. McLaughlin, Eds), Harvard UP, Cambridge/London, 1999.

31. Th. W. Adorno: *Kierkegaard: Konstruktion des Ästhetischen,* Tübingen, 1933 [Engl. Ed.: R. Hullot-Kenter (Ed.): *Kierkegaard: Construction of the Aesthetic.* Minnesota UP, 1989]

32. Benjamin, *Arcades, Op. Cit.,* p. 517, 650.

33. Benjamin, *Arcades, Op. Cit.,* p. 518, 519.

34. On the constitutive role of *division* and *partition* in understanding the human character, see: Jan M. Broekman: *Meaning, Narrativity, and the Real,* Springer 2016, Ch. 4 and 5.

35. Our streets filled with quizzing and twittering are perhaps surprisingly near to Ancient Athenian practices, where a special fund supported citizens to decide the prize-winning of dramas and tragedies as a sign of their more or less direct democracy based on insight and free decision. Ancient Greek *theoria* and its *theoric*

fund implied an appeal to grasp for a form of sovereignty. Legal theoreticians in the EU equally struggle with the question whether sovereignty is effective on a conceptual or an object level. Their political situation enforces them to accept sovereignty beyond a state level or—since EU Commission and ECJ are independent from the Union's Member States—a plural sovereignty. They bring to the fore that the social power of sovereignty touches on deep structures of solidarity. Any communal experience changes to the extent that sovereignty is understood as a constitutional or as a non-constitutional component of social and political life. The Athenians understood their *theoric* fund as a socially important source of support and power (Pericles) and thus as the last-mentioned (non-constitutional) form of sovereignty. See discussions between D. Grimm, Fritz W. Scharpf and Ulrich K. Preuß as well as the essay of Alain Supiot in: Johan van der Walt & Jeffrey Ellsworth (Ed.): *Constitutional Sovereignty and Social Solidarity in Europe*, Nomos Baden-Baden 2015, p. 39 f, 55 f, 193 f, 109 f. See also: Jürgen Habermas: *The Crisis of the European Union*, Polity Press, 2012 p. 53 f.

36. The Invisible Committee (2014): *To Our Friends*. (Trl. R. Hurley) Semiotext(e), 2015, Op. Cit., p. 199 f. See Giorgio Agamben: *La comunità che viene*, 1990. [Engl. Ed.: *The Coming Community,* M. Hardt, (Ed.) Minnesota UP, 1993].

37. "Regaining the commons" seems a powerful ideal of the "street." The influence of it is very strong. For instance the actual "*Degrowth*" movement embraces major forms of the *commons*, those limiting or even abolishing a general *commodity* thinking included. The movement's basic concept identifies "the social" with a general "bonding" (for instance in new forms of community/commune) as its foundation. That "bonding" is, however, a form of sovereignty or external power, which limits the unfolding of an actual walker's *Self*. The concept of the social includes, as the "street" concept illustrates, *non-bonding as a positive value*. A disregard of that value also misinterprets the *sign* function of the "street." The "street" favors the unfolding of multiple positions and attitudes when a *Self* walks the street. See: Giacomo D'Alisa, Federico Demaria & Giorgos Kallis: *Degrowth. A vocabulary for a new era.* Routledge, London 2014, Ch. 1.

38. This observation challenges the hidden romanticism in philosophical positions from *Benjamin* to the more recent *Invisible Committee*.

39. Lorenzo Chiesa and Raffaello Palumbo Mosca (Ed.): *Figures of the o/Other: Brother, Neighbor, Stranger, Enemy.* Genoa School of Humanities (GSH), 2016, write: "Christianity preaches the love of the neighbor, yet ultimately reduces him to a repetition of the self. Modern democracy rests on fraternity, but all too often distorts it into inconsistent ideologies of identity, which pave the way for more or less explicit forms of racism. The battle for the emancipation of woman runs itself the risk of succumbing to a global dispositive of sameness dominated by Capital and its ruthless values. Faced with unprecedented social, economical, and political crises, we are today increasingly urged to treat any kind of otherness that challenges our fragile egos as an enemy . . . our basic hypothesis is that there can be no sincere appreciation of the other as another subject without acknowledging a more profound, albeit immanent, kind of Other: the linguistic/discursive nature of the animal that speaks and writes; its structural in-completeness and parallel desire for completeness."

REFERENCES

Adorno, T. W. *Kierkegaard: Konstruktion des Ästhetischen,* Tübingen, 1933. [Engl. Ed.: R. Hullot-Kenter (Ed.): *Kierkegaard: Construction of the Aesthetic.* Minnesota UP, 1989].

Agamben, Giorgio. *La comunità che viene*, 1990. [Engl. Ed.: *The Coming Community,* M. Hardt, (Ed.) Minnesota UP, 1993].

Arendt, Hannah. *The Human Condition*, Chicago UP, 1958.

Austin, M. M., & P. Vidal–Naquet. *Economic & Social History of Ancient Greece,* California UP, 1977.

Benjamin, Walter. *The Arcades Project*, (H. Eiland & K. McLaughlin, Eds.), Harvard UP, Cambridge/London 1999.

Bergson, H. *Les deux sources de la moralité et de la religion,* 1932. [Engl. Ed.: Two Sources of Morality and Religion, 1935, 1977].

Bréal, Michel. *Essai de sémantique*, [Essay on Semantics] Paris 1897,

Brent, Joseph. *Charles Sanders Peirce; A Life*, Indiana UP, 1993.

Broekman, Jan M. *A Philosophy of European Union Law.* Leuven, 1999.

Broekman, Jan M. & Larry Catà Backer. *Signs in Law-A Source Book. The Semiotics of Law in Legal Education III*, Springer 2015: "Jacob Israel de Haan, the First Legal Semiotician."

Broekman, Jan M. "A Goddess for semiotics of law and legal discourse" in *DADA-Rivista di Antropologia post-globale*, A. Palmisano (Ed.) Trieste 2011, pp. 7–24.

———. "On the Origins of Legal Semiotics" in: *The Journal of Comparative Law,* London, Vol. VII, Issue One, 2012.

———. *Meaning. Narrativity, and the Real*, Springer 2016.

Butler, W. E. & P. T. Grier. "Legal Consciousness and the Legacy of I. A. Ilyin."

Chiesa, Lorenzo & Raffaello Palumbo Mosca (Ed.). *Figures of the o/Other: Brother, Neighbor, Stranger, Enemy.* Genoa School of Humanities (GSH), 2016.

D'Alisa, Giacomo, Federico Demaria & Giorgos Kallis. *Degrowth. A vocabulary for a new era.* Routledge, London 2014.

de Haan, J. I. "Essence and Task of Legal Significs," p. 55–73.

Ehrlich, E. *Grundlegung der Soziologie des Rechts* 1913, [Fundamentals of the Sociology of Law], W. Moll, Tr. 1936.

Grimm, D., Fritz W. Scharpf & Ulrich K. Preuß. as well as the essay of Alain Supiot in: Johan van der Walt & Jeffrey Ellsworth (Eds.): *Constitutional Sovereignty and Social Solidarity in Europe*, Nomos Baden-Baden 2015.

Habermas, Jürgen. *The Crisis of the European Union*, Polity Press, 2012.

Hansen, M. H. *The Athenian Democracy in the Age of Demosthenes*, Oxford/Cambridge Mass. Athenian Citizens 457–309, Vol VII, p. 172–189, 1991.

———. "Demographic Reflections on the Number of Athenian Citizens," in: *American Journal of Ancient History*, Vol. VII.

Jones, A. H. M. *Athenian Democracy.* Baltimore, 1957.

Kokosi-Ostrov, Ann Olga. "Dura-Europos: Water, Baths, Latrines, and the Goddess Fortuna in a Desert City" in Lisa R. Brody & Gail. L. Hoffmann (Eds): *Dura Europos. Crossroads of Antiquity.* McMullen Museum of Art, Boston College, 2011.

Mauthner, Fritz. *Beiträge zu einer Kritik der Spache*, Stuttgart, 1901.
Padel, Ruth. "Making Space Speak" in J. J. Winkler & F. I. Zeitlin. (Eds): *Nothing to Do with Dionysos?* Princeton UP, 1990.
———. *In and Out of the Mind: Greek Images of the Tragic Self.* Princeton UP, 1992.
Peirce, C. S. *Works of Ch. S. Peirce.* Victoria Lady Welby and others.
Pickard-Cambridge, Sir Arthur. *The Dramatic Festivals of Athens.* (J. Could & D. M. Lewis, (Eds. 2nd Ed.) Oxford UP, 1988.
Popper, Karl. *The Open Society and its Enemies, (1945),* (5th Ed.) 9 1966.
Sinclair, R. K. *Democracy and Participation in Athens*, Cambridge UP, 1988.
Starr, Chester G. The *Birth of Athenian Democracy*, Oxford UP, 1990; H. W. Parke: *Festivals of the Athenians*, London 1977.
Stjernfelt, F. *Natural Propositions: The Actuality of Peirce's Doctrine of Dicisigns.* Boston, 2014.
Taylor, Charles. "Atomism" in: Shl. Averini & A. De-Shalit. (Eds): *Communitarianism and Individualism*, Oxford UP, 1992.
Thüry, Günter E. *Müll und Marmorsäulen. Siedlungshygiene in der römischen Antike.* Mainz, Zabern, 2001.
Vernant, J. P. *Les origines de la pensée grecque,* Paris, 1962 [Engl. Ed.: *The Origins of Greek Thought* Cornell UP, 1982].
Weck, Hermann. *Die Sprache im deutschen Recht*, Berlin, 1913.

Chapter 2

Sharing Conflict

Law, Justice, and the Street

Andrea Pavoni

In this chapter I explore the immanent normativity of everyday life in the city by looking at the notion of *shared space*, an urban design approach that challenges the segregation between traffic circulation and social interaction in which urban streetscapes are usually split. Focusing in particular on its current evolution in UK, I critically analyze its theoretical underpinnings vis-à-vis urban dialectics of risk and safety, comfort and anxiety, freedom and responsibility, within the frame of the contemporary process of neoliberal urbanization. At the same time, I also explore its implicit assumptions as regards law, space and the city, by tying what I see as the main shortcomings of the *shared space* approach to its failure to face the conflictual, heterogeneous and post-human quality of the urban. Notwithstanding its flaws (exacerbated in its UK version), and the related danger for *shared space* to be co-opted into capitalistic processes of urban valorization, I argue that *shared space* remains a valuable experiment in urban normativity, at the conceptual and strategic level, to rethink the relation between law, space, and justice against the perils of the current neoliberal condition. I develop this necessarily open-ended suggestion in the concluding section, through the notions of spatial justice. Prior to discuss *shared space*, three sections introduce the foundations of my approach: a complex ontology of the urban; a related spatial understanding of law or, more precisely, the "spatiolegal"; the historical condition of the contemporary "post-political" city.

THE URBAN

On the escort of the various "turns" (spatial, affective, material, post-human) in social science and humanities, I understand the urban as an immanent coming-together of bodies, a dense ecology of objects, people, ideas, noises, expectations, affect, agencies, movements.[1] "Whereas no singular logic or unity may be assumed" to account for this complexity, "the result is no simple displacement of the local by the global, of place by space, of history by simultaneity and flow, of small by big scale, or of the proximate by the remote. Instead, it is a subtle folding together" of such oppositions.[2] Exploring this post-human landscape requires abandoning any anthropocentric bias as well as the presupposition of a substantial separation between physical and ideological spaces, abstract structures and concrete everyday life, flows and solid rocks, discourses and buildings.[3] What is important is the way these elements "get" and "hold" together, how different scales overlap and clash within the urban, simultaneously contributing to its solidification as well as opening the potential for its alteration. Crucially, this agonistic matrix made of heterogeneous assemblages of bodies, multiple scales and juxtaposed spatiotemporalities, is neither overdetermined by suprastructures nor denied by incontrollable flows. Order and disorder coexist and overlap in the urban space, and thus the challenge is to find a way to account consistently for how the urban is *tuned*—that is, how normative orderings emerge immanently out of the common spacing of being-together, without resorting to conceptual binary traps, cumbersome dichotomies or dialectical promises.[4] Space is never simply chaotic or a neutral, "culturally-relative flat ontology but a tilted, power-structured surface."[5] It is by looking at the asymmetrical tunings shaping (without determining) the urban that a properly "spatial" and "material" grasp on how law functions in the city can be gained.

THE SPATIOLEGAL

Exploring law through these lenses requires a shift from its traditional understanding as a set of rules we rationally, cognitively and pragmatically decide to follow, or as a merely "social" pressure, as the classic sociological approach would pretend.[6] Law is partially so, but at the same time is a material and affective force, moving and ordering people, producing connections, often independently from, and in any case irreducible to, its supposed "truth-value."

Law is simultaneously a *project* aimed at manipulating, governing and channelling the urban into precise categories, boundaries and definitions; and a *process* emerging out of the intermingling of human and non-human, tangible and intangible bodies, as such inseparable from this continuum.[7] "Not merely operating 'through normative space,'" therefore, law "is normative space and normative body and normative movement,"[8] simultaneously a glorious spectacle projecting an idea of order and precision, a capillary apparatus of techniques and technologies that seeks to keep together such a projection, and an immanent ordering inseparable from its own spatiality.

Let us qualify. *First*, there is law's pretence "to possess the capacity to realise the harmony" between law and justice, violence and equality, between its always traumatic application to the world and its self-description as neutral, objective and necessary.[9] A self-description which, evidently, is also a self-justification, namely law's attempt to evacuate the political nature of its own operation.[10] *Second*, there is the "machinery of non-legal governance," that is, the bureaucratic, securitarian, economical operations and ramifications into which law blurs and through which law produces its subjects.[11] "What generalizes the power to punish—Foucault famously observed—is not the universal consciousness of the law in each juridical subject; it is the regular extension, the infinitely minute web of panoptic technique."[12] *Third*, there is the immanent and diffuse normativity resulting from the frictional coming together between legal abstractions, sociotechnical apparatus and the contingency of space. Bodies are never isolated but always imbricated in the materiality of co-belonging, in a sort of "atmospheric tension" exercising a permanent attraction on the collective. A *nomotop,* in Sloterdijk intriguing term, that is, the normative architecture of co-existence, a "moral ether" holding together the urban as a tensegritous system of immanent tensions in permanent "action" upon bodies, made of customs, cultures, objects, rights, regulations, affects, relations of production, language games, forms of life, institutions, habitus, etc.[13]

Before such a complex spatiolegality the limits of the critique of legal abstraction *per se* are evident. This critique assumes legal abstractions as an impalpable grid of categories and boundaries that deny the contingency, heterogeneity and complexity of sociospatial relations. Abstractions therefore, in this understanding, are negatively opposed to a "concrete" and supposedly more authentic spatiality. What is in this way overlooked, however, is that abstractions are never merely "abstract." They are at the same time abstract forms (e.g., the notion of "private sphere") as well as the concrete and historically situated relations through which these are actualized (i.e., a given affective, material and semiotic sociospatial formation).[14] Against their understanding "as a mere mask, fantasy, or diversion," we need to account for "the generative role that abstraction plays in disclosing and giving consistency to different kinds of worlds."[15] As Peter Goodrich observes, the production of legal subjects by law is not to be understood as a simple "extraction" (the meaning of the Latin term: *abstrahere*) of abstract figures (*personae*) from the social, but as at the same time the ontological production of "the spectacular space of the social" in which the "persons [are] catapulted."[16]

Understanding the productive, world-making role of legal abstractions is crucial, if we are to avoid reproducing their functioning, while pretending to deconstruct them. This is particularly relevant in relation to the supreme legal abstraction: the presupposition of a separation between law and space. As Carl Schmitt wrote: "every general rule demands a regular, everyday frame of life to which it can be factually applied and which is submitted to its regulations . . . a *homogeneous medium*. There exists no norm applicable to chaos."[17] What this oft-misunderstood passage refers to is the fact that legal categories are never a mere "partitioning" of the social, but that their very definition rests on a more "originary spatialisation that governs and makes possible every localisation and every territorialisation."[18] The legal *project*, in other words, is always premised on a preliminary flattening of the complex heterogeneity of space into a *tabula rasa*.

The anarchic tropes of (pre-legal) chaos, indeterminacy and disorder, it follows, far from embodying a radical challenge to the legal project, are its direct presupposition, that is, the space of exception the legal project requires, both to justify itself as well as draw its boundaries. If Hobbes obviously comes to mind, this reasoning is equally applicable to any attempt to overcome society's malaise and alienation in the direction of a more "original" condition, posited either as anarchic chaos or as peaceful and consensual togetherness. This is the trap in which many urban critiques fall, implicitly or explicitly, remaining hypnotized by the spectacular façade of the Law and, under the effect, embarking on the search for some more authentic and genuine substratum supposedly lying beneath. We are to see soon how this problem resurfaces in the case of *shared space*. Prior to do that, however, the historical urban condition in which this occurs needs to be dealt with.

IMMERSION

Notwithstanding at times succumbing to the temptation of apocalyptic descriptions, post-political theorists have described efficaciously the current neoliberal condition, as the systematic colonization and neutralization of the *political* (assumed as the space of agonistic encounter, contestation and dissensus) by means of technocratic and consensual mechanisms of governance.[19] The "post-political" city is accordingly a post-conflictual, consensual and uneventful space of socioeconomic transactions where conflict, dissensus and risks are (sought to be) neutralized or removed.[20] This is a useful observation, as long as we do not assume it in a totalizing fashion. Abstractions are always actualized in the contingency of a given locale: they take place in the turbulent singularity of everyday life, which always resists being fully translated into them.[21] Exploring the post-political city thus requires accounting simultaneously for its abstract form (namely, the locus of de-politicized consensus) as well as the concrete sociospatial relations in and through which this form is concretely actualized in the urban space. Peter Sloterdijk offers a compelling way to understand conceptually and explore empirically this condition, by assuming it as the result of a process of *interiorization*.

Not one afraid of grand narratives, Sloterdijk conceives this process as the direct consequence of the claustrophobic closure of the world that globalization (as a physical, sociocultural and techno-mediated process) has brought about. If the prior epoch was one of *expansion*—exemplified in the unilateral movement towards the unknown of missionaries, conquerors, explorers—the current is one of *interiorization*, in which a novel "aesthetic of immersion" would recalibrate expansionists hubris into the projectual task of arranging our being-together within a dense and limited space.[22] Enter the society of comfort. Interiorization is the historical process of integration of social life into a series of technological, normative, affective and physical enclosures, as result of which the everyday life is increasingly molded within safe, comforting, commodified and entertaining spaces, relations and practices, from which any risk must be expunged. This historical evolution is directly shaped by an ontological "explicitation," that is, the gradual surfacing of a shared awareness about the common spaces on which life depends. What has become explicit, Sloterdijk explains, is our ontological essence as space-creating being, always "inhabiting the outside" through a "praxis of world-making," and thus co-producing tangible and intangible "interiors" whereby we guarantee our physical and affective immunity.[23] Although this awareness does not only belong to our epoch, it is in the latter (especially from the end of 19th century onwards) that it reaches a certain degree of consistency among various disciplines and practices, propelling the emergence of a properly "spatial" awareness. From chemical warfare to novel disciplines like interior design, from the emersion of stadia to the evolution of experience economy, from phenomenological thinking to installation art: different ideas, disciplines and practices thus converged in assuming the urban and its space, rhythms and atmospheres—hitherto intangible, implicit, invisible—as a tangible and explicit *field of mission*, immunization and projectuality, in which questions of control, entertainment, culture, market, aesthetics, sociality, politics, art and even death would be played out.[24] Such a novel awareness of the co-constitutive spatiality of co-existence signifies a renewed attention to our "co-fragile" condition, and thus the surfacing of a new immunitary ethos: the shift from a theological to an immunological paradigm.[25]

Whatever its limits and unavoidable simplifications, the significance of this narrative rests in offering a resolutely spatial lens to capture the convergence between immunity and consumption—or securitized safety and commodified comfort—in the contemporary city, whose everyday life is increasingly acclimatized by comfort, immunized by security and excited by entertainment. A convergence that, more prosaically, Thrift has captured with the notion of *security-entertainment complex*.[26] What is of peculiar interest for the present discussion is the resulting configuration of responsibilization and delegation. In a post-holistic world, Klauser suggests, "immunity and integrity are not to be gained from the submission to a larger whole, but must be achieved as the outcome of a personal effort of seclusion."[27] Hence the surfacing of what Dean terms a "new prudentialism," that is, "the multiple "responsibilization" of individuals, families, households, and communities for their own risks."[28] The urban dweller is thus required "constant preparedness" in the form of a pervasive need to rehearse one's capacity to perform and provide for one's own security: *do not become a crime victim*, as a common sign in the London underground effectively suggests.[29] At the same time this condition is tied to ever-wider possibilities for delegation. From the looming presence of surveillance technologies to the omnipresent possibility of litigation to the self-referential circularity of health and safety regulations, the urban space is populated by texts, devices, technologies and other legal proxies to which the responsibility to act vis-à-vis the unexpected may be delegated, in this way reducing redundancy and decreasing the "risk" of conflict. As a result, the very notion of risk undergoes a significant reformulation.

While danger may be described as the inherent potential for harm, adversity or injury in some person, event or thing, risk is a measure of that potential's likelihood and consequences/impact.[30] Although risk has always been at the core of governance, in the contemporary society we observe significant shift. Whereas Garland highlighted the transition of State from provider of welfare to manager of risk, Clear and Cadora add a useful qualification, by pointing out a further, social-control related shift from *risk management*—according to which the existence of risk and thus uncertainty is deemed inevitable and sought to be minimized—to *risk control*, according to which risk is not accepted, but rather must be prevented, avoided and erased, even to the detriment of individual life-choice.[31] Corollary is the absolutization of the value of safety and, with an apparently paradoxical consequence, the increase in the feeling of vulnerability.[32] Whether, as Hacking observes, risk could be understood as a modulator of the relationship between fear and harm, today these two elements are conflated, since fear (as well as anxiety) is singled out as a harm *per se*, with a corollary *right to be free from fear* surfacing.[33] Nowhere is this more evident as in Anti-Social Behaviour regulations, where what is criminalized is exactly a "conduct which caused or was likely to cause harm, harassment, alarm or distress."[34]

As a result, the ongoing self-responsibilization for one's own safety is matched by systematic delegation. Not only fear but even distress and discomfort are conditions whose resolution we are supposed to delegate to legal and security apparatuses.[35] As Sloterdijk argues, after Arnold Ghelen, this configuration is the very cypher of the comfort society: the constitution of a generalized system of "disburdening," or relief, from necessities and responsibilities.[36]

To understand this seemingly contradictory configuration of simultaneous responsibilization and de-responsibilization, let us take *Health and Safety Legislations.*[37] In these perfectly self-referential regulations, the matter of health and safety is not directly related to the achievement of *actual* health and safety but rather to the performance of "correct procedures." The key issue at stake here is the immunization of anyone from the risk of being "held responsible." This logic "demands a self-policing, premised not upon any sense of justice or responsibility, but *liability*, i.e., what one can get away with."[38] As a result, responsibility is reduced to the task of carving out spaces of delegation, via sociotechnical proxies, in which safety from the risk of being held responsible may be achieved. This condition of *horizontal separation via vertical delegation* systematically immunizes the urban against the ethical need to perform "responsible gestures" in reaction to unexpected occurrences. Although for long time urban thinkers have discussed the detrimental effects of this condition on ways of acting and being that may be defined as "ethical" and thus, we may argue, on the very possibility of justice in the city,[39] it is in the contemporary city that this seems to be most explicitly actualized. In the next part of this chapter this observation will be clarified by looking at the *shared space* approach, which emerges exactly as a challenge to existent dialectics of risk/safety, comfort/anxiety and freedom/responsibility in the contemporary city. The next section introduces the approach in the context of street traffic politics.

SHARING SEGREGATION

The "new mobilities paradigm" proposes to understand movement as the defining condition of modernity.[40] In the same way as geographers propose the notion of place to provide with sociocultural and material significance the abstract notion of location, so mobility is employed to shift from an abstract concept of movement (as a temporaneous condition of a body moving between two stable states) to a "socially produced motion," a condition that does not simply "move," but shapes and constitutes, the bodies in movement.[41]

Accordingly, people movement is not simply understood as the result of a voluntary decision of individual bodies, but as a process shaped by the interplay of images, regulations, affects, technologies and human and non-human bodies, organized in hierarchies, disparities and conflicts, whose complexity has an immediate sociopolitical significance. Traffic politics makes not exception. In the words of Kotanyi and Vaneigem, traffic circulation, which they define as the "supreme stage of city planning," is "the organization of universal isolation. As such, it constitutes the major problem of modern cities. It is the opposite of encounter: it absorbs the energies that could otherwise be devoted to encounters or to any sort of participation."[42] Putting aside its slightly grandiloquent rhetoric, the quote emphasizes the key aspect of the way traffic politics have evolved in the last century, that is, the fracture between (vehicular) circulation and (social) interaction. This was the direct result of a reductionist understanding of movement as point-to-point travel, whose key qualities are speed, efficiency and safety. This perspective prioritizes fastest forms of transport (i.e., motorized, especially cars), marginalizing other movements such a walking, as well as, more generally, other less purposeful ways to go about in the city, that are not directly connected with the cycle of production and consumption: from *flaneurie* to sitting and lying down (impaired by the routine removal of seating or the placing of pikes and other "hostile architecture" tools), from skating to simply "doing nothing," etc.[43]

As a result, the streetscape is split into a separation between pedestrian and cars, enforced through physical demarcations, legal regulations, security personnel and technological devices.[44] In UK, this trend towards binary segregation found its culmination, as well as the implicit germs of its subsequent contestation, in two influential reports: *Traffic in Towns*, published in 1963 by Colin Buchanan, and *Roads in Urban Areas*, by the Ministry of Transport in 1966.[45] As Hamilton-Baillie underlines, these reports reasserted the principle of segregation by keeping strictly separated the principal functions of the street (car traffic and social interaction).[46] Yet, at the same time Buchanan's work introduced a notion—"environmental areas," that is, residential areas insulated from car traffic, whose evolution would eventually morph into a challenge to the very logic of separation the report apparently sealed. Environmental areas are zones in which the criteria of "environmental capacity—referring to a series of attributes such as social activity, pollution, noise, pedestrians etc.—is to be prioritized in the definitions of road standards.[47] The idea of urban streets in which "the quality of living comes first" thus began to seep in.[48]

Although not well received in UK, the report would prove influential in the Netherlands, where it inspired Dutch engineers Nick de Boer and Joost Váhl to develop an approach that, besides being oriented to the quality of life of urban streets, did not take for granted the separation between traffic and social interaction.[49] The concept of *woonerf*, that is, "living yard," was thus coined. The *woonerf* is basically an area where a series of traffic calming measures are put in place, street and curbs are leveled so as to create a common surface for different users, and a set of aesthetic criteria (art, street furniture etc.) are implemented to increase comfort and livability.[50] Based on the logic of integrated uses, the *woonerf* provides "a type of "gestalt" message that streets belong to residents," without necessarily separating the space from car circulation.[51]

Applied in various instances around Europe, the concept was somewhat slower to migrate back into UK. Here, propelled by emerging works on "livability" that fostered a shift towards "social" criteria over strictly functional ones (efficiency, safety and speed) in street politics,[52] it would partially resurface in the notion of *home zones,* proposed by Barbara Preston in 1992.[53] In fact, the notion of *home zone,* conceived in the face of a worrying trend in child casualties on the street, did not address questions of street functions and design, and simply focused on the legal aspect: its proposal was to hold accountable any driver injuring child pedestrians in the designated zones. Although never fully implemented, the concept had a significant influence on local authorities, stimulating a series of more sensible approaches to the regulation and design of the everyday life in the street.[54] However, it would only be in 2007, with the *Manual for Streets for England and Wales,* that this tendency would take a more concrete shape, developing into the notion of *shared space*. Differentiating them from *roads*—"highways whose main function is accommodating the movement of motor traffic"—the *Manual* defines *streets* as areas "typically lined with buildings and public spaces" in which, "while movement is still a key function, there are several others, of which the place function is the most important."[55] Thus the place-making potential of streets is explicitly prioritized over transport, emphasizing their significance as places that "fulfil a complex variety of functions in order to meet people's needs as places for living, working and moving around in."[56] Although still employing the term *home zones*, this report sanctioned a decisive move in government thinking towards the *shared space* concept, officialized in 2011 with a homonymous *Local Transport Note.*[57]

As for the *woonerf*, the notion of *shared space* originated in the Netherlands. Introduced and experimented in the 80s in northeast Dutch villages by Hans Monderman and the Keuning Institute, the concept gained widespread popularity in the last decade, especially after becoming a European Cooperation Project (2004–2008) to be tested in seven EU nations. A radicalized version of the *woonerf* concept, *shared space* contrasts the notion of segregation with that of integration, by removing any separation and hierarchical differentiation between road users (car-drivers, pedestrians, cyclists), not only by lowering pavement to street level but also eliminating traditional traffic-control signs and devices (signs, street lights, zebra crossings), substituted with visual and tactile cues on the surface, such as different colors and textures.[58] The task, as the leading UK proponents Hamilton-Baillie puts it, is that of "re-writing the language of separation" by modifying the approach to planning, design, decision making, and more importantly to develop, in Monderman terms, "a common vision about how public space can work."[59]

The presupposition is that, for this to occur, it is required to move "away from regulated, legislated traffic toward space which, by the way it's designed and configured, makes it clear what sort of behavior is anticipated."[60]

At the culmination of a long-lasting shift in traffic thinking, *shared space* seems to comply with Bonham's wish for a street politics able "to take into account the many other motivations and meanings that people attach to their travel."[61] Yet, is this approach able to more radically call into question "the present day ordering and prioritization of certain travellers (specifically motorists)?"[62] Facing its surge in popularity, many quantitative and (rather less) qualitative studies have been carried out to assess its impact, with various and discordant results. Touching some of them, in the following pages I will explore the explicit as well as implicit theoretical assumptions informing this concept, vis-à-vis the understanding of the spatiolegal proposed above. By doing so, I will be able to show its key limits and, at the same time, its strategic potentials.

SHARING RISK

Himself one of the most vociferous proponent, John Adams' approach to risk is a key theoretical underpinning of the *shared space* model. Adams challenges the way in which in traffic politics the question of risk has been organized, according to a systematic deference of non-car vis-à-vis car users, tied to an increasing obsession for insurance claims, over-reliance on technical fixes and a culture of technological determinism, whose paramount concern is allowing for the highest possible volume of traffic in streets.[63] As we saw, the result is a streetscape shaped by the quest for maximum capacity and efficiency of traffic flows, calculated by traffic engineers and designed by highway engineers, where social interaction and encounter are unlikely to occur and "good accident record is purchased at the cost of community severance."[64] According to Adams, "safety literature almost universally ignores the potential loss of reward consequent on behaviour that is too safe. Its ambition is to eliminate all accidents."[65] Not only Adams emphasizes that what is valuable in the public space is not necessarily what is safer. His theory of "suitable risk" more ambitiously implies that danger, and more precisely the feeling of uncertainty that the removal of delegating proxies supposedly generates, is counter-intuitively conducive to greater safety.

Developing this argument around such regulations as those concerning the compulsory use of seat belts or cycle helmets, Adams explains that these legal, physical and semiotic devices actually shift the acceptable threshold of risk-taking, prompting more risky behavior on the account that a greater protection is offered. The subsequent increase in risk quickly compensates for the gain in safety provided by these devices in the first place. Seat belts and cycle helmets would thus function as delegating proxies by de-responsibilizing individuals from the need to take care of themselves and thus fostering ever-riskier behaviors.

Whereas street politics is normally grounded on the overarching assumption that "potential conflict and friction between different activities could be designed-out through planning and regulation."[66] Adams counters that it is the very removal of these elements, by means of producing a feeling of unease and insecurity, to ultimately increase mutual attention and thus safe behavior, re-responsibilizing individuals (especially car-drivers) for the safety of others. As a consequence, "drivers and pedestrians naturally become more attentive and engaged, prompting drivers to reduce speeds and drive more safely," in this way redistributing the burden of risk and "giving pedestrians more control."[67]

The reliance of *shared space* on environmental clues is implicitly informed by Gibson's theory of "affordance," according to which the environment would provide affordances that, though not determining, shape individual behavior by offering more or less preferable options for action.[68] On the one hand, the *shared space* approach can be understood as part of a wider "post-moral" shift in urban governance from *law-abiding* citizens to *efficient* users, most notably exemplified in UK with the concept of *nudging.*[69] Surfaced to popularity with New Labour, this strategy intends to prompt behavior modification by acting on the contextual affordances, representations and institutional practices that constitute the "local installations" of society, thus reconfiguring politics as "scientific" nudging enterprise.[70] On the other hand, however, *shared space* simultaneously appears to counter this trend. Its environmental design, in fact, does not aim to reduce and minimize anxiety and insecurity but rather to unleash them, thus severing the apparatus of vertical delegation and thus forcing individuals to re-responsibilize themselves, in this way countering the paternalistic *Nanny State* assumption of urban dwellers as being "completely oblivious to dangers in the environment around" them.[71] In this sense, *shared space* appears as a potential antidote to the post-political anaesthetization of modern urban life and its apparent necessity, in Chatterton Williams' polemical words, to revolve "around never feeling less than fully at ease."[72]

At the same time however, *shared space* appears to rely on some problematic implicit assumptions. First, the romantic presupposition of a somewhat more authentic form of being-together that would prevail once the alienating force of law is removed. Second, a reductive understanding of law as written texts and technical devices, as such unable to grasp the role law plays in shaping the immanent normativity of the urban. As result of these limits, we are to see, the political value of *shared space* is eventually neutralized and its model reduced to an aesthetic device easily co-opted by neoliberal logics of place valorization. Let us articulate this point in details.

SHARING DISCONTENTS

With its emphasis on the "human beings and their manifold activities," Hans Moderman was convinced, *shared space* would allow for "interpersonal understanding" to replace "priority rules" in the street.[73] Countering the neglect of human perspective that Adams diagnosed as the main flaw of safety literature, this would permit to progress "away from the regulating highway towards using the natural skills humans are blessed with to negotiate movement" and "to resolve potential conflict through informal protocols and human interaction prompted by clues from the built environment."[74]

It would be perhaps too much to expect a post-human language from *shared space* literature. Yet it is worth noting that in its conceptual elaboration the environment only appears as a background reality from which rational human beings are able to extract themselves, so as to take right decisions, stimulated by positive anxiety, prompted by built environment, and guided by mutual sympathy. However, interaction in the street is not simply among humans, not even simply between humans and non-humans, but rather emerges across an assemblage populated by complex bodies, spaces and structures that do not fall within such neat categories. This ontology is incompatible with the notion of freedom implicitly grounding *shared space* model, namely a de-spatialized, autonomous free will allowing to overcome uncertainty in rational and empathic fashion. Agency in the street is not centralized, unilateral, anthropocentric and intentional, but rather *distributed* across a complex, heterogeneous and post-human assemblage.[75] This is not to deny freedom but rather to prompt its reformulation. Philippopoulos-Mihalopoulos does it convincingly, following Spinoza:

> Freedom is a responsibility, and the responsibility of freedom is to unveil the illusion of freedom (in the sense of free will) and allow this to inform our knowledge of the causes for which bodies move the way they do. No body decides its own fate, not because there is a teleology that determines it, but because a body is part of a continuum.[76]

This understanding points to a situated ethics in which acting is always dependent on one's position within a complex assemblage. This strategic attitude opens up a complexity that should not "demotivate" action, as some argues, but rather emphasizes that action always occurs within a given spatial situation, against the perils that the illusion of abstract freedom produces.[77]

Illusion that, I argue, is directly responsible for SS's naïve understanding of conflict, and the consequent failure to acknowledge crucial power asymmetries in the street.

According to Department of Transport, "sharing" is "the ability and willingness of pedestrians, facilitated by the sympathetic behaviour of motorists and others to move freely around the street."[78] Such ideal depiction of urban interaction is opposed to the alienating effects of government intrusion and rule-making, usually in explicitly libertarian fashion. In the words of Monderman,

> . . . wherever you have the freedom in making your own choices without government interfering you learn what it means to be a free civilian in a free country. But whenever government takes over your decision, you can't develop your own evaluations anymore . . . rules diminish our opportunities to act as good citizens, so instead we get public space that is horrible and we get behaviour that is anti-social.[79]

Libertarianism, humanism and the belief in the good will of urbanites converge in this depiction of *shared space* as a sort of post-political "differential space" in which a more authentic, originary and post-conflictual (spontaneous, sympathetic . . .) interaction, lying beneath the rule-led urban alienation, will be restored by means of environmental design. *Shared space* proponents thus fall neatly within a well-worn urban theory path, where present-day alienation is contrasted through an oft-nostalgic yearning for more genuine ways of being-together (usually posited as pre-capitalist, pre-consumerist, pre-legal).[80] A position that rests on a series of problematic dichotomies (local vs. global, concrete vs. abstract, genuine vs. alienating, non-law vs. law etc.), which are theoretically unproductive, disturbingly moralistic and strategically de-politicizing, as well as unwittingly prone to co-optation by conservative politics, that on the priority of authenticity, roots and soil have always been grounded.

The implicit assumption here is that the removal of law's semiotic, physical and technical devices would unleash a homogenous, egalitarian and pre-legal space, in which individual autonomy would be reasserted, as a freedom to navigate frictionlessly in the consensual space of reason and common sense, overcoming uncertainty and disagreement through the sympathetic force of inter-subjective agreement. What is implied is that the productive effect of legal abstractions on the urban simply depends on law's operational devices (e.g., signs, demarcations, speed limits etc.). As shown above, however, the spatiolegal is more complex than that. Removing such devices won't unleash a utopian space of pre-legal sociality—just like, incidentally, it won't plunge the street into a "law of the jungle," as some critics rather too emotionally suggest.[81] Both interpretations belong to the same misunderstanding of space, and both testify for the hypnotizing force of legal abstractions. Space, in fact, is implicitly understood as an "innocent," homogenous and malleable matter, from which power relations can be decoupled and normative asymmetries flattened, so as to unfold a neutral substance to be re-modeled through design. Yet, space is not neutral or innocent but heterogeneous and asymmetrical, a tilted surface traversed by conflicts, power relations and normative tunings which can be challenged, reoriented, modified but never eliminated. This is, in the most radical sense of the spatial turn, what reinserting the "political" into space means. Ignoring this aspect, instead, equates to performing the symmetrically opposite move: namely, to "reframe the political as a purely *environmental* matter."[82]

This is evident for instance in the peculiar fact that both the "shared" and the "segregated" model seem to be informed by the same implicit assumption about conflict. Whereas the "traffic segregation" approach aims to prevent conflict and frictions through strict design- and rule-led segregation, *shared space* proceeds from the symmetrical assumption that the removal of segregating devices will lead, through uncertainty and anxiety, to pacific interaction. For all their apparent differences, eventually both models remain convinced of the possibility to expunge conflict from the urban. If the segregation model assumes and seeks to overcome conflict, *shared space* appears to go as far as dismissing its very possibility (conflict, in fact, is reduced to consensus-inducing uncertainty). Consequently, *shared space* appears eventually unable, as one critic observes, to "provide a mechanism or real political movement for challenging the dominance of the car in cities: it is overly theoretical and idealistic, and doesn't address real issues of power and intimidation."[83]

This emerges manifestly in the case of the most vulnerable category: blind people, obviously unable to employ the array of "visual cues" through which *shared space* re-organizes the streetscape.[84] As Rob Imrie argues, "the diverse subject-positions of vision-impaired people are neither recognized nor, consequentially, given a platform to influence, with any ease, the shaping of shared space."[85] Discrimination occurs both within shared spaces and at the level of decision-making. Consistent with the wider shift towards "participation" and "community engagement" in urban governance, also *shared space* is usually presented as grounded on an inclusive decision-making process. Post-political theorists have deeply deconstructed this rhetoric, showing its reliance on a claustrophobic notion of participation, namely as mere inclusion within a horizon whose parameters have already been set in advance, and real dissensus pre-emptively designed out.[86] UK-based *shared space* seems to make no exception to this pattern. In local debates, in fact, the desirability of *shared space*—tied to seemingly incontestable values such as "health, wellbeing and safety"—is usually positioned beyond contestation, with community participation reduced to "prosaic matters relating to specific design details to 'help identify any operational problems.'"[87]

To sum up, three are the main shortcomings of the *shared space* model. First—and mirroring what Bonham diagnosed as the main problem of the segregation model—the bodies that fall outside the *shared space* norm continue to be excluded and discriminated.[88] Second, the dogma of "inviolability of the automobile" remains unchallenged. As Imrie caustically observes, "shared space has appeal to politicians and policy-makers precisely because it does not destabilize, or challenge, the centrality of the motor vehicle's presence in the environment, or seek to displace or remove it from town centres."[89] Third, the de-politicization of *shared space* often leads to prioritize de-contextualized aesthetic principles over strategic and contextual "political" questions. Take for instance the Department for Transport's advice against "more conventional street design features" because they "may compromise the original vision and purpose of the scheme."[90] In the words of a blogger, "a pedestrian crossing is anathema to the "naked streets" tenet of the "shared space" philosophy . . . they are primarily concerned with making a street *look* attractive, rather than *making* it attractive."[91]

This seems to be particularly the case in UK model where the parable of *shared space* is akin to that of many initiatives that, starting with a somewhat radical impulse, are eventually de-politicized into merely aesthetic rhetorics to be standardly replicated on the urban. Nowhere as in UK, in fact, "from a neighbourhood and community based inclusive facility," *shared space* has been hurriedly "rolled onto highways and mainstream roads in town and city centres."[92] In this sense, the failure to keep into account both its historical origin and the specific contexts of application has led to dilute its significance, de-prioritizing its most subversive potential in favor of "the more artistic, creative and place-making aspects."[93] As a result, *shared space* risks becoming a (de-spatialized) "spatial fix," ironically not so dissimilarly from the very technological fixes Adams despises, and as such vulnerable to co-optation by neoliberal politics as a tool for the capitalistic valorization of public space.

What is there to be saved then? In the next, concluding section, I argue that notwithstanding these limits *shared space* should not be jettisoned, since it remains extremely valuable at both the conceptual and strategic level. To unfold this potential, however, its logic and application should be disentangled from any suspicious logic of liberation and tied to a fully strategic notion of (spatial) justice.

SHARING CONFLICT

Spatial justice is a recent and particularly promising attempt at conceptualizing the relation between justice and space.[94] In the last decades various concepts, mainly coming from the field of geography, have been mobilized for such purpose (e.g., territorial justice, environmental justice, just city, right to the city, etc.), instigated by the intent to insert a novel sensibility to the spatial dynamics of injustice, especially in the city. These notions provided a spatial perspective on social justice, as well as tool to spatialize political debates and social struggles, advocating for a geographically equitable distribution of resources, services, and access. However, for the most part they fell short of integrating the premises of the spatial turn, and thus an understanding of the urban in its heterogeneous and assembled, conflictual and post-human, asymmetrical and tuned nature. This often led to dilute the strategic potential of these concepts, making them vulnerable to co-optation, a fate arguably encountered already by notions such as participation, sustainability, social capital and the likes. Weakly crafted concepts easily become Trojan horses to foster consensus for conservative politics, while foreclosing more promising ones.[95]

This is also a risk spatial justice runs, whether it is assumed as mere shorthand for "social justice in space."[96] Contrary to that, and faithful to the radical impetus of the spatial turn, spatial justice is meant to wrest the "social" away from justice, by asserting justice's always-already spatial character. Spatial justice, in this sense, is meant to materialize the original meaning encapsulated in the Greek notion of *Dike*, as a persistent incompatibility with a given state of affairs. Not a matter of rearranging the status quo (e.g., distributive justice), but rather a possibility to rupture it, and strategically retune it. Not the post-conflictual utopia that notions such as "just city" gesture towards, or the "ultimate goal of many planning policies," as Marcuse defines it.[97] If there is anything the notion of justice should problematize is exactly the anxiety for "result" and "solution" that characterizes contemporary urban policies.[98] Rather than the "antidote" to spatial injustices many would wish for,[99] spatial justice is more fruitfully understood as a *pharmakon*: simultaneously a remedy and a poison, insofar as unfolding the inevitability of conflict, the impossibility to purge it from space, and the necessity to address it for any emancipatory politics.

Spatial justice is a way to *do justice* to space (in the sense of addressing its complex ontology) as well as *rescue justice* from its dilution into participatory and consensual post-political procedures. This is why it is *not* meant to be a solution. "While acknowledging and working through the impossibility of a solution—Philippopoulos-Mihalopoulos observes—spatial justice brings forth the conditions of such an impossibility, thereby allowing a flicker of possibility to stream through."[100] A simultaneously *modest* and *strategic* position thus ensues. Modest, not in the sense of a renunciation to act, but of asserting the awareness of our positional (ethical) responsibility vis-à-vis the assemblages in which we are. Strategic, since requiring a situated praxis aimed to *act* on the asymmetries, disparities and conflicts of the urban, rather than pretending to transcend them into post-conflictual utopias.

Giorgio Agamben defines as *destituent* a strategy according to which "something—a power, a function, a human operation—is made inoperose without being simply destroyed, but rather freeing the potentialities that there remained non-actualised, in this way allowing a different use of them."[101]

Crucially, this does not mean "liberating" some sort of neutral, power-free and authentic space lying beneath the alienating and violent world of power relations. Unplugging an existent configuration of power, means releasing a conflictual space in which negotiation must be responsibly carried out, so as to reorient the residual power towards alternative configurations, whose desirability cannot be postulated in advance, but requires to be assessed and tested every time.[102] *Unplug* and *reorient*: a formula for an urban strategy that does not endeavor to produce just cities according to criteria supposedly beyond contestation, conflict and politics—it rather seeks to release them. In fact, whether comfort societies, as we saw, are characterized by the production of spaces of consensual de-responsibilization in the city, then spatial justice, insofar as reasserting the situated, collective, post-human, and relational quality of responsibility, may be said to potentially emerge every time such apparatuses are deactivated, plunging bodies into a conflict that must be responsibly addressed. "Spatial justice is the movement out of this conflict while delving deeper into it," Philippopoulos-Mihalopoulos reminds.[103]

Therefore, whilst dismantling the pernicious effects of existent power structures is arguably the required step of any emancipatory politics, it is never an emancipatory more *per se*. This is where the limits of *shared space* emerge. By means of removing the semio-material proxies to which responsibility is routinely delegated, *shared space* dismantles the structure of disburdening that shapes contemporary street politics. It is a "re-burdening" enterprise, that is, which by restoring a situated responsibility, opens an epistemological space for conceiving an alternative approach to the question of urban vulnerability, as well as an ontological and thus ethical space for action in which delegation, so to speak, is re-territorialized onto the situation itself, and thus opened to the conflictual contingency of spatial justice. What is to be shared, here, is conflict itself. Yet, this is exactly the conclusion that *shared space* proponents ultimately miss. Its potential to retune the configuration of conflict, power and law in the urban space is in fact neutralized as *shared space* is understood as being conducive to an idealized togetherness from which exactly conflict, power and law would be apparently expunged. Hence the uncritical assumption of *shared space* as being *per se* conducive to a more desirable urban space. The approach risks to fail, in other words, exactly insofar as falling short of carrying out its radical potential.

Unplugging the spatial apparatus of segregation is not the end point but rather the beginning of an urban praxis that must be necessarily followed by the delicate task of strategically addressing the situation thus unleashed, so as to constructively retune it towards potentially emancipatory outcomes, whilst preventing suffocating power structures from resurfacing in other forms. What this may require, specifically, cannot be said in advance, but evidently such an endeavor can neither be left to spontaneity or aesthetic purism. At the same time, it should not indulge into the simple condemnation of the immunitary quest for comfort in the city—a temptation, moreover, whose Fascist nuances should warn us against.[104] The urban question is not one of liberating us from the conflict, stress and asymmetries that shape the city, but rather of dwelling into them in the effort to find emancipatory ways of tuning our being together, eschewing anarchic fantasies of anti-normativity, disorder and unpredictability, whilst remaining vigilant vis-à-vis the oppressive effects that any normative stabilization may produce.

NOTES

1. My understanding of body is inspired by the Deleuzian take on Spinoza: "a body can be anything: it can be an animal, a body of sounds, a mind or idea; it can be a linguistic corpus, a social body, a collectivity." Gilles Deleuze. *Spinoza, Practical Philosophy* (City Lights Books, 1988), 127.

2. Ash Amin and Nigel Thrift, *Cities: Reimagining the Urban* (Wiley, 2002), 150. Ash Amin, "Rethinking the Urban Social," *City* 11, 1 (2007): 103.

3. For example, Alan Latham and Derek P. McCormack. "Moving Cities: Rethinking the materialities of urban geographies." *Progress in Human Geography* 28, 6 (2004). Marcus Doel, *Poststructuralist Geographies: The Diabolical Art of Spatial Science* (Rowman & Littlefield, 1999).

4. On the notion of tuning see Andrea Pavoni, "Exceptional Tunings. Controlling Urban Events," PhD diss. *University of Westminster,* 2013.

5. Andreas Philippopoulos-Mihalopoulos, *Spatial Justice: Body, Lawscape, Atmosphere* (Routledge, 2015), 3.

6. Both positivist and socio-legal models, most famously Hart's notion of "social pressure," frame law only with reference to social power and/or mutual communication and conformity to pre-agreed rules by subjects—thereby missing the role played by its immanent and material normativity in "tuning" the social. H. L. A. Hart, *The Concept of Law* (Oxford University Press, 1997), 84.

7. The distinction between *project* and *project* is inspired by its use Moore's vis-à-vis Capitalism. Jason W. Moore, *Capitalism in the Web of Life: Ecology and the Accumulation of Capital*, (Verso, 2015).

8. Philippopoulos-Mihalopoulos, *Spatial Justice*, 69.

9. This is the "real nature" of law's hubris, according to Massimo Cacciari, *L'Arcipelago* (Adelphi, 1997), 51 (my translation).

10. See Costas Douzinas, Peter Goodrich, and Yifat Hachamovitch, *Politics, Postmodernity and Critical Legal Studies: The Legality of the Contingent* (Routledge, 1994).

11. Peter Goodrich, "The Theatre of Emblems: On the Optical Apparatus and the Investiture of Persons." *Law, Culture and the Humanities* 8, 1 (2012): 48.

12. Michel Foucault, *Discipline & Punish: The Birth of the Prison* (Vintage, 1995), 224.

13. Peter Sloterdijk, *Tome 3, Ecumes, Sphérologie plurielle* (Hachette Littératures, 2006), 420. Sloterdijk takes the notion of *tensegrity* from architect and theorists Buckminster Fuller, to refer to a "social" made by assemblages whose consistency does not depend on transcendent principles, abstract structures or metaphysical framework, but rather on the mutual tension between their components.

14. David Cunningham, "The Concept of Metropolis: Philosophy and Urban Form," *Radical Philosophy* 133 (2005).

15. The quotes are respectively from Alberto Toscano, "The Open Secret of Real Abstraction," *Rethinking Marxism* 20, 2 (2008): 274; and Derek McCormack, "Geography and Abstraction: Towards an Affirmative Critique." *Progress in Human Geography* 36, 6 (2012): 727.

16. Goodrich "The Theatre of Emblems," 59.

17. Carl Schmitt, *Political Theology: Four Chapters on the Concept of Sovereignty* (University of Chicago Press, 2006), 13 (my emphasis).

18. Giorgio Agamben, *Homo Sacer: Sovereign Power and Bare Life* (Stanford University Press, 1998), 111.

19. For example, Jacques Rancière, "Ten Theses on Politics," *Theory & Event* 5, 3 (2001). Slavoj Žižek, *The Ticklish Subject: the Absent Centre of Political Ontology* (Verso, 2000).

20. For example, Eric Swyngedouw, *Designing the Post-Political City and the Insurgent Polis* (Bedford Press, 2011).

21. Anna Tsing Lowenhaupt, "On nonscalability. The Living World Is Not Amenable to Precision-Nested Scales." *Common Knowledge* 18, 3 (2012).

22. Peter Sloterdijk, *In the World Interior of Capital: Towards a Philosophical Theory of Globalization* (Polity Press, 2013), 171.

23. "To inhabit always means to build spheres." Peter Sloterdijk, *Sfere I, Bolle* (Meltemi, 2009), 82 (my translation).

24. Sloterdijk, *Ecumes,* 443–463.

25. Sloterdijk, *Ecumes*, 477.

26. "A complex made up of two particular linked assemblages which have gained increasing purchase by feeding off each other." Nigel Thrift, "LifeworldInc—and What to Do About It," *Environment and Planning D: Society and Space* 29, 1 (2011): 7.

27. Francisco Klauser, "Splintering Spheres of Security: Peter Sloterdijk and the Contemporary Fortress City," *Environment and Planning D: Society and Space* 28, 2 (2010): 338.

28. Anders Fogh Jensen, *The Project Society* (Unipress, 2012). Michael Dean, *Governmentality: Power and Rule in Modern Society* (Thousand Oaks, 1999), 162.

29. James Hay, "Designing Homes to be the First Line of Defense," *Cultural Studies* 20, 4 (2006).

30. David Garland, "Risk," in *Risk and Morality,* ed. Richard V. Ericson and Aaron Doyle (University of Toronto Press, 2003), 50.

31. Todd R. Clear, and Eric Cadora, "Risk and community Practice," in *Crime, Risk and Justice*, ed. K. Stenson and R. R. Sullivan (Devon, Willan Publishing, 2001). Obvious reference here is Ulrich Beck, "The Terrorist Threat: World Risk Society Revisited," *Theory, Culture and Society* 19, 4 (2002).

32. Enter the safety-paradox: The more the society is controlled and normalised, the more "variations" from the norm are singled out as dangerous. Michalis Lianos and Mary Douglas "Dangerization and the End of Deviance: The Institutional Environment," *British Journal of Criminology,* 40 (2000).

33. Ian Hacking, "Risk and Dirt," in *Risk and Morality*, ed. Richard V. Ericson and Aaron Doyle (University of Toronto Press, 2003), 27. See also Peter Ramsay, "The Theory of Vulnerable Autonomy and the Legitimacy of the Civil Preventative Order." *LSE Legal Studies Working Paper,* 1 (2008).

34. *UK Crime and Disorder Act 1998* s1 (1). According to the UK police, the definition of "Anti-social behaviour covers a wide range of unacceptable activity that causes harm to an individual, to their community or to their environment. This could be an action by someone else that leaves you feeling alarmed, harassed or distressed. It also includes fear of crime or concern for public safety, public disorder or public nuisance," from "Anti-social behaviour," accessed March 10, 2017, https://www.police.uk/crime-prevention-advice/anti-social-behaviour/.

35. See for instance *Deneys Reitz v SA Commercial Catering and Allied Workers Union 1991*, where a workers' protest is forbidden on the ground that it was infringing the "right to peace and quietness" of the residents, in Johan Van der Walt, "Johannesburg: A Tale of Two Cases," in *Law and the City*, ed. Andreas Philippopoulos-Mihalopoulos (Routledge, 2007).

36. Stress itself, he continues, is to be understood as the artificial product of this condition: stress, in other words, would be "the disappointment of an expectation of relief . . . Irritations are perceived as stressory figures against a foundation of relief; they all have the form of re-burdenings that counteract a tendency towards relief. Means of relief, in turn, all take the form of stress-reducing measures." Sloterdijk, *In the World Interior of Capital*, 213.

37. Health and Safety Legislations are a set of regulations applying to all employers and workplaces. In UK they have been defined by the Health and Safety at Work etc. Act 1974, then complemented by further four regulations in 1992, one in 1998 and one in 1999.

38. Nathan Moore, "Icons of Control: Deleuze, Signs, Law," *International Journal for the Semiotics of Law* 20, 1 (2007).

39. Since the end of 19th century many urban sociologists and psychologists emphasised the detrimental effect of urban life, with its socio-psychological patterns of delegation, vis-à-vis the "duty to intervene" that qualifies responsible behaviour vis-à-vis the unexpected. Suffice here to mention the work of Stanley Milgram, whose notorious experiment showed the extent to which delegation can be detrimental to

social life. Stanley Milgram. *Obedience to Authority; An Experimental View*, (Harpercollins, 1974).

40. Mimi Sheller, and John Urry, "The New Mobilities Paradigm," *Environment and Planning A* 38, 2 (2006). John Urry, *Mobilities* (Cambridge, Polity, 2007).

41. Tim Cresswell, *On the Move: Mobility in the Modern Western World* (Taylor & Francis, 2006).

42. Attila Kotayani, and Raoul Vaneigem, "Elementary Program of the Unitary Urbanism Office" in *The Situationists and the City*, ed. Tom McDonough (Verso, 2009), 148.

43. Ian Toon describes effectively the "daily doing nothing" of urban youths and its incompatibility with the ethos of control of contemporary society, "Finding a Place in the Street: CCTV surveillance and young people's use of public space," in *City Visions* ed. D. Bell and A. Haddour (Harlow: Longman, 2000), 145. Jennifer Bonham, "Transport: Disciplining the Body That Travels," *The Sociological Review* 54, s1 (2006). The MacMillan dictionary defines hostile architecture as "the design of buildings or public spaces in a way which discourages people from touching, climbing or sitting on them," accessed March 10, 2017, http://www.macmillandictionary.com/buzzword/entries/hostile-architecture.html.

44. See Sean Dockray, Steve Rowell, and Fiona Whitton, "Blocking all Lanes," *Cabinet Magazine* 17 (2005), accessed February 7, 2016, http://www.cabinetmagazine.org/issues/17/blocking.php.

45. Colin Buchanan, *Traffic in Towns: A Study of the Long Term Problems of Traffic in Urban Areas* (Routledge, 2015 [1963]). Ministry of Transport, *Roads in Urban Areas* (London, HMSO, 1966).

46. Emma Clarke, "Shared Space—The Alternative Approach to Calming Traffic," *TEC* (2006), accessed February 7, 2016, http://www.hamilton-baillie.co.uk/_files/_publications/18—1.pdf.

47. Buchanan, *Traffic in Towns.*

48. "First, main traffic should be canalised into a 'primary road network.' Here traffic takes precedence. Second, the rest of the town should be planned as 'environmental areas.' Here the quality of living comes first." From the speech my Minister of Transport Lord Chesham, accessed March 10, 2017, http://hansard.millbanksystems.com/lords/1963/nov/27/the-buchanan-report-traffic-in-towns.

49. Dylan Passmore, "Evolving Streets: A Review of Contemporary Approaches to Street Design," April 12, 2005, accessed February 7, 2016, http://dylanpassmore.com/Passmore_(2005)_EvolvingStreets.pdf.

50. See Natalia Collarte, "The Woonerf Concept 'Rethinking a Residential Street in Somerville,' MA diss., Tufts University, 2012, accessed February 7, 2016, http://nacto.org/docs/usdg/woonerf_concept_collarte.pdf.

51. Norman E. P. Pressman, "The European Experience," in *Public Streets for Public Use*, ed. A. V. Moudon (New York, Van Nostrand Reinhold Company, 1987), 42, quoted in Passmore, "Evolving Streets," 9.

52. R. K. Jarvis, "Urban Environments as Visual Art or as Social Settings?: A Review," *The Town Planning Review* 51, 1 (1980). Donald Appleyard, *Liveable Streets* (Berkeley and Los Angeles, University of California Press, 1981).

53. Barbara Preston, *Cutting Pedestrian Casualties: Cost-Effective Ways to Make Walking Safer* (London, Transport 2000, 1992).

54. Tim Gill, "Home Zones in the UK: History, Policy and Impact on Children and Youth," *Children, Youth and Environments* 16, 1 (2006).

55. Department for Transport, *Manual for Streets for England and Wales* (London, Thomas Telford, 2007).

56. Ibid.

57. Department for Transport, "Shared Space," *Local Transport Note* 1/11 (DFT, London, 2011).

58. See Ben Hamilton-Baillie, "What Is Shared Space?," accessed February 7, 2016, http://www.hamilton-baillie.co.uk/_files/_publications/6—1.pdf.

59. Quoted in Emma Clarke "The Evolution of Shared Space," *TEC* (2006) accessed February 7, 2016, http://www.hamilton-baillie.co.uk/index.php?do=publications&action=details&pid=18.

60. "Hans Monderman," accessed February 7, 2016, http://www.pps.org/reference/hans-monderman/.

61. Bonham, "Transport," 71.

62. Ibid.

63. John Adams, "Streets and the Culture of Risk Aversion," in *What Are We Scared Of? The Value of Risk in Designing Public Space*, ed. J. Thrift (London, CABE Space, 2004).

64. Ibid., 41.

65. John Adams, *Risk,* (UCL Press, 1995), 20.

66. Ben Hamilton-Baillie, "Shared Space: Reconciling People, Places and Traffic," *Built Environment,* 34, 2 (2008): 166.

67. John Adams, quoted in Clarke "Shared Space," 291.

68. James J. Gibson, *The Ecological Approach to Visual Perception* (Hillsdale, NJ, Erlbaum, 1986).

69. Richard Thaler and Cass Sunstein, *Nudge: Improving Decisions about Health, Wealth and Happiness* (Penguin, 2009).

70. Saadi Lahlou, "How to Control and Change Individual Behaviour: The World as Installation," Talk given at LSE, October 26, 2009, available at http://www.youtube.com/watch?v=WdDmtpqt2hc].

71. John Adams, quoted in Clarke "Shared Space," 291.

72. Thomas Chatterton Williams, "How Hipsters Ruined Paris," *New York Times,* November 8, 2013, accessed February 7, 2016, http://www.nytimes.com/2013/11/10/opinion/sunday/how-hipsters-ruined-paris.html.

73. Hans Monderman, quoted in Rob Methorst, Jürgen Gerlach, Dirk Boenke and Jens Leven, "Sense and Nonsense about Shared Space-For an Objective View of a Popular Planning Concept," *Routes/Roads* 342 (2009).

74. Ben Hamilton-Baillie, "The Drive to Integrate Traffic with Other Users of Public Space Has Been a Hallmark of Dutch Urban Design since the Late 1960s. Now 'Shared Space,'" *Architecture Today,* February 5, 2008, accessed February 7, 2016, http://www.architecturetoday.co.uk/?p=5647.

75. For example, Ansell Pearson. *Germinal Life: The Difference and Repetition of Deleuze,* (Routledge, 1999).

76. Philippopoulos-Mihalopoulos, *Spatial Justice,* 63.

77. Clive Barnett, "Geography and Ethics: Justice Unbound," *Progress in Human Geography* 35, 2 (2011): 252.

78. Department for Transport, "Shared Space."

79. Quoted in Clarke "Shared Space," 291.

80. Relevant examples may be found for instance in the otherwise significant work of Richard Sennett [e.g., *The Uses of Disorder: Personal Identity & City Life* (W. W. Norton, 1992)], Michel de Certeau [*The Practice of Everyday Life* (University of California Press, 1984)] and Henri Lefebvre, who coined the notion of "differential *space*" [*The Production of Space* (Wiley-Blackwell, 1991)]. For a piercing critique of this concept and generally these "nostalgic" tendencies, see Doel, *Poststructuralist Geographies.*

81. Rob Methorst, Jürgen Gerlach, Dirk Boenke and Jens Leven, "Shared Space: Safe or Dangerous? A contribution to objectification of a popular design philosophy." (paper presented at the WALK21 conference, Toronto, October, 1–3 October 2007)

82. Douglas Spencer, "Architectural Deleuzism," *Radical Philosophy* 168, 9 (2011): 14.

83. "Byng Place and the influence of the anti-infrastructural "Shared Space" movement," *Vole O'Speed Blog,* July 1, 2011, http://www.voleospeed.co.uk/2011/07/byng-place-and-influence-of-anti.html. It should be noted that various critiques moved against *shared space* suffer similar limitations, which can be roughly gathered in two main tendencies. First, the common-sense line of argument: "there should be a reason for the highway code." As an interviewee exclaimed: "HONESTLY, THE PAVEMENT IS FOR PEDESTRIANS, THE ROAD IS FOR CARS" [quoted in Lord Holmes, "Accidents by Design," see the following note]. This position does not take into account the simple fact that the crystallization of relations into a stable forms is no guarantee of their desirability. Time does not dissolve but rather invisibilizes the power relations ingrained into legal apparatuses, whose "violence" does not disappear, but rather becomes structural. Here is a variation of this argument: *shared space* does not "recognise that many people do not want to have to 'negotiate' for space and safe passage: they wish to be protected by infrastructure and by laws" [in "Byng Place"]. Yet, is not this "protection" dependent on conceding a disproportionate space of manoeuvre to cars? In other words, does not such a protection protect more certain categories while making more vulnerable others? Second, the limited scope of both focus and methodology. Many works assessing *shared space* systematically avoid addressing its potential benefits (e.g., health, social interaction, quality of life etc.), and rather focus only on its impact vis-à-vis actual and perceived safety. This is clearly reductive, since it pretends to assess *shared space* exactly from the frame of efficiency and safety that *shared space* contests in the first place. Equally incongruous is the tendency to emphasise the negative impact of *shared space* on the perception of safety of street users: since *decreasing* the perception of safety, that is, creating a sense of unease and uncertainty, is exactly what is argued to be more conducive to *actual* safety by *shared space* theorists (this is the core of Adams' theory). These limits are paralleled by methodological approaches that, by relying on quantitative and short-term analyses, are clearly inadequate to grasp the effects of SS, which are qualitative and, moreover, requires long-term social adaptation by the society. If

certainly *shared space* is not beyond assessment, it cannot be assessed only from the very parameters of the model it is opposing.

84. Most notably Lord Holmes of Richmond MBE, "Accidents by Design: The Holmes Report on "shared space" in the United Kingdom," July 2015, accessed February 7, 2016, http://chrisholmes.co.uk/wp-content/uploads/2015/07/Holmes-Report-on-Shared-Space-.pdf.

85. Rob Imrie, "Shared Space and the Post-politics of Environmental Change," *Urban Studies,* 50, 16 (2013): 3448.

86. For example, Jacques Rancière, *Disagreement: Politics and Philosophy* (University of Minnesota Press, 1995).

87. Ibid., 3450, 3454 [internal quote from Department of Transport, "Shared Space," 23].

88. Bonham, "Transport," 70.

89. Imrie, "Shared Space," 3452.

90. Department for Transport, "Shared Space," 24.

91. "The delusion of 'shared space' as an urban transport panacea," *As Easy As Riding A Bike Blog,* July 12, 2001, https://aseasyasridingabike.wordpress.com/2011/07/12/the-delusion-of-shared-space-as-an-urban-transport-panacea/.

92. Unity Law, "#SharedSpaces: Blurred Lines," *Unity Law*, 2015. Accessed February 7, 2016, http://www.unity-law.co.uk/files/file/Unity_Law_Shared%20 Spaces_Report.pdf.

93. Mould is here referring to the notion of Tactical Urbanism but I believe this comment perfectly applies to this case as well. Oli Mould, "Tactical Urbanism: The New Vernacular of the Creative City," *Geography Compass* 8, 8 (2014): 536.

94. For an introduction to the concept a useful resource is the dedicated online journal: *Justice Spatiale/Spatial Justice* [accessed February 7, 2017, http://www.jssj.org/].

95. For example, Erik Swyngedouw "Apocalypse Forever? Post-Political Populism and the Spectre of Climate Change Theory," *Culture & Society* 27, 2/3 (2010).

96. Andreas Philippopoulos-Mihalopoulos, "Spatial Justice: Law and the Geography of Withdrawal," *International Journal of Law in Context* 6, 3 (2010): 204. For a critical discussion on the (mis)use of this concept, see Pavoni, "Exceptional Tunings"; and Philippopoulos-Mihalopoulos, *Spatial Justice*.

97. Peter Marcuse, "Spatial Justice: Derivative but Causal of Social Injustice." *Justices spatiale | spatial justice*, 2010, accessed February 7, 2016, http://books.openedition.org/pupo/420.

98. Which does not mean to simplistically and cowardly avert the task of achieving *a* result, but to pursue a trajectory freed from the anxiety of *the* result. See Nicola Masciandaro, "Becoming Spice: *Commentary* as Geophilosophy," in *Collapse Vol. VI: Geo/Philosophy* ed. Robin Mackay (Urbanomics, 2010), 52.

99. Thus is defined for instance in the presentation to the conference *New Urban Languages: Tales and Images of Spatial Justice*, Delft, June 24–26, 2015 [accessed February 7, 2017, https://nulconference.wordpress.com/new-urban-languages/].

100. Philippopoulos-Mihalopoulos, *Spatial Justice*, 184.

101. Giorgio Agamben, *L'Uso dei Corpi* (Neri Pozza, 2014), 345 (my translation).

102. "This is the challenge of spatial justice: to negotiate a con tested space without taking recourse to origins, central commands, outlines." Philippopoulos-Mihalopoulos

189. On the question of "unplugging" and "reorienting" see Eyal Weizman, "Political Plastic (Interview)," in *Collapse Vol. VI: Geo/Philosophy* (Urbanomics, 2010).

103. Philippopoulos-Mihalopoulos, *Spatial Justice*, 41.

104. Sloterdijk reminds of "Mussolini's dictum that Fascism is a horror of the comfortable life," *World Interior*, 221–222.

REFERENCES

Adams, John. "Streets and the Culture of Risk Aversion" in *What Are We Scared Of? The Value of Risk in Designing Public Space*, ed. J. Thrift, (London, CABE Space, 2004).

———. *Risk* (UCL Press, 1995).

Agamben, Giorgio. *Homo Sacer: Sovereign Power and Bare Life* (Stanford University Press, 1998).

———. *L'Uso dei Corpi* (Neri Pozza, 2014).

Amin, Ash, and Nigel Thrift. *Cities: Reimagining the Urban* (Wiley, 2002).

Amin, Ash. "Rethinking the urban social," *City* 11, 1 (2007): 100–114.

Appleyard, Donald. *Liveable Streets* (Berkeley and Los Angeles, University of California Press, 1981).

As Easy As Riding A Bike Blog. "The delusion of 'shared space' as an urban transport panacea," July 12, 2001. Accessed February 7, 2016, https://aseasyasridingabike.wordpress.com/2011/07/12/the-delusion-of-shared-space-as-an-urban-transport-panacea/.

Barnett, Clive. "Geography and ethics: Justice unbound," *Progress in Human Geography* 35, 2 (2011): 246–255.

Beck, Ulrich. "The Terrorist Threat: World Risk Society Revisited," *Theory, Culture and Society* 19, 4 (2002): 39–55.

Bonham, Jennifer. "Transport: Disciplining the body that travels," *The Sociological Review* 54, s1 (2006): 55–74.

Buchanan, Colin. *Traffic in Towns: A Study of the Long Term Problems of Traffic in Urban Areas* (Routledge, 2015 [1963]). Ministry of Transport, *Roads in Urban Areas* (London, HMSO, 1966).

Cacciari, Massimo. *L'Arcipelago* (Adelphi, 1997).

Certeau, Michel de. *The Practice of Everyday Life* (University of California Press, 1984)

Clarke, Emma. "Shared Space—the alternative approach to calming traffic," *TEC* (2006), accessed February 7, 2016, http://www.hamilton-baillie.co.uk/_files/_publications/18—1.pdf.

Clear, Todd R., and Eric Cadora. "Risk and community Practice" in *Crime, Risk and Justice*, ed. K. Stenson and R. R. Sullivan (Devon, Willan Publishing, 2001).

Collarte, Natalia. The Woonerf Concept "Rethinking a Residential Street in Somerville," MA diss., Tufts University, 2012. Accessed February 7, 2016, http://nacto.org/docs/usdg/woonerf_concept_collarte.pdf.

Cresswell, Tim. *On the Move: Mobility in the Modern Western World* (Taylor & Francis, 2006).

Cunningham, David. "The Concept of Metropolis: Philosophy and Urban Form," *Radical Philosophy* 133 (2005): 13–25.

Dean, Michael. *Governmentality: Power and Rule in Modern Society* (Thousand Oaks, 1999).

Deleuze, Gilles. *Spinoza, Practical Philosophy* (City Lights Books, 1988).

Department for Transport. "Shared Space," *Local Transport Note* 1/11 (DFT, London, 2011).

———. *Manual for Streets for England and Wales* (London, Thomas Telford, 2007).

Dockray, Sean, Steve Rowell, and Fiona Whitton. "Blocking all Lanes," *Cabinet Magazine* 17 (2005), accessed February 7, 2016, http://www.cabinetmagazine.org/issues/17/blocking.php.

Doel, Marcus. *Poststructuralist Geographies: The Diabolical Art of Spatial Science* (Rowman & Littlefield, 1999).

Douglas Spencer. "Architectural Deleuzism," *Radical Philosophy* 168, 9 (2011).

Douzinas, Costas, Peter Goodrich, and Yifat Hachamovitch. *Politics, Postmodernity and Critical Legal Studies: The Legality of the Contingent* (Routledge, 1994).

Fogh Jensen, Anders. *The Project Society* (Unipress, 2012).

Foucault, Michel. *Discipline & Punish: The Birth of the Prison* (Vintage, 1995).

Garland, David. "Risk," in *Risk and Morality,* ed. Richard V. Ericson and Aaron Doyle (University of Toronto Press, 2003).

Gibson, James. J. *The Ecological Approach to Visual Perception* (Hillsdale, NJ: Erlbaum, 1986).

Gill, Tim. "Home Zones in the UK: History, Policy and Impact on Children and Youth," *Children, Youth and Environments* 16, 1 (2006): 90–103.

Goodrich, Peter. "The Theatre of Emblems: On the Optical Apparatus and the Investiture of Persons." *Law, Culture and the Humanities* 8, 1 (2012): 47–67.

Hacking, Ian. "Risk and Dirt," in *Risk and Morality*, ed. Richard V. Ericson and Aaron Doyle (University of Toronto Press, 2003).

Hamilton-Baillie, Ben. "Shared Space: Reconciling People, Places and Traffic," *Built Environment,* 34, 2 (2008): 161–181.

———. "The drive to integrate traffic with other users of public space has been a hallmark of Dutch urban design since the late 1960s. Now 'shared space,'" *Architecture Today,* February 5, 2008. Accessed February 7, 2016, http://www.architecturetoday.co.uk/?p=5647.

Hamilton-Baillie, Ben. "What Is Shared Space?" Accessed February 7, 2016, http://www.hamilton-baillie.co.uk/_files/_publications/6—1.pdf.

Hart, H. L. A. *The Concept of Law* (Oxford University Press, 1997).

Hay, James. "Designing Homes to be the First Line of Defense," *Cultural Studies* 20, 4 (2006): 349–377.

Imrie, Rob. "Shared Space and the Post-politics of Environmental Change," *Urban Studies,* 50, 16 (2013): 3446–3462.

Jarvis, R. K. "Urban Environments as Visual Art or as Social Settings?: A Review," *The Town Planning Review* 51, 1 (1980): 50–66.

Klauser, Francisco. "Splintering spheres of security: Peter Sloterdijk and the contemporary fortress city," *Environment and Planning D: Society and Space* 28, 2 (2010): 326–340.

Kotayani, Attila, and Raoul Vaneigem. "Elementary Program of the Unitary Urbanism Office" in *The Situationists and the City*, ed. Tom McDonough (Verso, 2009).

Lahlou, Saadi. "How to Control and Change Individual Behaviour: the world as installation," Talk given at LSE, October 26, 2009, available at http://www.youtube.com/watch?v=WdDmtpqt2hc.

Latham, Alan, and Derek P. McCormack. "Moving cities: Rethinking the materialities of urban geographies." *Progress in Human Geography* 28, 6 (2004): 701–724.

Lefebvre, Henri. *The Production of Space* (Wiley-Blackwell, 1991).

Lianos, Michalis, and Mary Douglas. "Dangerization and the end of deviance: The institutional environment," *British Journal of Criminology,* 40 (2000).

Lord Holmes of Richmond MBE. "Accidents by Design: The Holmes Report on "shared space" in the United Kingdom," July 2015. Accessed February 7, 2016, http://chrisholmes.co.uk/wp-content/uploads/2015/07/Holmes-Report-on-Shared-Space-.pdf.

Marcus Doel. *Poststructuralist Geographies: The Diabolical Art of Spatial Science* (Rowman & Littlefield, 1999).

Marcuse, Peter. "Spatial Justice: Derivative but Causal of Social Injustice." *justicespatiale | spatial justice*, 2010. Accessed February 7, 2016, http://books.openedition.org/pupo/420.

Masciandaro, Nicola. "Becoming Spice: *Commentary* as Geophilosophy," in *Collapse Vol. VI: Geo/Philosophy* ed. Robin Mackay (Urbanomics, 2010).

McCormack, Derek. "Geography and Abstraction: Towards an Affirmative Critique." *Progress in Human Geography* 36, 6 (2012): 715–34.

Methorst, Rob, Jürgen Gerlach, Dirk Boenke and Jens Leven. "Shared Space: Safe or Dangerous? A contribution to objectification of a popular design philosophy." (paper presented at the WALK21 conference, Toronto, October 1–3, 2007).

———. "Sense and nonsense about Shared Space-For an objective view of a popular planning concept," *Routes/Roads* 342 (2009). Accessed February 7, 2016, http:// katana. hsrc. unc. edu/cms/downloads/Shared% 20Space_short_german-Eng. pdf.

Milgram, Stanley. *Obedience to Authority; An Experimental View* (Harpercollins, 1974).

Mohaghegh, Jason B., and Seema Golestaneh. "Haunted Sound: Nothingness, Movement, and the Minimalist Imagination," *Environment and Planning D: Society and Space,* 29, 3 (2011): 485–498.

Moore, Jason W. *Capitalism in the Web of Life: Ecology and the Accumulation of Capital* (Verso, 2015).

Moore, Nathan. "Icons of control: Deleuze, signs, law," *International Journal for the Semiotics of Law* 20, 1 (2007): 33–54.

Mould, Oli. "Tactical Urbanism: The New Vernacular of the Creative City," *Geography Compass* 8, 8 (2014): 529–539.

Passmore, Dylan. "Evolving Streets: A Review of Contemporary Approaches to Street Design," April 12, 2005. Accessed February 7, 2016, http://dylanpassmore.com/Passmore_(2005)_EvolvingStreets.pdf.

Pavoni, Andrea. "Exceptional Tunings. Controlling Urban Events," PhD diss. *University of Westminster,* 2013.

Pearson, Ansell. *Germinal Life: The Difference and Repetition of Deleuze* (Routledge, 1999).

Philippopoulos-Mihalopoulos, Andreas. "Spatial Justice: Law and the Geography of Withdrawal." *International Journal of Law in Context* 6, 3 (2010): 201–216.

Philippopoulos-Mihalopoulos, Andreas. *Spatial Justice: Body, Lawscape, Atmosphere* (Routledge, 2015).

Pressman, Norman E. P. "The European Experience," in *Public Streets for Public Use*, ed. Anne Vernez Moudon (New York, Van Nostrand Reinhold Company, 1987).

Preston, Barbara. *Cutting Pedestrian Casualties: Cost-Effective Ways to Make Walking Safer* (London, Transport 2000, 1992).

Ramsay, Peter. "The Theory of Vulnerable Autonomy and the Legitimacy of the Civil Preventative Order." *LSE Legal Studies Working Paper,* 1 (2008).

Rancière, Jacques. "Ten Theses on Politics," *Theory & Event* 5, 3 (2001).

———. *Disagreement: Politics and Philosophy* (University of Minnesota Press, 1995).

Schmitt, Carl. *Political Theology: Four Chapters on the Concept of Sovereignty* (University of Chicago Press, 2006).

Sennett, Richard. *The Uses of Disorder: Personal Identity & City Life* (W. W. Norton, 1992).

Sheller, Mimi, and John Urry. "The New Mobilities Paradigm," *Environment and Planning A* 38, 2 (2006): 207–226.

Sloterdijk, Peter. *In the World Interior of Capital: Towards a Philosophical Theory of Globalization* (Polity Press, 2013).

———. *Sfere I, Bolle* (Meltemi, 2009).

———. *Tome 3, Ecumes, Sphérologie plurielle* (Hachette Littératures, 2006).

Swyngedouw, Eric. "Apocalypse forever? Post-Political Populism and the Spectre of Climate Change Theory," *Culture & Society* 27, 2/3 (2010): 213–32.

———. *Designing the Post-Political City and the Insurgent Polis* (Bedford Press, 2011).

Thaler, Richard, and Cass Sunstein. *Nudge: Improving Decisions about Health, Wealth and Happiness* (Penguin, 2009).

Thrift, Nigel. "LifeworldInc—and What to Do About It," *Environment and Planning D: Society and Space* 29, 1 (2011): 5–26.

Toon, Ian. "Finding a Place in the Street: CCTV Surveillance and Young People's Use of Public Space," in *City Visions* ed. David Bell and Azzedine Haddour (Harlow: Longman, 2000): 141–165.

Toscano, Alberto. "The Open Secret of Real Abstraction," *Rethinking Marxism* 20, 2 (2008): 273–287.

Tsing-Lowenhaupt, Anna. "On nonscalability: The Living World Is Not Amenable to Precision-Nested Scales." *Common Knowledge* 18, 3 (2012): 505–524.

Unity Law. "#SharedSpaces: Blurred Lines," *Unity Law,* 2015. Accessed February 7, 2016, http://www.unity-law.co.uk/files/file/Unity_Law_Shared%20Spaces_Report.pdf.

Urry, John. *Mobilities* (Cambridge, Polity, 2007).

Vole O'Speed Blog. "Byng Place and the influence of the anti-infrastructural "Shared Space" movement," *Vole O'Speed Blog,* July 1, 2011. Accessed February 7, 2016, http://www.voleospeed.co.uk/2011/07/byng-place-and-influence-of-anti.html.

Walt, Johan Van der. "Johannesburg: A Tale of Two Cases," in *Law and the City*, ed. Andreas Philippopoulos-Mihalopoulos (Routledge, 2007).

Weizman, Eyal. "Political Plastic (Interview)," in *Collapse Vol. VI: Geo/Philosophy,* ed. Robin Mackay (Urbanomics, 2010).

Williams, Thomas Chatterton. "How Hipsters Ruined Paris," *New York Times,* November, 8, 2013, accessed February 7, 2016, http://www.nytimes.com/2013/11/10/opinion/sunday/how-hipsters-ruined-paris.html.

Žižek, Slavoj. *The Ticklish Subject: the Absent Centre of Political Ontology* (Verso, 2000).

Chapter 3

Everyday Jurisprudence in Urban Australia

Negotiating the Space of Legal Performances

Richard Mohr and Nadirsyah Hosen

TIME, SPACE, AND CULTURE

The theme of "street-level sovereignty" invites us to contrast the informality of law on the street with the formal authority of the sovereign power. Legal pluralists argue that that law can be informal and based in social formations other than the state.[1] Practitioners of the law, including judges, lawyers, and legislators, work with the assumption that state law has a unique status as an authoritative, knowable, and monolithic structure. Even for formal law, this has not always been the case: canon law, international law, customary law, and other legal regimes are still recognized in various jurisdictions. The laws people live by are more diverse still. Some of these are formal and written, even if they are tangential to state law, such as religious laws or industry codes and standards. Others are known, perhaps even viscerally or unconsciously, by the communities who adhere to them, as in taken-for-granted business practices or generally accepted codes of behavior toward others: queuing, keeping to the left or right on stairs and escalators.

We distinguish here between formal law, which is written and known by experts even though it may not be recognized by state law, and informal laws, recognized in practice, but unrecorded in any formal way. The intersection of various legal regimes, sometimes called "internormativity,"[2] raises a number of questions that will be addressed in this chapter. Central to these is the relation between informal law and state law: how the two coexist, compete, or constitute each other.[3] We explore the following questions through a study of the interaction of formal and informal laws in action on a Sydney street.

First, how are conflicts and transitions worked out between informal and formal laws? We may inquire whether state law always trumps the informal laws of everyday practices, or whether there are opportunities for the recognition of informal law. As will be seen in the case studies, the conflicts are not always between a monolithic formal law and a single underlying informal or "customary law." This question can be approached through the longitudinal study of legal application over time. Thus we may see whether formal law ultimately wins out by burying informal practices of law under the weight of authority and enforcement, or whether informal laws may persist over time, or perhaps even infiltrate the formal systems of state law.

Second, if formal laws comply with expectations that they be written, publicly known, and formally promulgated by state-recognized lawmakers, how are informal laws recorded? This question is related to that of time in the previous question, since a law can hardly be worthy of the name if it is ephemeral, changing day by day. Yet if it is not written down, in the manner of formal law, we may ask how is it known and how it persists over time. While some of the informal, or nonstate laws to be seen in these studies are written (industry codes, religious law) others are not. We will notice that space and spatial practice can perform some of the functions that writing has for formal law: we will explore the extent to which informal laws are "written" in places and the ways they are used.[4]

Third, what is the foundation or origin of informal laws? This is not a question about the founding legitimacy of the law, which is a mythomania that we leave to the exponents of the authority of state law. It asks, instead, about the cultural milieu that gives rise to and nourishes laws. That milieu, or provenance, of the law is well documented in the case of state law, with its roots in Roman law, common law or Napoleonic traditions. In this study we find informal laws' origins in cultural practices and ethnic diversity.[5] The juxtaposition of state law with customary law is often seen to be a duality of legal systems. A broader legal pluralism, we will suggest, is spawned by social and cultural diversity found in a multicultural society.

These introductory paragraphs open the tool kit to be used in this analysis: time, space, and culture. Time allows us to delve into the development, conflicts, and outcomes of competition between legal regimes, formal and informal. Space provides the fixed point and theater of social performances, where rituals, patterns and laws can be inscribed without the need for the formalities of writing. Cultures, in all the diversity seen in an inner suburban multicultural main street, propel the proliferation and cross-pollination of incipient or vestigial legal regimes. They introduce the seeds of normative orders that may have been formally inaugurated or better established in other times or places, whether those be the nations from which immigrants have arrived, or the "law of the land": the Indigenous legal substrate on which formal Australian settler law has been superimposed.[6] This chapter acknowledges the primacy of indigenous laws in Australia, even though they are not its focus. Studies of Australian customary laws contrast the Aboriginal laws of the land with the formally sovereign common law imposed by settler society, leading to the dualism noted above.[7] Because of the nature of the areas in this study, where there are more overseas immigrants than Aboriginal residents, the diversity of international cultures, and associated informal laws, are more conspicuous than the presence of indigenous laws.

LAWS ON THE STREET

This study centers on the inner south western suburbs of Sydney, and specifically on streets running off Canterbury Road (closer to the city called New Canterbury Road). They are in the adjoining local government areas of Marrickville and Canterbury, between 10 and 15 km (6–10 miles) from the city center. This was the axis of Sydney's manufacturing industries, which progressively extended three times further to the south west. In the 1950s–1970s immigrants were sought for industrial work, so these suburbs were heavily populated by successive waves of migration from southern Europe, then the Middle East and South East Asia. The areas along (New) Canterbury Road, which had been established along tram and train routes in the early 20th century, have become convenient and accessible inner suburbs in sprawling, automobile-based Sydney, prized for their public transport links and their multicultural vibe. The attraction of lower housing prices, which also drives gentrification, is diminishing in those parts of this area closer to the city, and is banishing even remotely affordable housing further and further from the city center.

The present chapter is based on two distinct experiences of these areas, separated by several decades. The first period was in the late 1970s, during intensive migration into the Canterbury local government area of people fleeing Lebanon's civil war which began in 1975 and lasted about 15 years. One of the authors worked in community health in the area, involving liaison and research with local and other levels of government, with other agencies and with the Lebanese community.[8]

The second period of research began in 2012, when a survey was made of all the food outlets in Marrickville Road, the commercial and civic main street of the eponymous local government area. In the street's 2.7 km (1.7 miles) length, there were 117 food outlets, bearing 17 different linguistic or national cultural identifiers. Our main focus in this chapter is on two blocks closest to New Canterbury Road, where there is a local shopping center with cafés, restaurants, fresh food shops, a bookshop, hairdressers, and other businesses which mainly serve the local community and people working in the area. Shops and restaurants within these two blocks at that time were identifiably Vietnamese, Pakistani, Lebanese, French, Italian, Turkish, Thai, Portuguese, and Greek.[9]

This area has been observed since 2012, with a second period of systematic research in 2014, updated in 2016. In the more recent time period, forty years after the influx of Lebanese immigrants, we report on research carried out at two yearly intervals, with ongoing informal observation in the intervening periods.

This study proceeds by way of three case studies which illustrate the interactions of formal and informal laws. The first looks at smoking at two pavement cafés. The second considers the availability of halal food, comparing the situation in the period of intensive migration from Lebanon in the 1970s with that in 2014, when there was a halal restaurant between the two cafés, and a halal butcher and convenience store around the corner in New Canterbury Road. In the third case study we compare experiences of crossing the street and regulation by speed humps and marked pedestrian crossings. In the first of these case studies, change took place within the 12–18 month period of observation. The other two case studies draw on comparative material from the earlier period for their longitudinal aspects over time.

THREE CASE STUDIES

Smoking at Outdoor Cafés

Outdoor tables and seating at cafés and restaurants in Marrickville Road is licensed by the local government authority, Marrickville Council. The Council is keen to encourage these uses of outdoor space, having widened footpaths for the purpose, and waived licensing fees. However, since this is publicly owned land controlled by Council, it can apply certain conditions. One is a blanket ban on smoking at any outdoor seating associated with cafés or restaurants, adopted with the Council's Smoke-free Outdoor Environments Policy in 2011.[10]

There is a widened section of footpath accommodating up to about 20 tables outside six premises on the north side of Marrickville Road, running some 20 meters east from Seaview Street in Dulwich Hill (see Figure 3.1). These premises included two cafés (at 471 and 469) and, in 2014, an upstairs restaurant. The cafés each use about half of the available footpath space. The corner of Seaview Street and Marrickville Road is a focal point for the Dulwich Hill shopping center. There is a council notice board on one side of the road, and pedestrian crossings over both streets. Round the corner in Seaview Street from the outdoor cafés there is a council library, opposite the high school.[11] At the corner there are two phone boxes, and council has provided bench seating, planting, and a water dispenser.

The widened section of footpath on Marrickville Road is fenced to the trafficable side, which is busy with passing cars, trucks, and buses (limited to 40 km/h). There are signs on this fencing, spaced about 3–4 meters apart,

Figure 3.1 Cafés on Marrickville Road. Seaview Street Corner in the Foreground, Looking East. (Richard Mohr, 2014, ink on paper.)

reading "This Is a No Smoking Area," with the usual symbol. The last one of these signs, at the eastern end of the fencing, has been graffitied to read "This Is a Smoking Area," with a tick. The change to the sign followed local custom, since smoking was better tolerated at the eastern end of the tables. The shopkeeper from the last shop in this row would walk directly from his door to one of these tables, and was one of the regular smokers and coffee drinkers there. In wet weather, when the last tables are exposed, the smokers generally retreated to the adjoining tables under the umbrella, still those furthest from the Seaview Street corner. At the end closer to Seaview Street it was very rare to see anyone smoking.

This case study highlights the interaction of formal and informal regulation of activity in a public space. While the formal council regulation applies equally throughout the area, informal regulation applies more strictly at one end than at the other. Entering this area from the corner of Seaview Street the tables are more visible, and form a more obvious "front" area to the civic space. The eastern end becomes an out-of-the-way back area, despite a similar amount of passing foot traffic, where transgression of the formal rules is more acceptable.

The Council gave reasons for the smoke-free zones policy: "healthier, cleaner and greener." There are good health reasons not to smoke including avoiding passive smoke, and less obvious environmental reasons, notably the impact of butts which "take up to 5 years to break down." Yet the extent of bans on smoking in public areas, notably outdoor areas, has an obvious aesthetic and sensory dimension. Contravention of nonsmoking regulations is first perceptible to the sense of smell; passing by, one will not notice (visually) the surreptitious cigarette, or even, unless you look for it, the packet or the lighter on the table. The smell alerts us to this transgression.

Despite uniform council regulations covering the whole extent of the outdoor seating and dining area, informal law dictated that smoking was tolerated at the eastern, but not at the western end of the footpath. The council regulation had been in force for 3 years in 2014, when this study was carried out, and was still consistently breached. Since that date, it has been noticeable that smoking has been eradicated from the entire area. Informal changes to the law, such as a change of management at the "offending" café did not seem adequate to explain this change. Research into the formal law did. While local councils in New South Wales have delegated authority over planning and land use, they have no constitutional recognition in Australia, and have few powers and no authority to police criminal or other such matters. From 2011 to 2014, council cautioned businesses that their license to use footpaths "will be conditioned." No other penalties were specified in the policy. In July 2015, however, the New South Wales government, with the major police enforcement power in the state, introduced amendments to the *Smoke-free Environments Act 2000*. These provided a $300 on the spot fine for customers smoking at outdoor cafés, and a possible $5,500 penalty for businesses where offences occurred.

We see here the interaction of three legal orders: the informal law of the street, which appeared to tolerate smoking further from the "civic" corner of Seaview Street, but without formal penalties; the local government regulation which banned smoking at all outdoor cafés in the Marrickville area, displaying signs and threatening conditions on licenses to use footpaths; and the State law of New South Wales, which provided direct penalties, including substantial fines applied to individual smokers and to business proprietors. It appeared that the soft approach of the local council did little to overcome the informal law, with its graded tolerance for smoking. Financial penalties levied by the State, however, were of sufficient deterrent force to eliminate smoking from all the tables of the outdoor cafés within six months of their implementation. Since the informal law continued to apply, despite council regulations, right up to the time of the legislation, it seems likely that this was the main factor that trumped the law of the street.

The Formalization of Halal Meat

At the time of the 2014 study the door between the two cafés on Marrickville Road opened to a flight of stairs leading to a halal Pakistani restaurant ("Jinnah's," seen in figure 3.1). Around the corner, in New Canterbury Road, was a halal butcher and convenience store. In each case, the status of the food sold was signified by the word "halal," in Roman or in Arabic script, displayed on signs at the front of the premises. This refers to religious law, indicating that the food has been prepared in accordance with Islamic principles: notably that pork is not served, and that other meat comes from animals that have been slaughtered in the correct manner by properly qualified people. The relationship between religious and state law has been formalized to a degree in recent years, though it was not always so. Practices, too, have changed, with the increasing formalization and availability of halal meat.

Here we broaden our inquiry, back in time to the early days of large scale immigration from Lebanon during the civil war there, and to consider also the neighboring local government area of Canterbury, which adjoins Marrickville less than 2 km (about 1 mile) south west of the area we are discussing. While only 2.7% of the population of the Marrickville local government area are Muslims (a little higher than Australia as a whole: 2.2%), 16.6% of the population of the Canterbury local government area state their religion as Islam.[12] While there had been Lebanese and Syrian migration[13] to that area, and to Marrickville, earlier in the 20th century, numbers of arrivals from Lebanon increased markedly following the outbreak of the civil war there in 1975.[14] While the immigrants had always included Muslims and Christians, the number of Muslims settling in the Canterbury area provided a population base for a mosque as well as numerous businesses catering to Muslims, including halal food outlets. Subsequently, Muslims from other countries gravitated to the area so that today there are more Muslims than Arabic speakers in Canterbury, and many times more than the number of persons born in Lebanon (many of whom are still Maronite Catholic or Eastern Orthodox).[15]

In the late 1970s, halal food was hard to come by in Australia, including in the south western Sydney areas of Canterbury and Marrickville. As coordinator of a state government community health service in Canterbury during that period, one of the present authors worked closely with the council and the Lebanese community. The slaughter of animals in suburban backyards came to the attention of council and the community health service. This practice was not uncommon in rural and semirural Lebanon, and was adopted in Australia as a means of ensuring halal meat was available, particularly during Eid celebrations. At that time there were few formal channels, such as halal abattoirs or widespread certification of halal meat. The practice of slaughtering animals in suburban backyards caused some consternation in council, perhaps more for cultural than for legal reasons.[16]

The legal situation surrounding slaughter of animals and halal certification has changed over the intervening forty years. This has involved a web of formal state and federal law, delegated powers allowing local governments to make certain orders, religious law, industry codes, and trade agreements.

At the time of writing, home slaughter is not illegal in Australia, but meat from animals killed "at home" is not allowed to be sold in a commercial context, that is, it is for home use only. Animal cruelty and human health seem to be covered by the response of the major animal welfare organization, the Royal Society for the Prevention of Cruelty to Animals: if you kill it you can eat it (at your own risk, as it were).

More recently than the historical events related above, Canterbury Council has adopted a Local Orders Policy on the "Keeping of animals," under section 124 of the *Local Government Act 1993* (NSW). The Act provides for a council to order a person to refrain from doing a thing under certain circumstances: this may include "not to keep birds or animals on premises, other than of such kinds, in such numbers or in such manner as specified in the order." So the Canterbury Council policy specifies the conditions under which various species may be kept. Sheep and goats, for example, must be kept on areas greater than 1500 square meters, and only on land where suitable grazing exists. Such conditions would not exist on private land in the densely populated Canterbury area, so even without any specific prohibition on slaughter, "keeping" the animal would breach these orders under the Act.

Halal slaughter is permitted under New South Wales (*Prevention of Cruelty to Animals Act 1979* s 24) and other states' legislation, while certification is regulated under a federal government initiative. Meat is certified as halal through the Australian Government Authorised Halal Program,[17] which recognizes some twenty Islamic organizations approved for "supervising the production and certification of halal meat for export." Establishments slaughtering and processing halal meat must have "Approved Arrangements," and slaughtermen must be registered and have an identity card, issued by Aus-Meat[18] (a body of the Australian meat and livestock industries) which notes the Approved Islamic Organisation responsible for training and oversight. Halal meat is thus highly regulated by a web of government, religious, and industry bodies. While these arrangements were put in place in 2005 to ensure the integrity of Australian halal meat exports, they also provide a clear and reliable foundation for halal certification for domestic consumption.

The overall impact of these interlocking formal, informal, and delegated laws has clarified the position of slaughter and halal certification. Backyard slaughter, a practice imported from the Lebanese countryside, is more clearly regulated, is less likely to be practiced due to the passage of time since migration, and has been rendered unnecessary to access halal meat. This is now sold in halal butcheries and served in halal restaurants. These "front" regions depend, as we have just seen, on a wide range of codes, orders, and procedures operating behind the scenes (as far "back" as the abattoirs and slaughtermen), so that customers can be confident that they are consuming halal products. Muslim shoppers can and do access halal food from the many shops catering to them in Canterbury and Marrickville.

Religious law can be observed either informally or formally; regulated by religious, industry, or state authorities; taken on trust, or on direct evidence; or by viewing a formal certificate. We see all these levels interacting in this case study. In the 1970s, the only authorities were religious, and the community ties were close-knit. Families knew the imam, or the local butcher or restaurateur. Animals slaughtered at home by the person known to be religiously authorized were directly seen, *experienced* to be halal. If the local food supplier was known to be honest and pious, then the community who knew this could take the food on trust as being halal.[19] Since the efforts of the national government to regulate halal meat in the interests of the export trade, a panoply of regulations has been introduced, involving state, religious, and meat industry players and resulting in a formal halal certificate for meat, which the consumer can see displayed at the point of sale.

Crossing the Street

Also dating back to the period of migration from Lebanon during the civil war, Ghassan Hage has documented the case of a particular Lebanese immigrant who had been traumatized during the war.[20] He developed a mania for going back and forth on a pedestrian crossing in Beamish Street in the Canterbury area, carried away by the power he had to make the traffic stop, so different from the closer encounters between cars and pedestrians he was used to in Lebanon. Pedestrian crossings, variously marked, exist in most jurisdictions, yet they are observed in very different ways. In Australia cars usually stop when a pedestrian indicates they are stepping off the curb. In most of Asia, the Middle East, and the Mediterranean, cars will slow or take evasive action so as not to hit a pedestrian, wherever on the road they happen to be, without necessarily coming to a halt.

Crossing Marrickville Road, in the block or two we are examining, is regulated by various laws, signs, barriers, and speed humps. There are fences at the edge of pavements which provide a barrier between the people at the cafés and restaurants and the passing traffic. They also stop pedestrians from jay walking and crossing too close to particular corners, while encouraging them to use the designated pedestrian crossings. The speed humps reinforce the speed limit by making excessive speed uncomfortable for the driver, and dangerous to the undercarriage of vehicles. The formal 40 km/hour speed limit is signaled by a red and black sign on a white ground: an official and standard form of legal notification. This is accompanied, on an extra panel on the side of the white sign, by the advisory note that this is a zone of "high pedestrian activity." (See figure 3.1, where a speed hump warning sign is positioned on a light pole before the "40" sign.) In addition to formal regulation of speed, and advice about the reason for the reduced speed limit, there is a moral persuasion in the form of an image showing pedestrians, particularly children. Pedestrian crossings are slightly raised, forming another speed hump, and are marked on the roadway in painted zebra stripes, together with a vertical yellow and black sign with a representation of a pair of walking legs.

In this proliferating forest of signs, and labyrinth of barriers, the pedestrian and the driver must draw on all their semiotic, interpretive, and urban survival skills. If a simple reading will help them to understand the intended and unintended meanings of the signs, further interpretation may be needed to discern the legal context and regulatory force of these signs. Their survival skills will impel them to stop reading and interpreting signs, in order to read the behavior of other pedestrians and of the car drivers. For all the regulation, only the most foolhardy pedestrian would step off the curb without first making eye contact with an approaching driver, or determining whether the car was slowing to a stop, speeding up, or simply cruising for a parking space, oblivious to the presence of pedestrians or of any signs other than those indicating the complicated parking restrictions.

Leone has catalogued many of the semiotic devices involved in crossing streets and ways of reading them.[21] Of particular importance is his recognition of their narrative and even intergenerational function. A street sign or a speed hump is erected to be permanent: it will be there even when there is no police officer. Yet the ways it is observed, interpreted or even transgressed are equally important in determining the regulatory culture of the street. Like any cultural expression supported by artifacts, it can be conveyed to newcomers, the young are raised into it, and the communications themselves are constantly circulating. Pedestrians observe each other, they observe drivers, who note each other's reactions and those of the pedestrians. The law inhabits the street in which it is observed. But of course this is not simply the formal law of the New South Wales traffic code. It includes the lore of the neighborhood and the accepted conventions of driving and crossing streets.

In different places and different cultures there are varying distances from the pedestrian at which the car will stop, whether the pedestrian has stepped off the curb, is walking purposefully toward the curb, or is simply thinking of crossing the street. One of the authors, when bringing his family to Haldon Street, Lakemba, in the heart of the Canterbury area, to eat and shop for the best Arabic and halal food in Australia, would warn them to forget their normal assumptions about the way traffic moved in the regional Australian city where they lived. To reinforce the different morés applying to traffic and crossing the street, his advice was to forget they were in Australia, and to assume an approach more familiar from Asia or the Middle East. Likewise, international students from Asia or the Middle East, driving on international licenses on a leafy university campus in the same regional city, take a different approach to marked pedestrian crossings than is customary in that refined environment. Particularly when there are more newly arrived students at the beginning of semesters, they can be seen to swerve around pedestrians already on crossings, and not to stop for others, about to step off the curb. One of the authors has had occasion to berate such drivers, in Arabic, even surprising himself, that he has become so "Australian."

Hage's example of the mania experienced when cars observe different informal laws than one is used to has its obverse in the sense of threat or offence when there is less distance or the limits are pushed further. The experience of one of the authors in crossing the street, just at the corner where the cafés are located, is illustrative of this inversion. Waiting for a bus to pass, and then another car or two that were travelling close behind, the pedestrian decided to enforce his right to cross at the crossing, and so interrupted the flow of traffic by stepping between cars. Perhaps this transgressed some recognized norm which is to avoid such discontinuity. Or perhaps the driver had been in Lebanon as recently as Hage's manic road-crosser. In any case, the shout from the car of "mash'Allah!" ("God is amazed!") was typical of the exasperated and ironic expressions reported all over the world from pedestrians and drivers whose normal routine or expectations are disrupted by transgressive activity.[22] It is hardly necessary to insist that the transgression involved has little to do with formal law (indeed, formally, the pedestrian had right of way): expectations of the enactment of informal law were transgressed.

In a more recent piece, Hage has revisited his analysis of the use made of a pedestrian crossing, in the context of a cross-cultural reading of informal law and urban activity. Having earlier referred to the pedestrian crossing as "an ethical structural fact," he had to rethink that definition in the context of Lebanese pluralism. The urban morés of Beirut, whether in queuing or jostling for a sandwich, or crossing the road, are more contested and socially interactive than the equivalent activities in Australia. Hage thus recognizes that sociality is negotiated, and not guaranteed by the state: "Negotiated sociality is a face-to-face 'horizontal sociality' that is not mediated 'vertically' by the law as a third party."[23]

With Hage, we suggest that such an observation always applies to urban street life, even in Marrickville. As we have seen in the case of smoking or crossing the road, strict state legality is always present, in signs, traffic codes, and speed humps, but is marginal to day-to-day activities. This may be more obvious in Beirut, Naples, or Teheran than in Sydney.[24] Yet the flow of peoples and cultures, whether these be the national cultures of immigration or the subcultures of class and age, provides constant challenges to a taken-for-granted interpretation and enactment of formal legal norms. Indeed, it may be that in a monocultural society (if such a thing exists) the ways law is negotiated horizontally are invisible: everyone "respects" the law and the lore in their own way. But since it is the way of all the other members of the society, any fault lines between formal and informal law are invisible. It is notable in the observations of Leone, Branco, and Hage, cited above, that the status of being an outsider, or a returning expatriate, stimulates the appreciation of the horizontality of informal norms, that is to say, of legal pluralism on the street.

DISCUSSION

Space

These case studies illustrate the interactions between formal and informal law and regulation in defining appropriate "region behavior."[25] Smoking is prohibited at all outdoor dining facilities, but it was informally tolerated at some more than others. It is safer to cross the road at a pedestrian crossing, but only if you recognize informal rules, closely observe cars, and negotiate your passage by eye contact with oncoming drivers. Animals need not be slaughtered in suburban backyards to meet halal standards: state, industry, and religious regulation and the practices of government, industry, and religious bodies now ensure that halal meat is available at "front of house," in restaurants and butcheries.

Smoking has been tolerated, but only at the "back" end of the café strip. Backyards are no longer spaces for halal slaughter: formally defined and carefully hidden back regions (abattoirs) now serve that purpose. The scandals that periodically erupt when animal rights activists penetrate the back regions of chicken factory farms or abattoirs, whether in Indonesia or Australia, indicate the significance of region differentiation. At the front—the restaurant or the suburban butchery—we see only the label certifying that what occurred at the "back" was halal, or met relevant health standards. When produce is properly and reliably certified—whether as organic, free range, or halal—we do not need, and probably do not want to see with our own eyes, or smell with our own nostrils what we savor with our mouth.[26] The interplay of formal and informal regulation of space and behavior removes the need for personal sensory experience or interpersonal trust. The certificate suffices.

Law, space and region behavior constitute each other. At the most formal level, statutes, planning instruments or council by-laws specify permitted land uses, conservation zones, pedestrian crossings and prohibited activities. These laws represent spaces and the activities that may or may not occur in them, clarified with signs or maps. At less formal levels, social interactions and habitus constitute the nature of spaces. They open, unveil, unleash or serve up pathways, sights, smells and dishes that are constituted by social relations, interacting with formal and informal codes of behavior. Spaces thus acquire their own regulatory force, so that we understand whether they are back or front, and what behavior is proper or improper to them.

In examining the informal as well as the formal law, we see more clearly the role of space itself as a marker and enforcer of standards and forms of activity. Rules, laws, or morés must, by definition, persist over time. Formal law in Europe, at least since the Roman and Visigothic administrations, relies primarily on written records or documents for its permanence.[27] Many historic formal law traditions also rely on space as a marker and reminder of the law: tombs in Rome,[28] the street processions of the Doge in Venice[29] or the bailiff in Amsterdam,[30] seisin and possession in 13th century England.[31] Space also serves informal law. Indeed, as formal law increasingly depends exclusively upon the written word, the language of spatial markers and patterns of spatial practice are increasingly abandoned to the realm of the informal.

Law is one of the social elements that produce space and regulate behavior. However, when we consider spatial practice and representational spaces, as they are understood by their inhabitants, we see that these are not always consistent with the legal and formal regulatory representations of space of local government and other authorities.[32] The accommodation between these conceptions of space is mediated through social activity and through a web of regulatory regimes that are not always apparent to a state-centered or "black letter" view of law. Urbanists, sociologists and architects, just like lawyers, can recognize that space, like law, is not always "black letter" space. That is to say, it is produced and represented by regulatory as well as behavioral systems that are not always formal and written, but are nonetheless effective. This perspective helps us to move away from a view of space as it is defined formally (as in written codes and regulations), and of activities as simply "compliant" or "transgressive," to a more modulated appreciation of the interaction of formal and informal codes with space and social activity.

Time

It has already been noted that laws must have permanence: ephemeral patterns of behavior and social activity are neither law-like nor lore-like. However, neither formal nor informal law is fixed and immutable. In the case studies we have observed formal law changing, through state legislation, and informal law coming into line with it, as in the case of smoking. We have seen the increasing importance of religious dietary law, both in regard to domestic demand and export markets, leading to changes in laws recognized by the state, as in the case of industry codes. And we noted the time lag between immigration, or arrival as an international student, and adoption of local laws—particularly informal ones—or the accommodation of the incoming informal law. In the meantime, each immigrant negotiates her or his own way to survive in an unfamiliar and alien legal regime. This may involve difficult experiences, such as trying to negotiate, from the assumptions of a different legal culture, with traffic police who enact their role as if it were the enforcement of a black letter law. Before *accommodation*, gaining access to halal food involves a process of *negotiation*, a process that may become easier as the laws and practices in the host country themselves negotiate new demands.

In rapidly changing situations, as for the immigrant or the multicultural society, or technological and scientific change, practice runs ahead of formal law. Texts slow down the law. Written at a specific point in time, they are then frozen and require increasingly flexible interpretations to cope with changing circumstances, both social and technological. Whether the text be a constitution, a holy book or a Napoleonic code, its pretensions to lay down the law for all time are constantly challenged. Both the circumstances of its enforcement and those of the "users" of the law change over time. The dangers of smoking, even passive smoking, are recognized, and social expectations, conditioned by both law and science, change; the law can change further. Cars go faster; speed limiting and detection devices are invented. Muslims migrate to new parts of the world without the established religious infrastructure; refrigeration and increasing speed of transport allow international trade in slaughtered meat; local meat producers, abattoirs, the imams, and ulama adjust to the demand; the state follows suit. Laws change in response to practices as they become established, while practices adapt to changing laws. This observation applies as much to informal as to formal law. Each dances with the other—formal law, practice, technique and informal law—in time and in place.

Places, like texts, help to slow down and position the law. Yet they do so without the explicit instructions of a text. It may be said that the law of a place is open to more flexible interpretation than that of a text. It follows repeated practice, rather than prescribing specific practices. Performances of the law always *take place*: they are situated. Here we see the constitutive theory of law in practice.[33] Repetition makes the law, while the law conditions iterations, but they are not condemned to be identical to each other.

"The performative needs to be rethought not only as an act that an official language-user wields in order to implement already authorized effects, but precisely as social ritual."[34] In noting the importance of ritual, Butler provides here a useful model to analyze and promote this formal-informal (re)iteration of law over time. Noting that Bourdieu fails to see the subversive possibilities of utterance and ritual, while Derrida assumes such to be inevitable, by combining elements of each she derives a liberatory analysis. This discovers the conditions for breaking out of the power of habitus through critical perspectives. Those critiques do not act purely at the level of language, but in social interactions, through "negotiated sociality." Each crossing of the street, each cigarette smoked, each halal transaction around food, references the previous ones and lays the groundwork for the next. This is how the social practice of law can be projected into the future.

Our illustrations from the demands of changing technology, health science, and trade show some of the channels by which law is opened to other institutional systems. Informal law is more malleable than formal or state law. It is quick to respond to new social facts, while being slowed down by habitual practices. Halal meat was regulated in the interests of international trade, but it was first popularized in Australia by Muslim immigrants. Prohibitions on smoking follow the discoveries of medical science on its dangers to health, yet they must interact with informal norms, and the interventions of the tobacco companies. Law reform is stimulated and challenged, slowed down or impelled by social practices, expressed in informal law, as well as by larger social realities including science, technology and economics.

By seeing the interpenetration of formal and informal law—in the provision of halal food and the practices of smoking, driving, and walking on the street—we catch a glimpse of the possibility of practice instituting formal as well as informal law. Even beyond constituting the law, Dardot and Laval have called this the "*praxis instituante*," the praxis that institutes the law: "the self-production of a collective subject in, and through, the continuous co-production of the rules of law." In their sketch for a revolution of the 21st century by which the common could overcome the monopoly of state power and the tyranny of the markets, it is only this instituting process which can establish "the common" in the social imaginary.[35]

Culture

Culture both nourishes law and is constituted by it. In the case studies we have seen legal cultures grow around street corners. We have seen cultures arrive in a new area and accommodate to, while also molding the laws of previously established cultures. The mix of cultures coming to the place form the basis for establishing new informal legal relations, renewed and renegotiated with each encounter. Each of us carries around a culture in our thoughts, actions and meaning systems. While culture is inculcated from our earliest years, this is not to say that we become, in adulthood, immutable products of a culture. Each of us carries culture into each encounter, from which new cultural understandings, practices and regularities emerge.

The assumptions of the model of indigenous "customary law," that we noted in introducing this chapter, suggest a timeless underlying law that has been superseded by the new sovereign law of the colonizers. Any "accommodation" is assumed to be on the terms of the colonists. This simple dualism is challenged when the presumptively monolithic sovereign law confronts new practices and informal legal regimes which arrive with, or spring from the legal cultures of a mix of new immigrants.[36] Each encounter of formal and informal law, or of one legal culture with another, is negotiated anew. The state plays a role in this process, but it is not the simple hegemonic act of "accommodation," the grudging and minimal acceptance of difference. The state cannot regulate every encounter. It *makes room* for the halal butcher not through *accommodation* but because the space is *taken up by* the new alternative.

"Accommodation" and "tolerance" are always top-down: they indicate what the state authority is prepared to accept or put up with. This study has shown both ethical and empirical reasons for preferring "negotiation." The citizens also have their own diverse opinions, habitus and cultural and legal expectations that suggest how far they can go in putting up with the state. Cultures and informal laws, like the immigrants themselves, insist on their own survival. This always involves negotiation: some recognition of formal or informal law is necessary to reach the other side of the road alive. This applies to the figurative road of living in a new country as much as the literal Marrickville Road or Beamish Street. The negotiations of law and culture pick their way among proliferating options: there are consequences as well as choices.

We follow Geertz in seeing that the comparative study of law is made up of cultural translation. He derives this conclusion from two principles that have also guided this study: "law is local knowledge not placeless principle and . . . it is constructive of social life not reflective, or at any rate not just reflective, of it."[37]

Each of the case studies illustrates the interaction of various levels of formal and informal law. The outcome of those interactions is always indeterminate, since every encounter is freshly negotiated. People may or may not smoke; cars may or may not stop; meat may be certified as halal or taken on trust. It is only in the outcome of each encounter that we can know which level of law, which combination of informal and formal laws, applied in a given situation. This negotiated sovereignty is a form of radical street-level positivism, based not on the solid foundation of a *Grundnorm*, but on the negotiated facts of empirical experience and the instituting praxis of law. These are patterns without certainty; indeterminate regularities that both make and break rules, always at the same time.

CONCLUSION

In this chapter we hope to have illuminated some central issues in the social, political, and material relations of law by exploring a few very specific places in the inner south west of Sydney. To restate our opening questions, in the broadest terms, we asked where laws come from, how they are recorded, and how conflicts among them are worked out. Throughout the chapter informal laws have been juxtaposed against formal, state laws. In the process, the lines between the formal and informal have become blurred.

Our focus on a multicultural and (post)colonial society has revealed a patchwork of legal regimes in operation. Invisible to this study, but preexisting and surviving beneath the surface of the laws we observed here, are the indigenous laws of Australia. The imposition of colonial common law, at federal and state level, laid down a formal platform of law, written and institutionalized. Overlaying and undermining the law of the colonial power are numerous informal laws, seen here to be operating at street level. They spring from traditions (both autochthonous and introduced), habits and alternative legal regimes.

At their least formal, these patterns of law-like behavior are expressed in everyday interaction: crossing the road, driving a car, sitting at outdoor cafés, buying food. They are performed against a backdrop of street-level laws and their signs. Some of these are state-sanctioned: the "no smoking," speed limit and pedestrian crossing signs. There are also signs that declare food to be halal, which derive from Islamic formal and written legal regimes, which have been incorporated over several decades into state and industry codes. So we see that the more formal of these laws have been inscribed into signs, codes and statutes. Others are inscribed in the human micro-geography—the regions—of the street: the visible, civic "front" corner where one does not smoke, as opposed to the "back" region where smoking was tolerated (and where the formal sign had been graffitied). The laws are recorded in action in space, in formal signs (in Arabic and English), and in graffiti as well as in codes and statutes.

Some of the activities on the street could be clearly seen to be transgressive, such as smoking in front of a "no smoking" sign, whether or not it had been graffitied. Most, however, fall into a gray area of negotiation, such as the interactive dance between the pedestrian and the car at the marked crossing, whether or not accompanied by ironic comments on unexpected behavior. Negotiation, we propose, is at the heart of all this street-level legal activity. In meeting their daily needs—to eat, smoke or cross the road—the local people go about their business in habitual ways. Habit, habitus and regularity come before regulation, before the law.[38] In this process laws, both formal and informal, carve out their own space, make room for actions, regularity and regulation, in a process that is less polite and less conscious than accommodation, yet more civil than competition or conflict.

Bodily practices in space and time precede legal regulation, but are not immune to it. Perhaps Legendre overstates it when he writes that there is "no difference between a legal codification and the encoding of the body" (as in dance).[39] De Certeau modulates more carefully when he identifies the dual functions of the planners and common people in the city, attributing to the former a panopticon urge to control, and to the latter a narrative (i.e., pedestrian) experience of the space, in which memory plays an important part. "In short," writes De Certeau, "space is a practiced place. Thus the street geometrically defined by urban planning is transformed into a space by walkers."[40] We see the same relationship between informal law, legal codes, and the habitus of daily life. Deep memories coded into bodies persist, new practices spring up in the urban environment, laws are created or respond through adaptation, prohibition, or negotiation.

If laws can come from below, from the street and from the coding and interaction of bodies, they can also channel the big ideas and interests of recent times or of long traditions.[41] Islamic law, medical science and economic interest have all been seen, in these case studies, to contribute to the outcomes of daily interactions: smoking is banned, and decreases as a social practice; halal meat becomes available, in accord with ancient laws and the demands of global trade. Yet even these big ideas are expressed on the street, in bodily habitus and suburban backyards, and in the signs that regulate and advertise activities of daily life, on their way to being law.

NOTES

1. Óscar Correas, *Pluralismo Jurídico, Alternatividad y Derecho Indígena* (Mexico DF: Fontamara, 2003); John Griffiths, "What Is Legal Pluralism?," *Journal of Legal Pluralism,* 24 (1986): 1-55.

2. Jean-Guy Belley, ed., *Le droit soluble. Contributions québécoises à l'étude de l'internormativité* (Paris: Librairie générale de droit et de jurisprudence, 1996); Roderick A. Macdonald, "Metaphors of Multiplicity: Civil Society, Regimes and Legal Pluralism," *Arizona Journal of International and Comparative Law*, 15 (1998): 69-91.

3. Sally Engle Merry, "Legal Pluralism," *Law and Society Review,* 22 (1988): 869-896.

4. Pierre Bourdieu, *Practical Reason: On the Theory of Action* (Stanford, CA: Stanford University Press, 1998), chapter 3; David Delaney, "Semantic Ecology and Lexical Violence: Nature at the Limits of Law," *Law Text Culture,* 5 (2001): 77-112; Gilles Deleuze and Félix Guattari, *A Thousand Plateaus: Capitalism and Schizophrenia* (London: The Athlone Press, 1988). chapter 11. In these citations, Deleuze and Guattari and Bourdieu examine the spatial origins and proliferation of

laws, including state laws (Bourdieu). Lefebvre and Blomley suggest other ways that laws are inscribed through spatial practice. Nicholas K. Blomley, *Law, Space and the Geographies of Power* (NY: Guildford Press, 1994): 190; Henri Lefebvre, *The Production of Space* (Oxford: Blackwell, 1991): 129ff.

5. Boaventura de Sousa Santos, *Toward a New Common Sense: Law, Science and Politics in the Paradigmatic Transition* (New York: Routledge, 1995): 148-151.

6. Henry Reynolds, *The Law of the Land* (Ringwood, Vic.: Penguin, 1987); Richard Mohr, "Shifting Ground: Context and Change in Two Australian Legal," *International Journal for the Semiotics of Law,* 15 (2002): 1-24.

7. Australian Law Reform Commission, The Recognition of Aboriginal Customary Laws. (Canberra: Australian Government Publishing Service, 1986). See further discussion of these matters at note 32, below.

8. Some of those experiences and findings, including inputs from other agencies, is included in Richard Mohr et al., *The Lebanese Community in the Canterbury Area,* (Canterbury Community Health Services). Sydney: Ethnic Affairs Division of the Premier's Department of NSW, 1978.

9. They were identifiable by the use of one of these languages, a depiction of a national flag, or by explicit reference to the cuisine or type of food available. In addition, there are other shopkeepers of these and other ethnicities, who do not advertise their linguistic or cultural background.

10. http://www.marrickville.nsw.gov.au/en/community/business/smoke-free-zones/ accessed March 3, 2016.

11. Since this was written in mid-2016, the library has moved and Marrickville Council has been amalgamated with other local authorities to form a larger council.

12. Australian Bureau of Statistics (ABS) 2011 Census from ABS, Canterbury and Marrickville Council websites, http://www.marrickville.nsw.gov.au and http://www.canterbury.nsw.gov.au accessed March 9, 2016.

13. Until the 1920s present-day Lebanon was part of Syria.

14. Mohr et al., *Lebanese Community.*

15. ABS data from Canterbury Council website http://www.canterbury.nsw.gov.au/Discover/Demographics-Statistics accessed March 9, 2016.

16. The backyard of a house in Belmore or Lakemba may have been considered to be private, a "back" region in Goffman's terms, by the Muslim residents. This was not the view of certain Anglo-Australian neighbours, or the council health authorities. They considered it sufficiently "public," or "front" to want to discourage or prohibit the slaughter of animals there.

17. http://www.daff.gov.au/biosecurity/export/meat/elmer-3/notices/2009/mn09—08 accessed August 28, 2014.

18. Aus-Meat is "an industry owned company operating as a joint venture between Meat and Livestock Australia (MLA) and the Australian Meat Processor Corporation (AMPC)." http://www.ausmeat.com.au/audits-accreditation/halal-information.aspx accessed August 28, 2014.

19. This informal system of trust continues to operate in large western cities: "Tayyabs, a popular Punjabi curry house in the London borough of Tower Hamlets, Britain's most Muslim area, does not even bother with certificates. The

manager says that he knows and trusts his suppliers and his customers know and trust him." "Food and Religion: A Meaty Question," *The Economist*, February 9, 2013, accessed February 12, 2013, http://www.economist.com/news/international/21571419-who-should-regulate-kosher-and-halal-food-meaty-question.

20. Ghassan Hage, *Against Paranoid Nationalism: Searching for Hope in a Shrinking Society* (Annandale NSW: Pluto Press, 2003), 144ff.

21. Massimo Leone, "Cruzando calles: Cosmos y caos en la semiótica urbana," *Revista L. I. S.* 14 (2015): 131-44.

22. Leone reports the "sarcastic courtesy" of an elderly pedestrian lady in Turin, cut off by a car: "vada pure, ne!" ("go right ahead!"). Leone, "Cruzando calles," 134.

23. Ghassan Hage, "Urban Jouissance in the Streets of Beirut, The Manufacturing of Happiness" (paper presented at the Johannesburg Workshop in Theory and Criticism, University of the Witwatersrand, Johannesburg, July 6, 2015).

24. In addition to Hage on Beirut, see also on Teheran, Leone, "Cruzando calles," 134–135, 142, and on Naples, Patrícia Branco and Richard Mohr, "Odore di Napoli: What if Jurisprudence Came to us through Smell?" *Non LIquet (Westminster Online Working Papers): Law and the Senses Series:* "Smell" (2015), 58–75, accessed November 10, 2015, www.westminster.ac.uk/data/assets/pdf_file/0009/376146/Smell.pdf.

25. Erving Goffman, *Relations in Public: Microstudies of the Public Order* (Harmondsworth: Penguin, 1971). Chapter 3, "Regions and region behavior."

26. Henshaw notes that in modern western cities "the smellscapes of city streets are turning into sterilized clones of one another." Victoria Henshaw, "Welcome to the Smellscape," 222 *New Scientist*, June 2014, 28.

27. Cornelia Vismann, *Files: Law and Media Technology* (Stanford, CA: Stanford University Press, 2008), 71–72.

28. Yan Thomas, "*Res Religiosae:* On the Categories of Religion and Commerce," in *Law, Anthropology and the Constitution of the Social: Making Persons and Things*, ed. Alain Pottage and Martha Mundy (Cambridge UK: Cambridge University Press, 2004).

29. Edward Muir, *Civic Ritual in Renaissance Venice* (Princeton, NJ: Princeton University Press: 1981), 192.

30. Agnes T. M. Schreiner, "So, This Is How It Is Done . . .," in *Ritual and Semiotics* ed. J. Ralph Lindgren and Jay Knaack (New York: Peter Lang, 1997), 123-43.

31. Frederic William Maitland, "The Mystery of Seisin," *Law Quarterly Review* 2 (1886): 481-96.

32. Lefebvre, *Production of Space*, 33 ff.

33. Karl Klare, "Law-Making as Praxis," *Telos* 40 (1979): 123–135.

34. Judith Butler, *Excitable Speech: A Politics of the Performative* (New York: Routledge, 1997), 142–159.

35. Pierre Dardot and Christian Laval, *Commun: Essai sur la révolution au XXIe siècle*. (Paris: La Découverte, 2014), 445–451.

36. The simple "customary law" model is equally challenged when indigenous peoples form new cultural and informal legal practices in response to colonization. This can occur through practices of resistance, through interpenetration and

innovation as a result of mingling of diverse indigenous and immigrant groups, or through creative adaptation and epistemic responses to settler law. See Mohr, "Shifting Ground," 1-24.

37. Clifford Geertz, *Local Knowledge: Further Essays in Interpretive Anthropology*. (New York: Basic Books, 1983), 218.

38. Charles Taylor, "To Follow a Rule . . . ," in *Bourdieu: Critical Perspectives*, ed. Craig Calhoun, Edward LiPuma, and Moishe Postone (Cambridge UK: Polity Press, 1993), 45-60.

39. Pierre Legendre, *La passion d'être un autre: Étude pour la danse*. Paris: Éditions du Seuil, 1978), 58.

40. Michel De Certeau, *The Practice of Everyday Life*, trans. Steven F. Rendall. (Berkeley: University of California Press, 1984), 117.

41. See also Richard Mohr, "Rethinking the Secular: Religion, ethics and science in food regulation," *Working papers of the Centre for International Governance and Justice, RegNet, ANU*, (2013), accessed April 18, 2016, http://regnet.anu.edu.au/research/publications/2749/working-paper-no-1-rethinking-secular-religion-ethics-and-science-food.

REFERENCES

Australian Law Reform Commission. *The Recognition of Aboriginal Customary Laws*. Canberra: Australian Government Publishing Service, 1986.

Belley, Jean-Guy, ed. *Le droit soluble. Contributions québécoises à l'étude de l'internormativité*. Paris: Librairie générale de droit et de jurisprudence, 1996.

Blomley, Nicholas K. *Law, Space and the Geographies of Power*. New York: Guildford Press, 1994.

Bourdieu, Pierre. *Practical Reason: On the Theory of Action*. Stanford, CA: Stanford University Press, 1998.

Branco, Patrícia, and Richard Mohr. "Odore di Napoli: What if Jurisprudence Came to us through Smell?" *Non LIquet (Westminster Online Working Papers): Law and the Senses Series* Smell: 58–75. Accessed November 10, 2015, www.westminster.ac.uk/data/assets/pdf_file/0009/376146/Smell.pdf.

Butler, Judith. *Excitable Speech: A Politics of the Performative*. New York: Routledge, 1997.

Correas, Óscar. *Pluralismo Jurídico, Alternatividad y Derecho Indígena*. Mexico DF: Fontamara, 2003.

Dardot, Pierre and Christian Laval. *Commun: Essai sur la révolution au XXIe siècle*. Paris: La Découverte, 2014.

De Certeau, Michel. *The Practice of Everyday Life*. Translated by Steven F. Rendall. Berkeley: University of California Press, 1984.

Delaney, David. "Semantic Ecology and Lexical Violence: Nature at the Limits of Law." *Law Text Culture* 5 (2001): 77–112.

Deleuze, Gilles and Félix Guattari. *A Thousand Plateaus: Capitalism and Schizophrenia*. Translated by Brian Massumi. London: The Athlone Press, 1988.

Geertz, Clifford. *Local Knowledge: Further Essays in Interpretive Anthropology*. New York: Basic Books, 1983.

Goffman, Erving. *Relations in Public: Microstudies of the Public Order*. Harmondsworth: Penguin, 1971.

Griffiths, John. "What Is Legal Pluralism?" *Journal of Legal Pluralism* 24 (1986): 1–55.

Hage, Ghassan. *Against Paranoid Nationalism: Searching for Hope in a Shrinking Society*. Annandale NSW: Pluto Press, 2003.

———. "Urban Jouissance in the Streets of Beirut, The Manufacturing of Happiness." Paper presented at the Johannesburg Workshop in Theory and Criticism, University of the Witwatersrand, Johannesburg, July 6, 2015.

Henshaw, Victoria. "Welcome to the Smellscape," 222 *New Scientist*, June 2014, 28–29.

Klare, Karl. "Law-Making as Praxis." *Telos* 40 (1979): 123–35.

Lefebvre, Henri. *The Production of Space*. Translated by D. Nicholson-Smith. Oxford: Blackwell, 1991.

Legendre, Pierre. *La passion d'être un autre: Étude pour la danse*. Paris: Éditions du Seuil, 1978.

Leone, Massimo. "Cruzando calles: cosmos y caos en la cotidianidad urbana," *Revista LIS* 14 (2015): 131–44.

Local Government Act 1993 (NSW).

Macdonald, Roderick A. "Metaphors of Multiplicity: Civil Society, Regimes and Legal Pluralism." *Arizona Journal of International and Comparative Law*, 15 (1998): 69–91.

Maitland, Frederic William. "The Mystery of Seisin." *Law Quarterly Review* 2 (1886): 481–496.

Merry, Sally Engle. "Legal Pluralism." *Law and Society Review* 22 (1988): 869–896.

Mohr, Richard, Leigh Deves, Roy Crino, Sam Choucair and Guler Peker. *The Lebanese Community in the Canterbury Area*. Sydney: Ethnic Affairs Division of the Premier's Department of NSW, 1978.

Mohr, Richard. "Rethinking the Secular: Religion, Ethics and Science in Food Regulation." Working papers of the Centre for International Governance and Justice, RegNet, ANU. Accessed April 18, 2016, http://regnet.anu.edu.au/research/publications/2749/working-paper-no-1-rethinking-secular-religion-ethics-and-science-food.

———. "Shifting Ground: Context and Change in Two Australian Legal Systems," *International Journal for the Semiotics of Law* 15 (2002): 1–24.

Muir, Edward. *Civic Ritual in Renaissance Venice*. Princeton: Princeton University Press: 1981.

Prevention of Cruelty to Animals Act 1979 (NSW).

Reynolds, Henry. *The Law of the Land*. Ringwood, Vic.: Penguin, 1987.

Santos, Boaventura de Sousa. *Toward a New Common Sense: Law, Science and Politics in the Paradigmatic Transition*. New York: Routledge, 1995.

Schreiner, Agnes T. M. "So, This Is How It Is Done . . ." In *Ritual and Semiotics*, edited by J. Ralph Lindgren and Jay Knaack, 123–143. New York: Peter Lang, 1997.

Smoke-free Environments Act 2000 (NSW).

Taylor, Charles. "To Follow a Rule . . ." in *Bourdieu: Critical Perspectives*, ed. Craig Calhoun, Edward LiPuma, and Moishe Postone, 45–60. Cambridge, UK: Polity Press, 1993.

Thomas, Yan. "*Res Religiosae:* On the Categories of Religion and Commerce." In *Law, Anthropology and the Constitution of the Social: Making Persons and Things*, edited by Alain Pottage and Martha Mundy, 40–72. Cambridge: Cambridge University Press, 2004.

Vismann, Cornelia. *Files: Law and Media Technology*. Stanford: Stanford University Press, 2008.

Chapter 4

The Seduction of Consent

Margaret Mott

STUDENTS FOR SURVEILLANCE?

The campaign to end sexual violence on college campuses provides an instructive counterexample to the relationship between policing and the street. Normally, when the law increases its surveillance over a specific population, such as with the stop-and-frisk policy, the communities under surveillance find ways to resist the law's authority. But in the case of increased surveillance of sexual encounters, the subject population appears to welcome the state's intrusion. Even as campus activists question the methods of most policing, particularly when it comes to the treatment of minority communities, they rarely question the methods of the state's campaign to end intimate violence on campus. As far as this group is concerned, they want more surveillance, not less.

For instance, when Vice President Joseph R. Biden Jr. announced, in April 2011, new Title IX guidelines for how colleges should handle students' reports of sexual assault, the response from students and student services was, "What took you so long?" While the procedural details of the 20-page "Dear Colleague" letter were vague, the message itself was clear: when it came to intimate violence on college campuses, the federal government would now be watching. From that point on, the state would use its multiple carrots and sticks to end a campus culture that promoted sexual violence. Thanks to the intervention of the Office of Civil Rights at the Department of Education, "rape culture" would be eradicated from American campuses.

Still, one might wonder why this generation of undergraduates is not skeptical of this federal oversight. Few undergraduates seem willing to raise concerns about due process or to question the underlying assumption that campuses promote a culture of rape. Instead, they accept the state's reasoning that women are more at risk of rape on college campuses than in other locations, and that the best way of ending this "rape culture" is through aggressive campus policing. Even as the rule changes offer less protections for the accused, there is little outcry from students against Title IX. This passivity is not surprising: If college administrators are reluctant to raise objections to this anti-rape campaign, then we should not be surprised that undergraduates are even more hesitant. Students who have been accused are unlikely to speak out, given the shame attached to those who engage in nonconsensual sex.

But there is more at play than just political timidity and shame. Consent trainings and sex positivity workshops convey the message that this new generation is ready for the adventures of sexual entrepreneurship without being marked as an offender. As long as these novice sexual actors successfully learn the rules of consent, they should be able to engage in casual sex without risking disciplinary action. The state campaign to end rape culture, they are told, will only affect the perverts. Consent is marketed as a get-out-of-jail card. A properly trained disciplinary panel will never punish the consenting sexual entrepreneur, only the sexual predator.

In actuality, the Dear Colleague letter greatly increased the chances of being charged and convicted for sexual misconduct. By broadening the definition of sexual violence to include any "physical sexual acts perpetrated against a person's will or where a person is incapable of giving consent due to the victim's use of drugs or alcohol," the category of what constitutes consensual sex was narrowed.[1] If the sexual encounter took place after a party, the "yes" could be compromised. Intellectual or other disabilities also compromised the effectiveness of using consent as a defense. If the complainant received an ADA accommodation, a panel could rightly question her capacity to consent.

Or so worried the adjudicators.

In the months following the Dear Colleague Letter, the Office of Civil Rights (OCR) was flooded with questions. Unprepared for the volume, the OCR was not able to respond with any clarifying details, leaving administrators to chart their own course. As Harvard Law professor Jeannie Suk explained, schools "weren't completely sure of exactly how to comply, and so in many cases they did more than they necessarily needed to do."[2] Confusion, and the threat of losing federal funding, caused many schools to lean more heavily in favor of victim's testimony. Given the new restrictions on consent, even if she had nodded her agreement, the presence of drugs or alcohol in her system weakened his defense.

As panels became more "victim-friendly," some aggrieved respondents claimed the proceedings suffered from a different type of gender discrimination. A story in *Inside Higher Ed* from 2013 reported that male students, who felt they had been falsely accused, were suing campus tribunals for violating their protections under Title IX. Claiming that the college's "guidelines and regulations are set up to disproportionately affect the male student population," these aggrieved respondents demanded relief.[3] But allegations of partiality and lack of due process did not diminish the Obama Administration's effort to fight campus sexual violence using aggressive tribunals. Even if they faced a gender discrimination lawsuit from male students, college administrators still had to make this problem go away.

A 2014 report from the White House Council on Women and Girls, titled "Not Alone," called for a "coordination among federal agencies to hold schools accountable if they do not confront sexual violence on their campuses."[4] Rather than address the problem of discrimination against men, the report instructed schools to follow a medical model. Sexual assault, explained the White House Report, "is a unique crime: unlike other crimes, victims often blame themselves; the associated trauma can leave their memories fragmented."[5] If her testimony was weak, disjointed or contradictory, the adjudicators must read that confusion as evidence that a traumatic event occurred. Rather than solving the problem of bias, the trauma-informed approach increased grounds for discrimination against men by providing special treatment for complainants. Although most respondents report being distressed by accusations of sexual misconduct, their psychological state was not factored into the proceeding. As a Title IX Coordinator from SUNY Albany confirmed at a recent Title IX informational panel, victims are traumatized, respondents are just "stressed."[6] Investigators and panelists should not treat respondents with the same sympathy and understanding as complainants.

"CHOOSING" CONSENT

If sex is adjudicated through the lens of trauma, sex is taught as a transactional business agreement. The former reduces the legitimacy of consent, while the latter promotes its lawfulness. For instance, at one BDSM (bondage, domination, sado-masochism) website, which promotes sex play that is "safe, sane, and consensual," participants are instructed in how to have safe and kinky sex. "Submissive partners," explains Sharon Glassburn, "are responsible for communicating their own limits."[7] If they start feeling violated or traumatized, they must make those feelings known. Dominators have the responsibility to check in with submissives by examining "the quality of their partner's face" and by looking "at his or her body language." But while these instructions appear simple, the constraints on reading each other's body language is challenged by the props of bondage. Dom(me)s are cautioned to "make sure your partner can breathe if you're using a ball gag or mask." The fact that this website even encourages masks and gags seems more like entrapment than realistic instruction. It only takes a frisson of trauma to turn the submissive partner into a complainant and the "dom(me)" into a respondent. The website, however, does not talk about the punitive aspect of the law, nor how a trauma-informed approach might adjudicate a ball gag. Instead, freedom of choice is promoted while the criminal risks are ignored.

Fortunately, most consent trainings do not encourage such risky behavior. Even so, the gap between what the law demands and how sex is taught is immense. In a 2012 Brown University training video, titled, "Brown Students Ask for Consent," individual students of various ethnicities, races, genders, and sexual orientations discuss the legalities of consent in sober and reasonable terms.[8] "Sex is great," explains one earnest female, "when it's consensual." Another young woman confides, "It's about talking about sex with my partner about how far I want to go, whether I'm in a relationship or just hooking up." Consent is "based on choice," says another confident undergraduate. It is "not drunk," "not passed out," and, spoken by a very tentative young woman, who pauses for effect, "not . . . silent." Consent means "giving permission without feeling pressured," explains one young woman. It means "positive cooperation and the exercise of free will," asserts the next smiling young man. "Consent is active and not passive," proclaims a serious young man. Each of the legal components of effective consent is presented as a matter of common sense.

Having laid out the legal components on consensual sex, the video addresses its pleasures. "Sex is great," says one actor alone in a screen, when it is "spontaneous," says another actor, or "comfortable," says another, followed by another who says, "when it feels good" and finally, "exciting." But while the script sounds convincing, the bodies seem remote from any sexuality. These intelligent young persons seem ready for a midterm exam, not for seduction. Passion is pointed to but never performed. None of the actors is aroused. Nor are any two actors on the screen at the same time. Consent, the video suggests, is most effective when no one else is around.

Indeed, according to a study conducted by behavioral economists at University of California, Berkeley, consent is most effective when the individual is not having sex. Male participants were first given a survey that asked them to predict how they would negotiate a sexual encounter. Would they pursue sex with someone who did not consent to their advances? Eighty percent of the participants answered in the negative. When the same participants answered the questions under the conditions of arousal (masturbating alone in a room while watching a pornographic video), forty-five percent predicted they would persist even without consent.[9]

Dan Ariely, who conducted the UC Berkley study, concludes that policymakers fail because "we all underpredict the degree to which arousal completely negates our superego and the way emotions can take control of our behavior."[10] Public policies fail because they wrongly assume that individuals are always rational. Instead, writes Ariely, "we are all less rational in our decision making than standard economic theory assumes."[11] Once we take into account our "predictably irrational" behavior, he argues, we should be able to design better policies. In this regard, consent trainings inevitably fail because they do not recognize the real conditions of human sexuality. We should not be surprised, then, that the statistics on campus sexual assaults have not changed since the campaign began. Indeed, some advocates will claim that the numbers are worse now than they were in 2011. But ineffectiveness is not the end of the story. Rather, by reinforcing the assumption that consent will protect sexual actors from investigation, these trainings provide undergraduates with false hopes.

Consent is also marketed as the way to transcend rape culture. Not just a means to avoid a disciplinary panel, consent is the practice that distinguishes the normal from the pervert. "We teach sexual consent as a way of subverting rape culture," explains the All Students for Consent (ASC) mission statement at Whitman College, "by recognizing that sexual scripting is rooted in, and thus perpetuates rape culture."[12] Like the Brown students, members of ASC believe that consent will give the intelligent undergraduate the tools to leave rape culture behind. Those who successfully navigate sexual encounters have transcended the past. Those who can't, are stuck in the mentality of rape culture, reinforcing the notion that those who are expelled are carrying the disease of rape culture within them.

All of this suggests that the true work of consent is the work of normalization. By creating two categories of students, those who can consent and those who can't, consent reinforces the legitimacy of the Title IX apparatus. Like the prison in Foucault's *Discipline and Punish,* the work of Title IX "is not intended to eliminate offenses, but rather to distinguish them, to distribute them, to use them."[13] According to this logic, the work of the consent trainings is to distinguish those who can have legal sex from those who can't. The work of the Title IX apparatus, according to a Foucaultian analysis, is not to end sexual assault on college campuses but to control the population. The specter of the sex offender is useful in this regard; it defines the norms of the sexual entrepreneur. The sex offender, explains legal scholar Joseph Fischel, makes it possible for consent "to do the sex work we want it to do."[14] The sex offender allows tribunals to uphold the regime of "national sexual normativity," a normativity that used to be characterized as heterosexual and is now "adult consensuality."[15] The fiction of freedom cloaks a system that is merciless.

College students are indoctrinated into this world view by appealing to their aspirations to be recognized as better adults than their parents' generation. The Brown University video championed each student's individual choice. The BDSM championed the pleasures of kinky and consensual sex. Neither of these promotional materials pointed to increased state surveillance or the slipperiness of consent under pressure. Rather consensual sex was both the practice and the reward of the sexual entrepreneur, someone whose sex would never be adjudicated.

THE SEXUAL ENTREPRENEUR

Sex, for the sexual entrepreneur, does not involve entanglements or distractions. Rather it is a brief release from the hard work of college. The term for this norm is "hook up," a phenomenon that became more recognizable after the financial collapse of 2008. Speaking with a *New York Times* reporter, one University of Pennsylvania junior explained that she wasn't interested in romance or in something as incalculable as "the meeting of two souls."[16] Indeed, she and her hook up "don't really like each other in person, sober" They "literally can't sit down and have coffee," although they can have sex after a few beers. Other female interviewees described the advantages of casual sex, based on "'cost-benefit' analyses and the 'low risk and low investment costs' of hooking up." These ambitious women report they don't have time for the burdens of a relationship. They would rather have sex with someone they don't like than risk emotional attachment.

Still, there is the issue of those beers.

The idea that a five-year plan is more compelling than romance points to the very different norms operating in the early 21st century. While her grandmother's generation might have gone to college to find a husband, and her mother's generation might have gone to college to further the feminist agenda, her generation follows the norms of the entrepreneurial subject, someone who makes strategic decisions in a competitive marketplace. The idea that sex serves market interests is not unexpected. As political theorist Wendy Brown explains, "neoliberal rationality disseminates the *model of the marke*t to all domains and activities."[17] Even sexuality, she argues, has been reduced to market terms. Referring to upscale online dating sites, Brown notes how "one might approach one's dating life in the mode of an entrepreneur or investor, trying to generate, accumulate, or invest monetary wealth in this domain."[18] Relationships are only worth it when they maximize individual resources.

But online dating is not subject to the same surveillance as the sexual encounters of college students. Female students who report getting drunk in order to "wrap up" a sexual encounter could, upon reflection, determine they were actually traumatized. The 2013 *New York Times* article described how one "girl" made sense of the fact that "her encounters freshman and sophomore year often ended with fellatio." She may have agreed to go back to a guy's room when she was drunk, but by the time she arrived she was "starting to sober up and didn't want to be there anymore, and giving the guy oral sex was an easy way to wrap things up and leave."[19] According to the standards of Title IX, the comment "didn't want to be there anymore" suggests that the sex was not consensual.

What is interesting about this 2013 article is that none of these entrepreneurial subjects described their ambiguous encounters as rape. Rather, the emphasis is on individual choice and efficient transactions. Since then, however, an entire industry of Title IX consultants and student activists is raising the specter of trauma. Upon reflection, should she determine that the fellatio was not a free act but a coerced performance, the sexual entrepreneur will be encouraged to see herself as a traumatized victim.

THE TRAUMA TECHNOCRACY

In September 2014, the faculty and staff of my small college were inducted as Campus Security Authorities (CSA) during a compulsory training, part of our annual compliance for Title IX and other federal regulations. As newly deputized CSA's (since then the term has been changed to Responsible Employees), we were required to complete an incident report for the federal government when any student alluded to a sex act that was nonconsensual.

"But what if we're not sure that the allegations are true?" asked a Writing Professor, who often hears lurid details of dorm life in first-year essays.

"For purposes of Clery," explained the Survivor Advocate and Sexual Respect Educator, "any allegation is assumed to be true. Victims have been traumatized. They need to know that they will be believed. They don't need any questions. They need to know they can trust you."

A photography professor, who often takes students on extensive field trips, raised his hand. "I've been in this situation before," he explained, "both parties have their own story." Other faculty members nodded in agreement. How could we file a crime report without any assurance that a crime had actually occurred?

The Survivor Advocate patiently explained that victims must be believed. That's what a "trauma-informed approach" required. Raising objections too early would cause her to doubt herself, making it less likely that she would report the crime.

"But what if it isn't a crime?" asked a frustrated faculty member.

"If he didn't get consent," she explained, "it was sexual assault." Although more hands shot up in the audience, the Survivor Advocate clicked on the next slide in her presentation.

As CSA, we were expected to engage in active listening, use appropriate language, avoid investigation, and demonstrate empathy. "You want to listen to her story, not tell her what happened to you once," explained the Survivor Advocate. "And you want to use language that makes it clear that you are concerned about her and her safety, language that doesn't have any judgment in it." Trauma, the advocate explained, makes it hard for victims to talk. Sometimes, she told us, their stories won't make a lot of sense. We should avoid asking questions about facts. We were not investigators; our job was to be supportive. If a student told us about a sexual experience and we were uncomfortable, we should explain to the student that we were unskilled in this matter and take him or her to the Survivor Advocate's office. Should the sexual encounter have a whiff of nonconsensuality, we must deliver the victims to specially trained providers.

The contradiction between the freedom of transactional sex (whether a hook up or BDSM) and the surveillance of college students (through the deputization of faculty, staff, and peer leaders) has produced a highly constrained discourse when it comes to discussing sex. On the one hand, students are assumed to be mature sexual entrepreneurs. On the other hand, once they have been marked by a nonconsensual sexual experience, all further conversations must comply with federal regulations. Not surprisingly, once an allegation of nonconsensual sex is voiced, both parties lose their autonomy. The accused becomes a sexual predator, incapable of understanding the niceties of consent. But even the person harmed loses the capacity to advocate for herself.

In an April 2016 law review article, law professor Aya Gruber lays out an extensive critique of the trauma-informed approach. The "trauma narrative," she explains, "plays a prominent role in campus advocacy and politics."[20] Unlike discussions of trauma in clinical or academic settings, where different types of trauma are analyzed with respect to recovery, the trauma narrative on college campuses serves the agenda of a militant anti-rape movement. Should we be concerned, asks Gruber, "when women students, months after an incident, decide to file a report because they talked to a counselor, professor, administrator, or activist who help them determine an ambiguous or barely remembered sexual situation was actually a traumatic rape?"[21] This "trauma technocracy," argues Gruber, "contextualizes women's sexual experiences for them."[22] Given the culture of "rampant mandatory report, we can expect more and more troubled but ambivalent students to meet with politically resolute campus personnel."[23] Rather than asking complainants what they want, campus personnel explain their feelings to them.

Not surprisingly, many complainants report feeling unheard throughout the proceedings. Complainants may feel ambiguous about the encounter, but the trauma technocracy will only hear their distress. Complainants may want expressions of sympathy, but panelists are only looking for indicators of trauma. When complainants reject the label of trauma, their feelings are dismissed as false consciousness. The trauma narrative, argues Gruber, "construes sexual assault complainants as devastated (or self-deluding) and female students as incapable of self-management, in order to presage a trauma-informed infrastructure involving extreme caution, mandatory report, and intense intervention."[24] Once she is identified as a victim, her testimony will be parsed through the logic of trauma. If she hesitates to bring a complaint, her hesitancy will be further evidence of trauma. If she says she is confused or ambivalent, that will be read as evidence that sexual misconduct actually occurred. If she later decides to opt out of a process, a teacher or a residential assistant may provide testimony that supports her initial allegation. If she says it was a misunderstanding, campus personnel will tell her she must hold him accountable. After all, it was his responsibility to get consent.

STATE FEMINISM

This state of affairs, where complainants are shoehorned into a narrow, traumatized stereotype and respondents are recast as monsters, follows the logic of dominance feminism. Catharine Mackinnon had provocatively argued that male sexuality is, by definition, the violation of women, an argument that took on "dramatic" legal proportions in the 1990s.[25] Feminists in the battered women's movement threw their considerable political power and organized networks behind President Clinton's 1994 Crime Bill, carving out a special realm of feminist jurisprudence that focused on the dangerousness of the male violence and the helplessness of the traumatized victim. At the time of the law's enactment, the proposed bill was promoted by white, middle-class feminists and rejected by women of color and women from immigrant communities; lines that had everything to do with each group's relationship to the police.

State feminism, however, was not inevitable. In the 1970s and 1980s, advocates who worked in shelters or on crisis hotlines were suspicious of any forms of social control, patriarchal or professional.[26] With the passage of VAWA, a major split took place in the movement. Women of color and women from immigrant communities backed out of the movement, turning the battered women's movement into a white, middle-class movement. And while some shelters tried to remain at arm's length from the DA's office, few shelters were in a position to refuse the federal funding that came with cooperation. Only towns and cities that promoted a "community-coordinated response" to domestic violence were assured of continued financial support.[27] As a result, advocates for battered women, who used to organize independently of the state through safe houses and international networks, were coerced into working with state prosecutors and police.

VAWA changed not only the strategies of the battered women's movement, but also of prosecutors. Prosecutors began to use the "Power and Control Wheel" to broaden the definition of what constituted abuse. Sexual assault statutes were broadened to allow for more convictions. "[F]eminists of the 1980s and '90s," explains law professor Leigh Goodmark, "were enormously successful in restructuring the legal response to domestic violence, a feat made possible only by virtue of their political power and their willingness both to assert that power and to seek partnerships with others that would maximize that power."[28] Feminists encouraged funding for special victim advocates in the offices of district attorneys and encouraged police departments to arrest more batterers.

In moving away from a community-based approach and toward a criminal justice approach, the battered women's movement lost touch with a key component of the women's movement: taking women seriously. "The movement went from being woman-centered to victim-centered, from self-help to saving, from working with women to generate the options that best met their needs to preferring one option," explains Goodmark.[29] Women were no longer considered able to negotiate healthier options; rather they became victims in need of state protection. But state feminism didn't just need victims, it also needed a steady stream of perpetrators of sexual violence to legitimize its illiberal methods of control.

In providing justifications for increased state surveillance over intimate violence, the battered women's movement played into the hands of a state that was increasingly using the criminal justice system to solve all social problems. According to political scientist Kristin Bumiller, the neoliberal regime coopted the movement in order to legitimate a "highly rationalized form of social control."[30] Intimate violence performed a key function of control by creating two categories of people in need of state surveillance: victims, who are "medicalized, controlled, and reformed"; and perpetrators, who are "removed beyond the territory of a civilized society."[31] Intimate violence was particularly useful at gaining public support for criminalization because "sex crimes generated diffuse fears that justified more punitive action by the state."[32] As with other issues on the "crime control agenda," explains Bumiller, "the link to an actual rise in the crime rate was less significant than how violence against women shaped a generalized fear of disorder and the image of habitual and recalcitrant criminals."[33] As long as the population remained afraid of sex crimes, this neoliberal system of control would remain in place.

Similarly, as long as undergraduates believe that rape culture exists, there will be no challenge to Title IX's system of control. As long as the majority of college students believe that only the bad guys will get picked up, they will continue to support these illiberal policies. Instead of demanding due process or a more restorative response, students will continue to demand punitive policies that hold rapists accountable. Fear of sex crimes, as Bumiller points out, inevitably strengthens the legitimacy of punitive state policy. By constantly invoking the evils of a rape culture, the Title IX apparatus gives its critics little ground for dissent.

ANOTHER PATH TO JUSTICE

In the last couple of years, however, the alliance between the punitive state and victim advocates is showing signs of stress. As more Americans consider the effects of mass incarceration on communities and families, victim advocates outside of college campuses are beginning to reconsider the strategy of punishment. Certainly books like *The New Jim Crow* by Michelle Alexander and *Just Mercy* by Bryan Stevenson are giving voters reasons to question the justice of a punitive state. But it's not just the experience of the incarcerated that is getting a second look. Many of the critiques of the criminal justice system are framed in terms that focus on the needs of the victim.

"Not all survivors have benefitted from the criminal justice system," explained Karen Tronsgard-Scott, Executive Director of the Vermont Network against Domestic and Sexual Violence, at the "Re-Imagining Criminal Justice Symposium" in December 2016. That was not a statement she would have made five years ago. Indeed, when she first read some of the feminist challenges to state feminism, she responded defensively. However, knowing first-hand the history of VAWA, particularly how women of color and women in immigrant communities had rejected the premise that the criminal justice system could make women safer, she decided to own up to the truth. "We were wrong," she told an audience of law students, public defenders, prosecutors, state's attorneys, formerly incarcerated, and victim advocates at the Vermont Law School. VAWA was a "well-intentioned undertaking," but it created a false reality. "People should not be defined by the worst thing they've done," said Tronsgard-Scott "We used a fear-based approach; what was needed was a love approach."

Something approaching a love approach is being used by proponents of restorative justice. In the United Kingdom, researchers found that restorative justice gave "voice to the real harms of sexual offenses . . . in a manner not possible in the conventional adversarial justice process."[34] Arizona's RESTORE program uses a victim-centered, community driven process that provides "carefully reasoned, safe, and respectful alternatives" for sexual assault survivors as long as "we collaborate, consult and listen to the needs of our constituencies."[35] In the RESTORE program, victims are part of the solution, deciding what will work best for all parties involved. Instead of being reduced to a trauma, devoid of any agency, survivors in the RESTORE program are given a chance to discuss *all* their emotional responses, which may include concern for the respondent. By treating victims as capable of advocating for themselves, restorative justice challenges the assumption that trauma restricts autonomy.

By treating the accused as capable of change, restorative justice challenges the assumption that sex offenders must be marked for life. At the Dalhousie University Dental School in Nova Scotia, a circle of accountability was created to address misogynistic Facebook postings. The fourth-year male dental students involved were eligible for dismissal under Dalhousie's policy on sexual harassment, but the victims of the harassment did not want such a harsh penalty imposed. Instead, Dalhousie used a restorative process that balanced a circle of support with a separate circle of accountability. Through the circle of accountability, the respondents came to understand how their actions affected others. They also came to realize that "we are not innocent, nor are we monsters."[36] At the end of the process, the class was able to graduate together.

Restorative justice operates on the assumption that human beings can heal through a community-based process that encourages self-reflection, vulnerability, courage, and second chances. Restorative justice, explains Linda Mills, "is grounded in spiritual traditions that believe in the potential of human beings to heal."[37] That healing takes place in a relational setting, where feelings are important and the myriad effects of an action are considered. To speak in relational terms on an American college campus right now is to invite the rage of victim advocates and Title IX consultants. Some of that rage may be fueled by an industry whose legitimacy depends on maintaining the narrative that a rape culture persists, that sexual monsters lurk in the dorms, and that victims are too traumatized to think for themselves.

On the campus quad, then, state feminism remains sovereign. If female students feel violated after a sexual encounter, then the response must be punitive. If male (and lesbian) students feel nervous that they cannot defend themselves against an accusation of sexual misconduct, then their understanding of consent is inadequate. The rhetoric of rape culture legitimizes an entire apparatus of trainers, consultants, advocates and student activists. Without the repeated invocation of a rape culture, there would hardly be work for the trauma technocracy and the consent industry. That these efforts do not address the actual circumstances of ambiguous sex between young adults seems of little importance. Rather, the student population seems to accept the twin processes of victimization and criminalization. Harsher punishment is welcomed as the necessary cost of a permissive sexual marketplace.

But it is not just fear of sex crimes that bolsters state feminism on college campuses, it is also the hopes attached to consent. As long as these young sexual actors believe themselves free to hook up, free to engage in bondage, and free from prosecution, they have no reason to protest the policing of sex. Consent, then, conforms to the logic of law under neoliberalism: only those who fail in their sexual encounters will be punished. Those who are successful have nothing to fear. Consent trainings prepare them for the neoliberal regime, not for the risks of being sexual. That they accept this order says something profound about the street-level experience of law when it comes to sex crimes.

NOTES

1. Russlyn Ali, Assistant Secretary for Civil Rights, "Dear Colleague," United States Department of Education (April 4, 2011). Available at https://www2.ed.gov/about/offices/list/ocr/letters/colleague-201104.html.

2. Jeannie Suk, cited in Sara Ganim and Nelli Black, "An Imperfect Process: How Campuses Deal with Sexual Assault," *CNN* (December 21, 2015). Available at http://www.cnn.com/2015/11/22/us/campus-sexual-assault-tribunals/.

3. Allie Grasgreen, "Going on Offense with Title IX," *Inside Higher Ed* (August 9, 2013). Available at https://www.insidehighered.com/news/2013/08/09/accused-rape-men-allege-discrimination-under-title-ix.

4. "Not Alone," White House Council on Women and Girls (April 2014), 16. Available at https://www.justice.gov/ovw/page/file/905942/download.

5. "Not Alone," 3.

6. Chantelle Cleary, "Community Meeting and Informational Session on Title IX," (February 8, 2017) Marlboro College, Marlboro, VT.

7. Sharon Glassburn, "Safe, Sane, and Consensual: The Bedrock Ethics of BDSM," *Good Therapy* (March 16, 2015). Available at http://www.goodtherapy.org/blog/safe-sane-consensual-the-bedrock-ethics-of-bdsm-0316155.

8. Brown University Health Education, "Brown Students Ask For Consent," (July 18, 2012). Available on YouTube at https://www.youtube.com/watch?v=8lRIWWItLx4.

9. Dan Ariely, *Predictably Irrational: The Hidden Forces That Shape Our Decisions* (New York: Harper Collins, 208), 89–108.

10. Ibid., 99.

11. Ibid., 249.

12. Leah Soule, "All Students for Consent, Whitman College," http://knowyourix.org/all-students-for-consent-whitman-college/.

13. Michel Foucault, *Discipline and Punish: The Birth of the Prison,* translated by Alan Sheriden (New York: Vintage, 1995), 272.

14. Joseph J. Fischel, *Sex and Harm in the Age of Consent* (Minneapolis: University of Minnesota Press, 2016), 11.

15. Ibid., 75.

16. Kate Taylor, "Sex on Campus: She Can Play That Game Too," *New York Times* (July 13, 2013), ST 1.

17. Wendy Brown, *Undoing the Demos: Neoliberalism's Stealth Revolution* (New York: Zone Press, 2015), 31.

18. Ibid., 31.

19. Kate Taylor, op. cit.

20. Aya Gruber, "Anti-Rape Culture," *Kansas Law Review* (April 13, 2016), 101–127, 114–115.

21. Ibid., 117.

22. Ibid., 117–118.

23. Ibid., 118.

24. Ibid., 123.

25. John Brigham, "Rape Culture, Due Process, and State Feminism," in *Wrongful Allegations of Sexual and Child Abuse,* edited by Ros Barnett (New York: Oxford University Press, 2016), 68.

26. See, *For Shelter and Beyond*, 2nd ed. Boston: Massachusetts Coalition of Battered Women's Groups, 1992.

27. National Task Force to End Sexual and Domestic Violence, "The Violence against Women Act: 10 Years of Progress and Moving Forward," (2004). Available at http://www.ncdsv.org/images/VAWA10YearsProgress.pdf.

28. Leigh Goodmark, *A Troubled Marriage: Domestic Violence and the Legal System* (New York: New York University Press, 2012), 16.

29. Ibid., 28.

30. Kristin Bumiller, *In an Abusive State: How Neoliberalism Appropriated the Feminist Movement against Sexual Violence* (Durham, NC: Duke University Press, 2008), 13.

31. Ibid., 13.

32. Ibid., 7.

33. Ibid., 7.

34. Clare McGlynn, Nicole Westmarland, and Nikki Goden, "'I Just Wanted Him to Hear Me: Sexual Violence and the Possibilities of Restorative Justice," *Journal of Law and Society* 39 2 (June 2012), 213–214.

35. Mary Koss, "Restorative Justice for Acquaintance Rape and Misdemeanor Sex Crimes," in James Ptacek, *Restorative Justice and Violence against Women* (Oxford: Oxford University Press, 2010), 219.

36. Jennifer J. Llewellyn, Jacob MacIsaac, and Melissa MacKay, "Report from the Restorative Justice Process May 2015 at the Dalhousie University Faculty of Dentistry," Available at https://www.dal.ca/cultureofrespect/report-from-the-restorative-justice-process.html.

37. Linda G. Mills, *Insult to Injury: Rethinking Our Responses to Intimate Abuse* (Princeton: Princeton University Press, 2003), 135.

REFERENCES

N. A. *For Shelter and Beyond.* 2nd ed. Boston: Massachusetts Coalition of Battered Women's Groups. October 1992.

Ariely, Dan. *Predictably Irrational: The Hidden Forces That Shape Our Decisions.* New York: Harper Collins, 2008.

Associated Press. "Gov. Jerry Brown signs landmark 'yes means yes' law. *San Jose Mercury News* (September 24, 2014).

Brigham, John. "Rape Culture, Due Process, and State Feminism." In *Mistaken Monsters: Wrongly Accused of Child Abuse and Sexual Crimes,* edited by Ros Barnett. New York: Oxford University Press, 2016.

Brown University Health Education Services. "Brown Students Ask for Consent." Uploaded to YouTube (July 18, 2012). https://www.youtube.com/watch?v=8lRIWWItLx4.

Brown, Wendy. *Undoing the Demos: Neoliberalism's Stealth Revolution.* New York: Zone Press, 2015.

Bumiller, Kristin. *In an Abusive State: How Neoliberalism Appropriated the Movement Against Sexual Violence.* Durham, NC: Duke University Press, 2008.

Fischel, Joseph J. *Sex and Harm in the Age of Consent.* Minneapolis, MN: University of Minnesota Press, 2016.

Foucault, Michel. *Discipline and Punish: The Birth of the Prison.* Translated by Alan Sheriden. New York: Vintage Press, 1995.

Ganim, Sara and Nelli Black, "An Imperfect Process: How Campuses Deal with Sexual Assault," *CNN* (December 21, 2015). Available at http://www.cnn.com/2015/11/22/us/campus-sexual-assault-tribunals/.

Glassburn, Sharon. "Safe, Sane, and Consensual: The Bedrock Ethics of BDSM," *Good Therapy* (March 16, 2015). Available at http://www.goodtherapy.org/blog/safe-sane-consensual-the-bedrock-ethics-of-bdsm-0316155.

Goodmark, Leigh. *A Troubled Marriage: Domestic Violence and the Legal System.* New York: New York University Press, 2012.

Grassgreen, Allie. "Going on Offense with Title IX," *Inside Higher Ed* (August 9, 2013). Available at https://www.insidehighered.com/news/2013/08/09/accused-rape-men-allege-discrimination-under-title-ix.

Gruber, Aya. "Anti-Rape Culture," *Kansas Law Review* (April 13, 2016), 101–127.

Jaschik, Scott. "Title IX Victory for Man Suing Over Sex Assault Finding," *Inside Higher Ed* (August 1, 2016). Available at https://www.insidehighered.com/news/2016/08/01/federal-appeals-court-revives-title-ix-suit-male-student-challenging-sex-assault.

Koss, Mary. "Restorative Justice for Acquaintance Rape and Misdemeanor Sex Crimes," in James Ptacek, *Restorative Justice and Violence against Women.* Oxford, UK: Oxford University Press, 2010.

Llewellyn, Jennifer J., Jacob MacIsaac, Melissa MacKay, "Report from the Restorative Justice Process May 2015 at the Dalhousie University Faculty of Dentistry." Available at https://www.dal.ca/cultureofrespect/report-from-the-restorative-justice-process.html.

McGlynn, Clare, Nicole Westmarland, and Nikki Goden, "I Just Wanted Him to Hear Me: Sexual Violence and the Possibilities of Restorative Justice," *Law and Society* 39 2 (June 2012).

Millis, Linda G. *Insult to Injury: Rethinking Our Responses to Intimate Violence.* Princeton, NJ: Princeton University Press, 2003.

National Task Force to End Sexual and Domestic Violence. "The Violence against Women Act: 10 Years of Progress and Moving Forward." (2004). http://www.ncdsv.org/images/VAWA10YearsProgress.pdf.

Soule, Leah. "All Students for Consent, Whitman College." Available at http://knowyourix.org/all-students-for-consent-whitman-college/.

Taylor, Kate. "Sex on Campus: She Can Play That Game Too," *New York Times* (July 13, 2013).

White House Task Force to Protect Students from Sexual Assault. "Not Alone." Washington, DC: 2014. https://www.notalone.gov/assets/report.pdf.

Chapter 5

Asphyxia

Naming Police Violence as Street-Level Sovereignty

Andrés Fabián Henao Castro

ASPHYXIA IN THE TIME OF NECROPOLITICS

According to the Malcolm X grassroots organization's report, *Operation Ghetto Storm*, 313 extrajudicial killings of black individuals perpetrated by the police, security guards, or vigilantes in the United States were reported in 2012. The number, which also registers the brutal frequency of this violence—one killing every 28 hours—is actually higher, because, as the coauthor of the report, Arlene Eisen, asserts, "police department and government agencies throughout the United States go to great lengths to hide the data on extrajudicial killings, particularly the race of the murder victims."[1] I first came across this report after joining a protest in the streets, organized by the Black Lives Matter Movement against the governmental decision to not press charges against Darren Wilson for the 2014 killing of Michael Brown in a street of Ferguson, a suburb of St. Louis, Missouri.[2] One week and two days after making public such decision, the impunity with which police officers could kill unarmed black young citizens was confirmed on December 3, 2014, when, amidst widespread national mobilization, the charges against the New York City police officers responsible for the lethal chokehold of Eric Garner in the streets of Staten Island on July 17, were also dropped.

The banality of the acts that first motivated the policing interpellation (Althusser 2012) of black people confirms, again and again, that the attributed "danger" lay not in the acts triggering the surveillance but on the racialized construction of those bodies that the surveillance itself perpetuated.[3] The result manifests a dramatic disproportion between the extreme violence used by the police in response to the least threatening activities—in the case of Garner, for example, selling cigarettes per unit in the street. The economic marginalization of people of color, noticeable in the activities motivating their disciplinary surveillance, is not just a structural condition making them more vulnerable to state-sanctioned violence; class exploitation plays a greater role in the direct reproduction of this violence. Based on a report issued by the nonprofit lawyers' group ArchCity Defenders, Michael Daly claimed—in an article following the killing of Michael Brown—that the fines and court fees imposed on poor people of color made the Ferguson's municipal court "the city's second-biggest source of revenue."[4] To the ways in which the system feeds off the poor, to echo the title of Daly's article, one should add the enormous profits reported by the private-industrial complex of incarceration developed in the United States, which, according to Michelle Alexander "has the highest rate of incarceration in the world," and whose "most striking feature" is its racial dimension, given that "no other country in the world imprisons so many of its racial or ethnic minorities."[5]

This paper seeks to understand and name the racist violence that characterizes the exercise of sovereignty at the street-level, that is, the lethal violence the police exercises today against racialized bodies. In Gilmore's now famous formulation, racism is "the state-sanctioned or extralegal production and exploitation of group-differentiated vulnerability to premature death."[6] Vulnerability to premature death is, thus, the converging result of two processes: on the one hand, new forms of capital exploitation (including the prison industrial complex) rendering racially differentiated bodies disposable and, on the other hand, the lethal repression exercised by different apparatuses of the state turning black and brown people as the most frequent victims of the old sovereign right to kill. Asphyxia is the name that I give to this police violence, which I understand as bringing together the lethal poles of the two economies of power that Michel Foucault conceived as antithetical in the 18th century: the right to "take life or let live" of classical sovereignty, and the right to "make live and let die," of modern biopolitics.[7] Necropolitics—Achille Mbembe's intervention into Eurocentrism of the discourse on biopolitics—refers to the original integration of the sovereign right to take life and the biopolitical right to let die in a single economy of massive production of death in the colonial spaces of the global south, the one experienced by both indigenous communities in the *encomiendas* and enslaved blacks in the plantation systems.[8] Asphyxia, however, refers to the specificity of police violence in the times of neoliberal hegemony, which I understand not just as a set of macroeconomic policies but also as a regime of power, which articulates a particular form of governmental rationality that extends an economic logic to previously noneconomic spheres.[9] Within this neoliberal context asphyxia names the current linkage of a negative notion of power that represses with a positive notion of power that produces lives that are expulsed from the new global order.[10]

There is, however, an additional theoretical agenda with the term asphyxia. This paper also emerges in response to the uneven attention given to the very same state-sanctioned lethal violence that black and brown women, especially transgender or gender nonconfirming, have suffered; and if the names of Trayvon Martin, Michael Brown, Eric Garner, Tamir Rice, and Freddie Gray had become well known to the American public, as a result primarily of black grassroots' activism, the same did not happen with the names of Tanisha Anderson, Rekia Boyd, Miriam Carey, Michelle Cusseaux, Shelly Frey, and Kayla Moore, just to name a few. Their names only entered the national scene after the vigil, under the banner of, "Say Her Name," was organized in the streets of New York on May 20, 2015, and replicated across the country in the weeks and months that followed.[11] Through street-level activism, the public now knows that Rekia Boyd was killed by an off-duty Chicago police detective on March 21, 2012, while she was standing in an alley with her friends.[12] That an off-duty sheriff shot Shelly Frey on December 6, 2012, in Houston, who "suspected her friend to be shoplifting from a Walmart store."[13] Miriam Carey was a "34-year-old dental hygienist and suburban mother," killed by the police on October 3, 2013, after allegedly speeding away from a White House checkpoint.[14] Michelle Cusseaux was shot in her home, on August 13, 2014, while the police "were attempting to take her to a mental health facility."[15] Something similar happened to Tanisha Anderson, who was not shot in her home but slammed against the concrete sidewalk by the police on November 13, 2014, in Cleveland, after her family "reached out for assistance to calm their daughter during a mental health crisis."[16] Finally, Kayla Moore, a black transgender woman, was killed by the Berkeley police on February 12, 2013, "in response to a call for help from her roommate because Moore was experiencing a mental health crisis."[17] Actually, black transgender women remain the most invisibilized, never appearing in the national media nor motivating comparable levels of national political mobilization, as happened again with the case of Deeniqua Dodds, killed on July 4 of last year, the fifteen transgender person killed on that year by then. If, as Foucault argues, the sovereign right "is essentially the right of the sword,"[18] asphyxia names this right from the perspective of the rope. Nicole Loraux was perhaps the first one to trace the historically different ways of gendering lethal violence back to Greek antiquity through the different strategies of "the rope and the sword."[19] In her account, the sword operates as the phallic symbol for the lethal violence that is exercised through the opening of an orifice whereas the rope functions as the feminized symbol of the lethal violence that is exercised through the closing of an orifice. The figure of the rope thus privileges the violence done to women and, as the dominant device of asphyxiation, has also a stronger link to the racialized history of lethal violence in the United States through lynching, which journalist Ida B. Wells documented extensively, and which also participates in the feminization of the black male body within a broader historical social co-constitution of race and gender as processes that feed off each other.[20]

Asphyxia thus problematizes and conceptualizes a set of continuities rendering both the life and death of black and brown women less relevant to public redress. It names the form of violence that, at a societal level, targets the free circulation of racialized bodies with the suffocation of their conditions of livability, a form of violence that is as characteristic of the police use of tear gas to disperse protestors in the street as it is of austerity measures imposed by financial institutions to control entire populations and keep them off the streets. Asphyxia, then, names the dominant form of everyday violence experienced primarily by black and brown women in the time of necropolitics, in which the increasing marginalization of their conditions of livability by means of neoliberal policies coincides with their lesser public visibility after their lethal encounters with a militarized police.[21]

A THEORETICAL GENEALOGY OF THE POLICE

If asphyxia names police violence, as the materialization of street-level sovereignty, it is important to define the police beyond the confines of the institution that bears the name. In *Disagreement*, Jacques Rancière claims that what we generally understand as politics, that is, the "set of procedures whereby the aggregation and consent of collectivities is achieved, the organization of powers, the distribution of places and roles, and the systems for legitimizing this distribution," we should rather understand as the police.[22] Rancière immediately recognizes his debt to Michel Foucault's attempt at understanding the police, not as a particular institution, but as the collective mode of governmentality that, during the seventeenth and eighteenth centuries in Europe—where Foucault misplaced its emergence as I argue below—was supposed to regulate "everything pertaining to men's *happiness*" (emphasis in the original).[23] It is my claim that neither Rancière nor Foucault's work, arguably two of the most theoretically influential texts on the police today, fully account for the racialized and gendered genealogies of this mode of governmentality.

The police, of which Rancière and Foucault speak, is irreducible to the repressive apparatus of the state with which it is most frequently identified, and which, Rancière adequately claimed, "is just a particular form of a more general order that arranges that tangible reality in which bodies are distributed in community."[24] Despite the similarities in their more extensive uses of the term, Foucault's historical investigation is quite different from Rancière's theoretical conceptualization. Historically, and most notably in his reading of von Justi's *Elements of the Police*, Foucault traced the very same distinction between politics and the police with which Rancière first opened his own definition of this term, but with a very different idea of politics in mind. Von Justi distinguished the negative form of power, *Politik*, which consisted in "the state's fighting against its internal and external enemies," from the positive form of power, *Polizei*, which "foster both citizens' lives *and* the state's strengths" (emphasis in the original).[25] Von Justi's distinction would resonate, later on, with the institutional differentiation between the juridical-political space of the military, as the institution in charge of protecting the nation-state from external and internal enemies—the domain of sovereignty—and the administrative space of the police, as the institution in charge of preventing crime, a de-politicized space internal to the strengthening of the nation-state's resources: capital and labor—the domain of biopolitics.[26] In synthesis, the police was never just an institution but a program of governmental rationality, one that operated in a de-politicized domain according to the parameters of the bourgeois state.

The police, however, never intersected with the racialized history of the body in Foucault's genealogy, when he considered that modern society was no longer a society "where power spoke *through* blood" (emphasis original), but had become rather a society of sex, a society whose "mechanisms of power [were] addressed to the body, to life, to what causes it to proliferate."[27] And yet, what allowed the right to kill to survive the transition from "a *symbolics of blood* to *an analytics of sexuality*" (emphasis in the original), that is, from sovereignty to biopolitics, was racism: the protection of "the purity of the blood" as the ensuring of "the triumph of the race."[28] As Hall, Critcher, Jefferson, Clarke and Roberts demonstrate, racism was not alone in occupying this in-between position that made it possible for the classical sovereign right to kill to be transformed into the modern biopolitical right to let die; the police was the institution that occupied that very same space, situating itself between normalizing, disciplinary apparatuses and the regulatory, governing apparatuses.[29] State racism and policing only met in Foucault's genealogy in the 20th century because they were never explored beyond the European territory, in the plantation system, the *encomiendas*, and all the other colonial spaces in which enslaved populations were controlled and where *Policing the Crisis* sought for a larger genealogy.[30] Foucault did recognize that racism was not invented at this time (17th and 18th century), that "it had already been in existence for a very long time" but functioning "elsewhere."[31] This is not just Eurocentric blindness, however, making race only politically and theoretically relevant once it entered the European space, as Alexander Weheliye rightly contests.[32] The problem lies in not having seen the other structure that was developing in that "elsewhere": that of necropolitics in the co-constitutive history of modernity and colonialism.[33]

The sovereign police of the plantation system, the introduction of sovereign power (the right to kill) into the figure of the police—which Agamben conceives as characteristic of today's renaming of imperial interventions as "policing operations" resembling an administrative function of law enforcement—required another transformation with regards to the temporal features of its punitive practices.[34] Lethal violence no longer functioned according to the temporal constrictions of the law, in the economy of sovereign excess, but according to the temporal extension of the norm, in the form of the everyday life. Unlike the limited economy of the law, whose "murderous splendor" could only last so long, a line no longer separated the prohibited from the allowed in the universe of the norm, which was invested in measures, spectrums and degrees. In other words, the norm extended—as in Foucault's famous analysis of the disciplinary power in the prison—the exercise of power because power was pluralized and distributed in the immanent microcosm of multiple apparatuses.[35]

Foucault's first years of research were devoted to this dimension of power. *Les Anormaux*, Foucault's 1974–1975 lectures, were an attempt at tracing the power of normalization that resulted from the integration of the juridical and the biological into the pathological figure of the "abnormal," in which criminality was no longer to be decided in the deed but in the character of the doer, in which psychiatry had constituted a sort of "psychologico-ethical double of the offense."[36] Foucault traced the genealogical formation of the "abnormal" as the integration of three previously discontinuous political figures: (i) the human monster of classic sovereignty; (ii) the individual to be corrected in disciplinary institutions, and (iii) the masturbating child of the new sexualized bourgeois family, the same distinction we find in his future lectures between sovereignty, discipline and biopolitics.

The black enslaved in the *territoire d'autre mar* was the body that first articulated all the figures accumulated in Foucault's character of the "abnormal."[37] The "negro" was technologically fabricated as the monster, the incorrigible, and, if not the onanist of the bourgeois/nuclear family, the hyper-sexualized subject that acted as its most abject distortion. If the "great masturbator" of the Republic revealed in the micro-physic of sexual transgressions the potential criminality of an incontrollable desire, real criminality was attached to black women's "nature" in particular, as sexually ungovernable, an excess ultimately affecting the grammatical overdetermination of the black female subject.[38] Such was the function played by the mythical figure of Jezebel when the Judeo-Christian iconography of sin first racialized abject bodies in the so-called "New World." Named after the biblical wife of King Ahab, Jezebel was the prototype of the hypersexualized and immoral black female subject that functioned as the iconic figure of racial degeneracy.[39] And it is the monster "*d'autre mar*" who returns in the lethal violence inflicted on black women today, ultimately rendering such violence unreadable within the grammars of humanism and anti-humanism, a binary from which they were excluded since the very historical formation of "the human" in that "elsewhere" rested on the radical de-humanization of their being, reduced to the status of an object to be exchanged in the market.[40]

STREET-LEVEL SOVEREIGNTY, RACIALIZED INTERPELLATION, AND NEOLIBERALISM

In the presence of the abject, historically unreadable racialized body beyond the scope of humanism, the most concrete form of policing through interpellation inevitably changes. The theory of interpellation was originally developed by Althusser in 1970 in order to investigate the production of the subject by state apparatuses through forms of police hailing.[41] Following on Althusser's work, Jacques Rancière has tried to analyze the most anti-political features of this policing, reconsidering the utterance as a form of securing a distribution of the visible in the field of politics:

> The police is not the law which interpellates individuals (as in Louis Althusser's "Hey, you there!") not unless it is confused with religious subjection. It consists before all else, in recalling the obviousness of what there is, or rather of what there is not, and its slogan is: "Move along! There's nothing to see here!" The police is that which says that here, on this street, there's nothing to see and so nothing to do but move along. It asserts that the space for circulating is nothing but the space of circulation. Politics, by contrast, consists in transforming this space of "moving-along," of circulation, into a space for the appearance of a subject: the people, the workers, the citizens.[42]

The policing utterance in the street becomes exemplary of the policing logic that Rancière first identified as irreducible to the repressive institution. The utterance, however, somehow emblematizes the distributive logic that informs its governmental function: that of seeing that "a particular activity is visible and another is not, that one speech is understood as discourse and another as noise."[43] Indeed, when black people gathered in front of the Ferguson Police Department to demand justice for Brown's death, as they did in New York to demand justice for Sandra Bland, mainstream media join the policing logic in shifting the public discourse from a concern with structural racism to a concern with looting—police's main focus. "Profit over people," was the motto of the policing utterance, "people over property," was that of the movement. Rather than political protestors, the media refer to "the mob" or "the thugs." However, the efficacy of the police's slogan, "Move along! There's nothing to see here!" was not accomplished through the verbal utterance but through the indiscriminate use of tear gas when facing black bodies in the street. The strategy was considerably more violent and Ferguson's West Florissant Avenue was turned into a war zone, with police brutality escalating in the following days.

From violence in the field of speech to violence in the field of what makes speech possible, the circulation of air, the anti-political character of the police becomes more radical when it targets black and brown people, it becomes necropolitical in a double sense, as it also entails the death of the political space itself, no longer breathable as a result of asphyxia. If, as Rancière claims, even the most violent utterance still recognizes, against its grid, potential equality in the communicate presupposition that the order of the masters must be understood by the slaves, the recourse to tear gas destroys even the tenuous possibility of such a space. If politics is the struggle over ways of doing, being, and saying that define that which is perceptible for the community, tear gas renders being, doing and saying impossible, as the material conditions that support the space are precisely what is first extinguished. A space of appearance, Arendt argues, does not preexist the coming together of the people in the manner of speech and action, the acts by which a public space is made public, and yet, the very existence of that space rests in material conditions that are not exclusively those of human bodies coming together and that, if affected, render this spatial re-signification impossible, notably by making the air un-breathable.[44] The police no longer utter an order, as they need to wear masks—the mechanical prosthesis that makes possible for the body to survive the conditions of asphyxiation within which it now guarantees the order. The enunciation can only come from the body that suffers the asphyxia, and their first words are devoted to a demand for the conditions that make that space possible, the "I can't breathe!" that Eric Garner cried eleven times on the day of his lethal asphyxiation by the police.[45]

As Judith Butler, Robert Pfaller, and Ghassan Hage rightly emphasize, what is crucial in Althusser's theory of interpellation is not the enunciated content but the performative gesture of the calling, the turning around beyond the boundaries of the ideological content.[46] This means that Althusser's "effet-sujet" includes, as part of the interpellation the very gesture "of calling into question the identity conferred on me by way of interpellation."[47] When police hailing faces black and brown bodies in the street, however, there is no space for such a calling into question of identity, as the imaginary identity conferred upon these subject never produces, as one of its effects, empty subjectivity beyond the imaginary attribution. Black and brown bodies are, historically, the material filling of that ideological imaginary, rendering that empty space inaccessible to them, thus collapsing the gap between the subject of enunciation and the subject of the enunciated, which is essential to the production of subjectivity. In other words, there is no properly speaking an "effet-sujet" when police interpellation faces racialized bodies, as there is no recognizable gap between being and doing. Instead of an "effet-sujet" there is only the continuous "locking into a suffocating reification (*objectivité écrasante*)" that turns black and brown people into "objects among other objects," and one that explains, in the event of the racialized mis-interpellation, why the turning around is always already perceived as a death-threat from which society must be defended by the police, even before the actual turning has taken place.[48]

This explains why the police no longer demands invisibility and inaudibility to be uncritically accepted by the *demos* (people), it enacts its violence through the destruction of the vulnerable body's conditions of livability, contaminating the air that grants material support to human inter-locution. The impossible slogan of the tear gas is not "there is nothing to see!" even if the cloud of smoke also renders everything invisible, the unpronounceable slogan is "there is nothing to breathe!" Marx's representation of capitalism's disenchanting force: "all that is solid melts into the air!" acquires a deadlier connotation in the context of the racialized poor.[49] Tear gas is not really gas, but a solid that gets turned into an aerosol and "melts" into the air. The most often chemical use is oleum capsicum, whose active ingredient, capsaicin, triggers pain receptors in the body. Against these particles the body reacts with tears and bronchial spasms that make it difficult to breathe, forcing it, literally, to "move along!" The commandment to move along is no longer verbally demanded but materially inflicted, and the melting of the solid compelling people to face, although no longer with sober senses but tears in their eyes and bronchial spasms in their chests, their real conditions of unlivability and the utmost loss of their political existence.[50] Asphyxia, thus, names the coincidence, in the contamination of the air, of the simultaneous death of physical and collective life, the literal end of politics, the destruction of the conditions of possibility for the public sphere to exist in its very materiality.

"There is nothing to breathe!" highlights racialized poverty in another sense, that of structural environmental racism. Greater exposure to disease, contamination of water, improper housing, underfunded welfare systems, among many others, coerce these bodies to sites of literal un-breathability.[51] They also redistribute the costs of repairing such breathability on the bodies of black and brown women, who are once again the primary caregivers of the global economy, hence the most affected by asphyxia.[52] Institutional precariousness reproducing forms of "letting them die," is coupled with a state-sponsored killing every 28 hours, marking the normalization of this form of lethal violence, blurring the distinction between sovereignty and policing control, integrated into the same de-politicized administrative space of law enforcement at the street-level. Asphyxia names the normalization of taking life and letting die, pluralized in a variety of systems—repressive and ideological—in charge of reproducing the conditions of unlivability primarily for black and brown women. That is so, because the rope that asphyxiates also refers to the shrinking and dismantling of public infrastructure through neoliberal privatization, once again forcing racialized women to become the sub-proletarian household that sustains the reproduction of capital.[53] As Brown argues, in the paradoxical conflation of neoliberalism and neoconservatism the ideology of "'responsabilization' in the context of privatizing public goods uniquely penalizes women to the extent that they remain disproportionately responsible for those who cannot be responsible for themselves."[54] The ways in which this policing order renders women invisible is dual, as the ability of women of color to leave the household depends on the very public infrastructure that is threatened, at the same time that the reproduction of capital, as Dunaway (2002) argues, continues to be grounded on the invisible source of cheap labor that women of color provide, redoubled by granting less public attention to their losses to state sanctioned violence in the streets.[55] Black and brown women are preemptively kept away from the street, through the unique penalizations effected by neoliberal policies, and actively kept away through the lethally sanctioned violence of the police, less publicly contested in their cases, moreover for transgender and gender nonconforming. Here we come to understand the political significance of another medical discovery, credited to James Rooney in the late 70s, that bleeding is caused by asphyxia. The rope precedes the sword, and it is always the killing of the political being what renders normal and inconsequential the physical killing of the individual body. You must be first disenfranchised, rendered insignificant, second-class, and invisible, for your life not to matter.

THE POLITICAL AGAINST NECROPOLITICAL ASPHYXIA

Asphyxia names the policing logic that makes the air in the public space no longer breathable in more than one sense of the word.[56] Un-breathable air threatens the conditions of possibility for the public to appear and the very life of the bodies seeking to occupy it. The political subject that contests those conditions refers to the phonetic de-*monst*-ration that exceeds the racialized erasure of the semantic demonstration. A de*monst*ration is the way in which the *demos* gives to itself a space of appearance, from the Latin *monstrare*—to show—the people give to themselves a stage in which to show and affirm their differentially experienced racialized existence and to publicly contest the asymmetric organization of their mattering. If the role of theory is to contribute to a history of the present, asphyxia is a way of naming that present, the necropolitical collapse of repression and production in a single economy of destruction and destitution: neoliberalism, as the dominant mode of production rendering the air un-breathable primarily for black and brown women, who are confined to the household, the *maquiladora*, the mental facility, and the prison-industrial complex, and doubly erased when public silence follows their killing in the streets for daring to contest their conditions of confinement.

Such a present also refers to the time in which the Black Lives Matter Movement says "No!" to the policing production of their worthlessness, contesting the conditions that Fanon first described as those of an "occupied breathing."[57] This movement, furthermore, centers their leadership around those who have been marginalized within Black liberation movements, that is, the black queer, transgender, disabled, undocumented, and with records, enacting a stronger break with the logic of the police, as the political fight for them to be seen, act, and exist as a people recognizes the plurality and different positionalities that converge in the people(s). "Bad air, bad air!" said Nietzsche with contempt for the democratic push towards equality that rendered people as something no longer to be feared, if only because such fear had been sublimated into a mythical indebtedness towards God that could no longer be paid off.[58] Having substituted god for capital, in the current melting of everything solid into the financial derivatives of the stock market and the public debt, such fear has become the everyday life affect that supports modern sovereignty with its hyper-Hobbesian obsession with security(zation). In this weather, as Christina Sharpe wonderfully articulates, "antiblackness is pervasive *as* climate" (emphasis in the original).[59] Clean air is the condition of possibility for the political itself, and it can only exist today as a result of changing the climate, of defeating the asphyxia of antiblackness in the present confrontation between the new liberation movements led by the black queer, transgender, disabled, undocumented, and with records, against police brutality.

NOTES

1. The report can be downloaded from the website of the Malcolm X Grassroots Movement, I consulted it for the last time on June 24, 2015. See https://mxgm.org/operation-ghetto-storm-2012-annual-report-on-the-extrajudicial-killing-of-313-black-people/.

2. The Black Lives Matter Movement was created in 2012, after Trayvon Martin's murderer was acquitted for his crime, see "Black Lives Matter Movement," last modified June 2016. http://blacklivesmatter.com/.

3. See Louis Althusser, "Ideology and Ideological State Apparatuses (Notes towards an Investigation)." In *Mapping Ideology*, ed. Slavoj Žižek (London: Verso,

2012). As Lise Marie Cacho puts it, not only the U.S. law targets their being, rather than their behavior, the law depends upon the permanent criminalization of the black body, making criminal activity "*unrecognizable* without a black body" (Lisa Marie Cacho, *Social Death: Racialized Rightlessness and the Criminalization of the Unprotected* (New York: New York University Press, 2012), 2–6.

4. See Daly. "Ferguson Feeds Off the Poor: Three Warrants a Year per Household," last modified August 22, 2014, in *The Daily Beast*, consulted for the last time on June 23, 2015, http://www.thedailybeast.com/articles/2014/08/22/ferguson-s-shameful-legal-shakedown-three-warrants-a-year-per-household.html.

5. Michelle Alexander, *The New Jim Crow: Mass Incarceration in the Age of Colorblindness* (New York: The New Press, 2013), 6. Actually, entire states, like that of California, have been built by building prisons, as Gilmore demonstrates by tracing the ways in which surplus finance, capital, land and labor were molded "into the workfare-warfare state" (Wilson Gilmore, *Golden Gulag: Prisons, Surplus, Crisis, and Opposition in Globalizing California* (Berkeley: University of California Press, 2007), 86). I thank the reviewer for leading me to this important reference. On the historical link between the prison system and sexual violence against black people see Marilyn Buck, "The Effects of Repression on Women in Prison." In *Warfare in the American Homeland: Policing and Prison in a Penal Democracy*, ed. Joy James (Durham: Duke University Press, 2007) and Jessi Jackson, "Sexual Necropolitics and Prison Rape Elimination." In *Signs* 39 (2013).

6. Gilmore, *Golden Gulag*, 28.

7. Michel Foucault, *Society Must Be Defended: Lectures at the Collège De France, 1975–1976*, trans. David Macey (New York: Picador, 2003), 240–241.

8. Achille Mbembe, "Necropolitics." *Public Culture* 15 (2003). I give a broader analysis of necropolitics in Andrés Fabián Henao Castro, "From the 'Bio' to the 'Necro': The Human at the Border." In *Resisting Biopolitics: Philosophical, Political and Performative Strategies*, eds. Stephen Wilmer and Audronė Žukauskaitė (New York: Routledge, 2015), 237–253.

9. Wendy Brown, *Undoing the Demos: Neoliberalism Stealth Revolution* (New York: Zone Books, 2015).

10. Saskia Sassen, *Expulsions: Brutality and Complexity in the Global Economy* (Cambridge: Harvard University Press, 2014).

11. Kimberlé Crenshaw and Andrea Ritchie, *Say Her Name: Resisting Police Brutality Against Black Women* (New York: African American Policy Forum, 2015). The report can be downloaded from the site of the African American Policy Forum (AAPF). I consulted the site for the last time on October 3, 2015. See http://www.aapf.org/sayhernamereport/.

12. Ibid., 20.

13. Ibid., 12.

14. Ibid., 10.

15. Ibid., 16.

16. Idem.

17. Ibid., 17.

18. Foucault, *Society Must be Defended*, 240.

19. Nicole Loraux, *Tragic Ways of Killing a Woman* (Cambridge: Harvard University Press, 1991).

20. Ida B. Wells, *On Lynching* (New York: Dover, 2014). As happens with current police brutality, the visual history of lynching in the U.S. has also under-visibilized the violence inflicted on the black female body, see Amy Louise Wood, *Lynching and Spectacle: Witnessing Racial Violence in America, 1890–1940* (North Carolina: University of North Carolina Press, 2009). For a more intersectional exploration of the (homo) erotics of lynching see Aliyyah Abdur-Rahman, *Against the Closet: Black Political Longing and the Erotics of Race* (Durham: Duke University Press, 2012), 51–80.

21. For a broader historical understanding of the new militarization of the urban space see also Leslie Wood, *Crisis and Control: The Militarization of Protest Policing* (London: Pluto Press, 2014); and Stephen Graham, *Cities under Siege: The New Military Urbanism* (New York: Verso, 2011).

22. Jacques Rancière, *Dis-Agreement: Politics and Philosophy*, trans. Julie Rose (Minneapolis: University of Minnesota Press, 1999), 28.

23. Michel Foucault, "*'Omnes et Singulatim'*: Towards a Critique of Political Reason." In *The Essential Foucault*, ed. Paul Rabinow and Nicholas Rose (New York: The New Press, 2003), 198.

24. Rancière, *Dis-Agreement*, 28.

25. Foucault, "*'Omnes et Singulatim,'*" 199.

26. Here Foucault follows the Hegelian location of the police—along with the corporation—at the level of the social (civil society), prior to the ethical level of the state (political). See Hegel, *The Philosophy of Right*, trans. H. B. Nisbett (Cambridge: Cambridge University Press, 1991), 262. Like Marx, however, Foucault understood the bio-political location of the police not as the institutional reconciliation of the particular with the universal at the level of the social (Hegel), but as the disciplinary "adjustment of the phenomena of population to economic processes," that was "an indispensable element in the development of capitalism." Michel Foucault, *History of Sexuality Vol. I: An Introduction*, trans. Robert Hurley (New York: Vintage Books, 1990), 140–141.

27. Foucault, *History of Sexuality*, 147.

28. Ibid., 148.

29. Stuart Hall, Chas Critcher, Tony Jefferson, John Clarke, and Brian Roberts, *Policing the Crisis: Mugging, the State, and Law and Order* (Hampshire: Macmillan Press, 1978).

30. Hall, Critcher, Jefferson, Clarke, and Roberts, *Policing the Crisis*, 362–388.

31. Foucault, *Society Must Be Defended*, 254.

32. Alexander G. Weheliye, *Habeas Viscus: Racializing Assemblages, Biopolitics, and Black Feminist Theories of the Human* (Durham: Duke University Press, 2014), 57.

33. On the historical link between the institution of the police, state violence, and racism in the U.S. see Joy James, *Resisting State Violence: Radicalism, Gender, and Race in the U.S.* (Minneapolis: University of Minnesota Press, 1996); and Mumia Abu-Jamal, *To Protect and Serve Who? Organizing a Movement to Abolish Police Violence* (Open Media Series: City Light Books, 2015).

34. Giorgio Agamben, *Means without End* (Minneapolis: University of Minnesota Press, 2000).

35. Michel Foucault, *Discipline and Punish: The Birth of the Prison* (New York: Vintage Books, 1979). Dipesh Chakrabarty is right when he claims that Marx anticipated this basic theme of Foucault's *Discipline and Punish*, apropos the move from sovereign power to disciplinary power that capitalism introduced, when Marx described "how the 'overseer's book of penalties replaces the slave-driver's lash [in capitalist management].'" Dipesh Chakrabarty, *Provincializing Europe: Post-Colonial Thought and Historical Difference* (Princeton: Princeton University Press), 56.

36. Michel Foucault, *"Abnormal" Lectures at the Collège De France 1974–75*, trans. Graham Burchell (New York: Picador, 2003), 16.

37. See Sylvia Wynter, "Unsettling the Coloniality of Being/Power/Truth/Freedom: Towards the Human, After Man, Its Overrepresentation—An Argument." *The New Centennial Review* 3 (2003); and Marlene Daut, *Tropics of Haiti: Race and the Literary History of the Haitian Revolution in the Atlantic World, 1789–1865* (Liverpool: Liverpool University Press, 2015).

38. Hortense Spillers, "Mama's Baby, Papa's Maybe: An American Grammar Book." *Diacritics* 17 (1987).

39. Dorothy Roberts, *Killing the Black Body* (New York: Vintage, 1997), 11.

40. On the historical tracing of contemporary surveillance back to transatlantic slavery see the great work of Simone Browne, *Dark Matters: On the Surveillance of Blackness* (Durham: Duke University Press, 2015). On the problematic representations of violence against the black body see Saidiya Hartman, *Scenes of Subjection: Terror, Slavery, and Self-Making in nineteenth-Century America* (Oxford: Oxford University Press, 1997), 3–14; Fred Moten, *In the Break: The Aesthetics of the Black Radical Tradition* (Minnesota: University of Minnesota Press, 2003), 1–24; and the very important work of Jared Sexton and Huey Copeland, "Raw Life: An Introduction." *Qui Parle* 13 (2003), where Sexton and Copeland introduce the notion of "raw life," to indicate how it is that forms of violence targeting bodies at the inter-section of racialized, gendered and sexualized compound forms of oppression fall outside the scope of humanism and its representational forms.

41. Althusser, "Ideology," 2012.

42. Jacques Rancière, *Dissensus: On Politics and Aesthetics*, trans Steven Corcoran (New York: Bloomsbury, 2013), 37. It is the merit of Judith Butler to have shown that if the subject is one of the products in Althusser's theory of interpellation, the police are the other, as the subject also produces the police through its active seeking for it. See Judith Butler, *The Psychic Life of Power* (Stanford: Stanford University Press, 1997), 106–131. Such co-performative result, as Sexton has persuasively argued, encounters a limit in the historical experience of black positionality, as it is the structural violence inflicted in the black body in particular, the origin from which racial profiling organizes its performative capacities. See Sexton, "Racial Profiling and the Societies of Control" In *Warfare in the American Homeland: Policing and Prison in a Penal Democracy*, ed. Joy James (Durham: Duke University Press, 2007), 197–218.

43. Rancière, *Dis-Agreement*, 29.

44. Hannah Arendt, *The Human Condition* (Chicago: Chicago University Press, 1998), 199.

45. For a broader analysis of the affective politics of racial interpellation see Ghassan Hage's helpful distinction between: (i) non-interpellation (racism linked to invisibility); (ii) negative interpellation (a hailing with all the racist attributes) and (iii) mis-interpellation—a drama in two acts, in which "the racialized person is first interpellated as belonging to a collectivity 'like everyone else,'" only to then be brutally reminded that "they are not part of everyone: 'No, I wasn't talking to you. Piss off. You are not part of us'" (Ghassan Hage, "The Affective Politics of Racial Mis-Interpellation," *Theory, Culture & Society* 27 (2010), 121–122. My own formulation, perhaps closer to a variation of the second model of negative-interpellation, does perform a racial hailing, yet one that substitutes the linguistic space of the verbal utterance with the militarized one of the lethal weapon.

46. Judith Butler, *Psychic Life of Power: Theories in Subjection* (Stanford: Stanford University Press, 1997), 107, Robert Pfaller, "Negation and Its Reliabilities: An Empty Subject for Ideology?" In *Cogito and the Unconscious*, ed. Slavoj Žižek (Durham: Duke University Press, 1998), 239; and Hage, "The Affective Politics," 121–122.

47. Pfaller, "Negation and Its Reliabilities," 239.

48. Frantz Fanon, *Black Skin, White Masks*, trans. Richard Philcox (New York: Grove Press, 2008), 89.

49. Karl Marx, "Manifesto of the Communist Party." In *The Marx-Engels Reader*, ed. Robert Tucker (New York: W. W. Norton & Company, 1978), 376.

50. There is no negotiation between bodies in this space, not even the kind of non-deliberative-post-humanist negotiation among bodies that Andreas Philippopoulos-Mihalopoulos has in mind when he develops his notion of spatial justice, as both the space that different bodies seek to occupy and their conflicting desires to occupy it are incommensurable. See Andreas Philippopoulos-Mihalopoulos, *Spatial Justice: Body, Lawscape, Atmosphere*. (New York: Routledge, 2015).

51. David Camacho, ed., *Environmental Injustices, Political Struggles: Race, Class and the Environment* (Durham: Duke University Press, 1998); and Volker Eick and Kendra Briken, *Urban (In)Security: Policing the Neoliberal Crisis* (Ottawa: Red Quill Books, 2013). Environmental racism and material un-breathability are as old as the colonial invention of the concept of race with the institutionalization of modern slavery. As Hartman reconstructs historically, the floor of the dungeon in which the slave was born was covered with human waste, and slaves were forced to sleep in the very same bare floor in which excrement and floor debris accumulated, making dysentery a commonplace and "the leading cause of death in confinement." Saidiya Hartman, *Lose Your Mother: A Journey along the Atlantic Slave Route* (New York: Farrar, Straus and Giroux, 2007), 120. Unsanitary conditions did not change in the belly of the ship, or in the plantations in which death also awaited the slave.

52. Wilma Dunaway, "Commodity-Chains and Gendered Exploitation: Rescuing Women from the Periphery of World-Systems Thought." In *The Modern/Colonial/Capitalist World-System: Global Processes, Antisystemic Movements, and the Geopolitics of Knowledge*, ed. Ramón Grosfoguel and Ana Margarita Cervantes-Rodriguez (Westport: Greenwood Press, 2002).

53. Joan Smith and Immanuel Wallerstein, *Creating and Transforming Households: The Constrains of the World-Economy*, ed. Joan Smith and Immanuel Wallerstein (Cambridge: University of Cambridge Press, 1992).

54. Brown, *Undoing the Demos*, 105.

55. Dunaway, "Commodity-Chains," 2002.

56. Fanon, *Black Skin, White Masks*, 201.

57. Frantz Fanon, *A Dying Colonialism*, trans. Haakon Chevalier (New York: Grove Press, 1994), 65.

58. Friedrich Nietzsche, *On the Genealogy of Morality*, trans. Carol Diethe (Cambridge: Cambridge University Press, 2007).

59. Christina Sharpe, *In the Wake: On Blackness and Being* (Durham: Duke University Press, 2016), 106.

REFERENCES

Abdur-Rahman, Aliyyah. *Against the Closet: Black Political Longing and the Erotics of Race*. Durham: Duke University Press, 2012.

Abu-Jamal, Mumia. *To Protect and Serve Who? Organizing a Movement to Abolish Police Violence*. Open Media Series: City Light Books, 2015.

Agamben, Giorgio. *Means without End*. Minneapolis: University of Minnesota Press, 2000.

Alexander, Michelle. *The New Jim Crow: Mass Incarceration in the Age of Colorblindness*. New York: The New Press, 2013.

Althusser, Louis. "Ideology and Ideological State Apparatuses (Notes towards an Investigation)." In *Mapping Ideology*, edited by Slavoj Žižek, 100–140. London: Verso, 2012.

Arendt, Hannah. *The Human Condition*. Chicago: Chicago University Press, 1998.

Brown, Wendy. *Undoing the Demos: Neoliberalism Stealth Revolution*. New York: Zone Books, 2015.

Browne, Simone. *Dark Matters: On the Surveillance of Blackness*. Durham: Duke University Press, 2015.

Buck, Marilyn. "The Effects of Repression on Women in Prison." In *Warfare in the American Homeland: Policing and Prison in a Penal Democracy*, edited by Joy James, 238–249. Durham: Duke University Press, 2007.

Butler, Judith. *The Psychic Life of Power*. Stanford: Stanford University Press, 1997.

Cacho, Lisa Marie. *Social Death: Racialized Rightlessness and the Criminalization of the Unprotected*. New York: New York University Press, 2012.

Camacho, David (ed.). *Environmental Injustices, Political Struggles: Race, Class and the Environment*. Durham: Duke University Press, 1998.

Crenshaw, Kimberlé and Ritchie, Andrea. *Say Her Name: Resisting Police Brutality Against Black Women*. New York: African American Policy Forum, 2015.

Daut, Marlene. *Tropics of Haiti: Race and the Literary History of the Haitian Revolution in the Atlantic World, 1789–1865*. Liverpool: Liverpool University Press, 2015.

Dunaway, Wilma. "Commodity-Chains and Gendered Exploitation: Rescuing Women from the Periphery of World-Systems Thought." In *The Modern/Colonial/Capitalist World-System: Global Processes, Antisystemic Movements, and the Geopolitics of Knowledge*, edited by Ramón Grosfoguel and Ana Margarita Cervantes-Rodriguez, 127–146. Westport: Greenwood Press, 2002.

Eick, Volker and Briken, Kendra. *Urban (In)Security: Policing the Neoliberal Crisis*. Ottawa: Red Quill Books, 2013.

Fanon, Frantz. *A Dying Colonialism*. New York: Grove Press, 1994.

———. *Black Skin, White Masks*. New York: Grove Press, 2008.

Foucault, Michel. "'*Omnes et Singulatim*': Towards a Critique of Political Reason." In *The Essential Foucault*, edited by Paul Rabinow and Nikolas Rose, 180–201. New York: The New Press, 2003.

———. *"Abnormal" Lectures at the Collège De France 1974–75*. Translated by Graham Burchell. New York: Picador, 2003.

———. "Lives of Infamous Men." In *The Essential Foucault*, edited by Paul Rabinow and Nicholas Rose, 279–293. New York: The New Press, 2003.

———. *Discipline and Punish: The Birth of the Prison*. New York: Vintage Books, 1979.

———. *History of Sexuality Vol. I: An Introduction*. New York: Vintage Books, 1990.

———. *Society Must Be Defended: Lectures at the Collège De France, 1975–1976*. Translated by David Macey. New York: Picador, 2003.

Gilmore, Ruth Wilson. *Golden Gulag: Prisons, Surplus, Crisis, and Opposition in Globalizing California*. Berkeley: University of California Press, 2007.

Graham, Stephen. *Cities under Siege: The New Military Urbanism*. New York: Verso, 2011.

Hage, Ghassan. "The Affective Politics of Racial Mis-Interpellation." *Theory, Culture & Society* 27 (2010): 112–129.

Hall, Stuart, Critcher, Chas, Jefferson, Tony, Clarke, John, and Roberts, Brian. *Policing the Crisis: Mugging, the State, and Law and Order*, Hampshire: Macmillan Press, 1978.

Hartman, Saidiya. *Lose Your Mother: A Journey Along the Atlantic Slave Route*. New York: Farrar, Straus and Giroux, 2007.

———. *Scenes of Subjection: Terror, Slavery, and Self-Making in nineteenth-Century America*. Oxford: Oxford University Press, 1997.

Henao Castro, Andrés Fabián. "From the 'Bio' to the 'Necro': The Human at the Border." In *Resisting Biopolitics: Philosophical, Political and Performative Strategies*, edited by Stephen Wilmer and Audronė Žukauskaitė, New York: Routledge, 2015, 237–253.

Jackson, Jessi. "Sexual Necropolitics and Prison Rape Elimination." In *Signs* 39 (2013), 197–220.

James, Joy. *Resisting State Violence: Radicalism, Gender, and Race in the U.S.* Minneapolis: University of Minnesota Press, 1996.

Loraux, Nicole. *Tragic Ways of Killing a Woman*. Cambridge: Harvard University Press, 1991.

Marx, Karl. "Manifesto of the Communist Party." In *The Marx-Engels Reader*, edited by Robert Tucker, 469–500. New York: W. W. Norton & Company, 1978.
Mbembe, Achille. "Necropolitics." *Public Culture* 15 (2003): 11–40.
Moten, Fred. *In the Break: The Aesthetics of the Black Radical Tradition*. Minnesota: University of Minnesota Press, 2003.
Nietzsche, Friedrich. *On the Genealogy of Morality*. Translated by Carol Diethe. Cambridge: Cambridge University Press, 2007.
Pfaller, Robert. "Negation and Its Reliabilities: An Empty Subject for Ideology?" In *Cogito and the Unconscious*, edited by Slavoj Žižek, 225–246. Durham: Duke University Press, 1998.
Philippopoulos-Mihalopoulos, Andreas. *Spatial Justice: Body, Lawscape, Atmosphere*. New York: Routledge, 2015.
Rancière, Jacques. *Dis-Agreement: Politics and Philosophy*. Translated by Julie Rose. Minneapolis: University of Minnesota Press, 1999.
———. *Dissensus: On Politics and Aesthetics*. Translated by Steven Corcoran. New York: Bloomsbury, 2013.
Roberts, Dorothy. *Killing the Black Body*. New York: Vintage, 1997.
Sassen, Saskia. *Expulsions: Brutality and Complexity in the Global Economy*. Cambridge: Harvard University Press, 2014.
Sexton, Jared and Copeland, Huey. "Raw Life: An Intrdocution." *Qui Parle* 13 (2003): 53–62.
Sexton, Jared. "Racial Profiling and the Societies of Control." In *Warfare in the American Homeland: Policing and Prison in a Penal Democracy*, edited by Joy James, 197–218. Durham: Duke University Press, 2007.
Sharpe, Christina. *In the Wake: On Blackness and Being*. Durham: Duke University Press, 2016.
Smith, Joan, and Wallerstein, Immanuel. *Creating and Transforming Households: The Constrains of the World-Economy*, edited by Joan Smith and Immanuel Wallerstein, 3–26. Cambridge: University of Cambridge Press, 1992.
Spillers, Hortense. "Mama's Baby, Papa's Maybe: An American Grammar Book." *Diacritics* 17 (1987): 64–81.
Weheliye, Alexander G. *Habeas Viscus: Racializing Assemblages, Biopolitics, and Black Feminist Theories of the Human*. Durham: Duke University Press, 2014.
Wells, Ida B. *On Lynching*. New York: Dover, 2014.
Wood, Amy Louise. *Lynching and Spectacle: Witnessing Racial Violence in America, 1890–1940*. North Carolina: University of North Carolina Press, 2009.
Wood, Leslie. *Crisis and Control: The Militarization of Protest Policing*. London: Pluto Press, 2014.
Wynter, Sylvia. "Unsettling the Coloniality of Being/Power/Truth/Freedom: Towards the Human, After Man, Its Overrepresentation—An Argument." *The New Centennial Review* 3 (2003): 257–337.

Chapter 6

Haircuts and Power

Sovereignty and the Military

Allen Linken

How can law be, simultaneously, nearly unseen, omnipresent, *and* materially affecting lives? Certainly the simultaneous presence of two of the three factors is plausible. Law can be both omnipresent and materially affecting a person.[1] Equally true, law can be nearly unseen and all-powerful,[2] or unseen and materially affecting lives.[3] The simultaneous presence of each of those three factors will strike most readers, at least initially, as being incompatible with at least one of those factors; that is, what aspires to be nearly unseen, omnipresent, and materially affecting lives must sacrifice one of those characteristics for the benefit of the other two.

Yet, such an improbable trifecta of law is found every day, in the lives of military members. The different character of the military community lends itself to the shared presence of what would ordinarily be inapposite ideals. The overt, yet hidden law stands as the backbone of a unique culture with an equally unique purpose, permitting the existence, and indeed, reinforcement, of a construct that affects every second of every minute of every hour of every day of those governed by it, but in a manner that goes largely unseen. This unique confluence of law and authority create the environment wherein the military can affect such a prominent role in the lives of its members, but also wherein civilian judges deeply defer to the rules and policies created by the military, resulting in weakened constitutional scrutiny as it relates to the military.

The reason is a very different mentality—the military mentality. It is necessary to understand that lens, with the goal of seeing law as authority and authority as controlling. This chapter will argue that the authority that the military derives and uses is not based in legal-rational grounding. Rather, by examining the power from the eyes of the street-level soldier, the power that the military wields becomes clear, evidencing strength and authority through tradition and imbuing that tradition in culture and law. By examining the theoretical underpinnings of military authority, this chapter will examine the source and nature of law that is leveraged upon the on-the-ground Soldier.

German legal sociologist Max Weber, and the concepts of authority and space will resonate throughout this chapter. The distinctive structure and form of the military will be introduced in order to provide the background necessary for this analysis. Next, the legal structure of the military will be examined, with a specific focus on the deference afforded decisions by military courts and commanders as evidence of the difference between military and civilian life. The moral underpinnings of the military emphasize its distinctive nature as does the everyday life of a military member to show the pervasive effect of the legal and moral structure on the individual. There is a well-connected macro-micro linkage between the doctrine of the military and its individual members. Using Army basic training as a case study, this chapter argues that the lenses of bureaucracy, law, power, and the rationalization of education and training ground the argument that the military, at the most basic level, operates under a different form of legitimacy, which permits the omnipresence of law, despite the fact that it is largely hidden from view.

THE MILITARY

This section will be an introduction to the military, followed by a legal, moral, and everyday understanding of the military, in an attempt to weave a tapestry that, in tandem with an unpacking of the theory of Max Weber, evidences law being concurrently unseen, as it is veiled in military authority, omnipotent, as it forms the backbone of order and discipline, and materially affecting the military member, as their every action is subject to a rule or code. At its conclusion, Weber is introduced and an analysis is performed of the various understandings relative to Weberian constructs and forms of authority.

The Military Command Structure

There is a certain understanding upon entering the military service that the individual becomes part of the organization and that the organization gains—and maintains—a degree of control over the individual. This degree of control extends so far as to include when the military member will work and when s/he will have free time, whether or not the military member will deploy into a hostile environment, and the amount of privacy that the military member has, to provide just a few examples.

The military chain-of-command is one of the building blocks of military culture and organization. The highest-ranking unit is responsible for several intermediate units, and each of those intermediate units is responsible for several smaller units. Likewise, with individual military members, the highest-ranking member is responsible for several members below him/her, and each of those members are responsible for more junior members, and this continues until the lowest ranking member is accounted for, and taken care of.

With those hierarchal relationships come responsibility over subordinate units, and with responsibility comes action on that responsibility. It is commonplace for a superior command or supervisor to inquire of the subordinate unit or member information. While this may seem intrusive on the part of the superior command, it is in line with what is normally expected. That is, that the superior command understands what its junior commands are doing, and if they are responsible for their activities and movements, that they account for those activities and movements and coordinate them as part of their larger mission. This is commonly known as "intrusive leadership," where the leader involves herself in the professional and personal lives of her military subordinates.

Somewhat axiomatically, leadership and management in the military are taken seriously, and the traditional civilian boss-subordinate relationship differs in many ways from the degree of military management that each individual is expected to achieve over each of their charges.

The Inference of Legality

It can be rationally inferred that military orders are presumed, and assumed to be, valid. However, the steps to have a lawful order and the legal basis for that inference merit discussion. The inference of lawfulness is directly derived from the Manual for Courts Martial, in the "Explanations" section of Punitive Articles, paragraph 14 (Article 90, Assaulting or willfully disobeying a superior commissioned officer), and is directly referenced by Punitive Articles, paragraph 16 (Article 92, Failure to obey order or regulation).

For an order to be lawful, there is an initial inference of legality, and three criteria that subject that inference to scrutiny. *Ab initio*, an order is inferred to be valid. After that initial inference, the three criteria that must be satisfied to have that order deemed legal are that the issuing officer must have valid authority, the order must bear a relationship to military duty, and there must not be a conflict between the order and the statutory or constitutional rights of the person receiving the order (10 U.S.C. §890 (c)(2)(a)(1)). Each of these criteria will be examined.

Taken verbatim from the Manual for Courts Martial, "an order requiring the performance of a military duty or act may be inferred to be lawful and it is disobeyed at the peril of the subordinate. This inference does not apply to a patently illegal order, such as one that directs the commission of a crime" (10 U.S.C. §890(c)(2)(a)(1); Marsh 1953).

With regard to the authority of the issuing officer, intuitively, the officer issuing the order must have the authority to give such an order. To that end, authority "may be based on law, regulation, or custom of the service" (10 U.S.C. §890 (c)(2)(a)(2); Keenan 1969; Schultz 1969). Without inquiry, there is a rebuttable presumption of an order's validity, but with all three of these criteria present, the order will very likely be held to be valid.[4]

LAW IN ACTION

Structure

Military law draws its basis from federal law. The military's criminal code is codified in federal law via Title 10 of the United States Code. However, while the military's law is contained within the same title as the civilian, federal code, there are numerous differences both in its content and in its understanding.

Perhaps one of the most telling statements about the difference between the structure of the military and its civilian counterparts relative to law is the aphorism that being late to work isn't a federal crime. Within the military, this adage holds true. "Any member of the armed forces who, without authority—(1) fails to go to his appointed place of duty at the time prescribed shall be punished as a court-martial may direct" (10 U.S.C §886). That is, being late to work—failing to go to the member's appointed place of duty at the appointed time—really is a federal crime! This adage represents only the tip of the iceberg with regard to what actions are criminalized within the Uniform Code of Military Justice (UCMJ), but do not have equivalent codification in civilian federal forums. Three categories of crimes that are exclusively found within the military are wartime crimes, disrespect crimes, and appearance crimes.

Wartime crimes are, as the title would lead one to believe, crimes committed during wartime. The providence of the military being reasonably exclusive during wartime, only a certain class of people can be convicted of these crimes, which class excludes (for the most part) civilians.[5] These crimes include mutiny (10 U.S.C. §894), sedition (10 U.S.C. §894), misconduct as a prisoner (10 U.S.C. §905), and malingering (10 U.S.C. §915). Describing conduct that is generally against the interests of the United States during wartime, these crimes due to that semi-exclusive province, are without equal in the civilian realm.

Another set of crimes that are codified within the military, but are not found in civilian forums are what can be termed "disrespect" crimes. These crimes revolve around disrespect towards someone, and have a uniqueness to them as against what is thought of as rude, crass, or commonplace behavior in the civilian realm. For example, within this category are contempt towards officials (10 U.S.C. §888) and disrespect towards a superior commissioned officer (10 U.S.C. §889). While the first is somewhat nebulous, the latter is analogizable to civilian life. Disrespect of a superior commissioned officer, per the elements of the crime, requires the disrespect to occur at any time and in any place, regardless of whether the officer is present. This strikes as being much akin to a group of employees gathered together and complaining about a supervisor or speaking derogatorily about a boss, even if (and usually when) that supervisor or boss isn't present. However, it is striking to think about that break room conversation being a criminal act. It is easy to comprehend the reaction to that act as being a warning, or a written counseling, or even a suspension at the extreme end, but certainly not a crime.

The final type of military-exclusive crimes are appearance crimes. These crimes might include conduct unbecoming an officer and a gentleman (10 U.S.C. §933), adultery (10 U.S.C. §934), wrongful cohabitation (10 U.S.C. §934), and fraternization (10 U.S.C. §934). The theory behind these crimes is that while the act is not in itself criminal, the appearance of the act is prejudicial to good order and discipline, thus weakening the fabric of the military. While a business transaction with one's supervisor is likely innocuous and would not advantage that employee in evaluations, the danger is that it *could*, or more importantly, that other employees would see that relationship as privileged and the subordinate employee as benefitting from it, even if it is not the case in reality. It is the appearance, and not the reality, of these crimes that matter, and they are, again, without equal in civilian society. Beyond that, however, it is evidenced in the legal treatment of military decisions that it is the good order and discipline—the legal fabric of the military—that is crucially important and a significant part of the rationale behind decisions involving military action or policy.

The uniqueness of military law does not necessarily equate to distinct treatment from its civilian counterparts, but it is argued, that it contributes to the military's distinct treatment by civilian authorities, and especially civilian courts. The difference in treatment of military decisions and policies by civilian courts is the basis of the military deference doctrine. To the greater point of this work, these unique rules and laws guide and bind the conduct of the members of the military, overtly placing guidelines on that conduct.

Morality

Morality is more difficult to evidence than legal culture. It is often seen as the difference between what is right and wrong, but that seems to both blur the line between legality and morality and juxtapose individual values onto the institution of the military. To align the institutional morality with something more descriptive than what is right and wrong, this work asserts that morality can be overlaid on chivalry. The qualities included within this concept include those qualities idealized by knights, such as bravery, courtesy, honor, and integrity.

The notion of the military being deeply connected to chivalric concepts is well-established. It is engrained in literature, in custom, and in law. Within military ethos, chivalry originated in the medieval period (Sweeney 1983). From that period, the ancient code of chivalry parallels nicely to what actions and behavior are celebrated in military life today. This ancient code includes such qualities as loving one's country, never lying, not recoiling before an enemy, not showing cowardice and the preference to die fighting rather than showing weakness, and always being right and good against evil and injustice (Gautier 1891).

Within medieval literature, the concept of chivalry is further defined, typically being categorized as duties to countrymen, duties to God, and duties to women, representing itself as warrior-chivalry, religious-chivalry, and courtly-chivalry. Examples of warrior-chivalry might include Sir Gawain, who is one of the bravest Knights of the Round Table or Henry V, as depicted by Shakespeare, and described by the protagonist to possess great bravery, compassion, loyalty, and honor.

Moving chivalry forward from literature and the Middle Ages to the modern period, chivalry is reflected throughout the progression of time to the modern period and in the military's ethos and its laws. In both the military's Code of Conduct and the UCMJ, chivalric influence is evident, and incorporated into the training, ritual, and understanding of the members of the military. The Code of Conduct states:

(1) I am an American, fighting in the forces which guard my country and our way of life. I am prepared to give my life in their defense.
(2) I will never surrender of my own free will. If in command, I will never surrender the members of my command while they still have the means to resist.
(3) If I am captured, I will continue to resist by all means available. I will make every effort to escape and aid others to escape. I will accept neither parole nor special favors from the enemy.
(4) If I become a prisoner of war, I will keep faith with my fellow prisoners. I will give no information or take part in any action which might be harmful to my comrades. If I am senior, I will take command. If not, I will obey the lawful orders of those appointed over me, and will back them up in every way.

(5) When questioned, should I become a prisoner of war, I am required to give only my name, rank, service number, and date of birth. I will evade answering further questions to the utmost of my ability. I will make no oral or written statements disloyal to my country and its allies or harmful to their cause.

(6) I will never forget that I am an American, fighting for freedom, responsible for my actions, and dedicated to the principles which made my country free. I will trust in my God and in the United States of America (Executive Order 10631; Executive Order 12017; Executive Order 12633).

These six elements of the Code of Conduct harken into the medieval code, preserving integrity, defending the nation, acting with honor, and tilting instead of cowering, and are reinforced both through culture and the codification of law. These articles of the Code of Conduct can also be seen as a basis for professionalization and standardization. In one sense, "professionalization" can be understood as ones who fought, "not because of social obligation, or duty, to fight, but for money" (Trim 2003: 4)—essentially creating a professional army, but in another sense, it can be seen as the rationalization of education and training (Weber 1921: 650), which can be reduced to criteria for the development of the military institution. Those criteria can be defined as including a discrete occupational identity, formal hierarchy, permanence, a formal pay system, or distinctive expertise and means of education, efficiency in execution of expertise, and a distinctive self-conceptualization (Trim 2003: 7–8). Analyzed through the lens of professionalization of the institution and its members, the Code of Conduct stands to establish occupational identity in the form of self-awareness, reinforce formal hierarchy and military structure, and reinforce permanence through its enduring nature.

Beyond the Code of Conduct and its overt harkening to a code of chivalry, there are also punitive articles in the UCMJ that essentially codify chivalry. Article 133 (10 U.S.C. §933), "Conduct Unbecoming an Officer and a Gentleman," and Article 134 (10 U.S.C. §934), sometimes termed the "General Article," are at the same time, both extraordinarily vague in meaning and interpretation and narrow in what they proscribe. Both Articles 133 and 134 have been constitutionally challenged as being void for vagueness, but they both have survived attack (Franz 1953; Grafton 1907; Ex parte Mason 1881; Dynes 1858). Each of these articles prohibits conduct that is prejudicial to the good order and discipline of the military, but why? As noted in the discussion on the legal culture in the military, these appearance crimes, if committed, lower the prestige of the military. An individual act would be attributed to the whole, lowering confidence in that entity. Therefore, the specificity in each of these articles derives from the professionalization of the military, and the desire to maintain its power and chivalric aura. That is, the law, and indeed, the military, is imbued with chivalry, and this value undergirds how law and authority are interpreted.

Drawing the discussion forward to incorporate gendered examinations of the military, the Manual for Courts-Martial (MCM), which is the single-source document for the Rules of Court-Martial and the UCMJ, continues notions of chivalry in a new sense. With women serving in the what is traditionally understood as a male-dominated culture in the military (Dunivin 1994; Herbert 1998), and in the past twenty years with sexual assault in the military being a hot-button issue, it is worth reevaluating the chivalric nature of the military and the rules that undergird it. While programs have been created and adapted to better train and equip servicemembers to be aware of their legal rights and the associated legal consequences concerning sexual assault, and several statutes that govern sexual contact have been amended, an argument can be conceived that, due to high-level comments about the military justice system,[6] and a possible amendment concerning procedure, having been discussed and debated in Congress,[7] the chivalric code may be pushed aside for one that keeps notions of respect, but abandons the gender stereotypes of chivalry. However, this argument does not gain strength when examined in the context of the UCMJ, and its evolution over the past thirty years. Articles 133, conduct unbecoming an officer and a gentleman, and 134, the general article, which require crimes to be connected to violations of "good order and discipline," remain largely untouched, despite complete revisions to the MCM in 1984 (MCM 1984), 1994 (MCM 1994), 1995 (MCM 1995), 1998 (MCM 1998), 2000 (MCM 2000), 2005 (MCM 2005), 2008 (MCM 2008), and 2012 (MCM 2012), and further amendments in 2013 (Executive Order 13643), 2014 (Executive Order 13669), and 2015 (Executive Order 13696). While the interpretation of "gentlemen" in Article 133 now includes women, the verbiage remains the same. The UCMJ continues to reflect chivalric values, despite the change in gendering, mirroring values in the Code of Conduct.

Intrusive Leadership

As previously mentioned in the introduction, the military employs a unique style of leadership that is intrusive to the personal affairs of its members. That intrusive leadership is a necessary consequence of a heavily hierarchical system. That is, leadership is performed by leaders, and the structure provided by the military, and its hierarchy, is quite intense, for several reasons that will be discussed.

The primary involvement of the military hierarchy is extensive. It includes official involvement in the medical, physical, legal, and family readiness of individual servicemembers, whether they be Soldiers, Sailors, Airmen, or

Marines. While many will understand the following four areas of intrusion to be normatively "good" or "desirable," for the servicemember, the following actions and involvement are mandatory, and disobedience is at the jeopardy of the individual who disobeys. Medical involvement in the lives of servicemembers can include the ordered receipt of vaccinations, physical examinations, and other individualized treatments for the general welfare of the individual or the unit. Physical involvement can involve an order to exercise with a unit, and to take physical fitness tests with that unit, for the purpose of ensuring that members are fit enough to deploy, if necessary, and to meet service weight and appearance standards, generally. Legal involvement is more difficult to pin down because a commander cannot order an individual to get legal advice, but can order an individual to report to a place where legal services are performed. The command discipline program requires that the unit leadership process alleged offenders, both minor and major at the appropriate forum (administrative, quasi-judicial, or judicial). Legal readiness, as differentiated from the command discipline program drives at making sure that service members receive any necessary powers of attorney, wills, or legal advice necessary to keep the unit ready to deploy. Finally, family involvement ranges from ordering servicemembers to provide financial support to their family, to specifically briefing them regarding deployments. Additionally, this family involvement includes ensuring that that single parents arrange for the safe care of their children should an incident occur, and that the family is generally taken care of through a variety of instructions and mechanisms. This involvement can even extend to where they live, with many military installations having family housing, maintaining communities of families on base.

The lawful authority of commanders to issue orders which must be obeyed is the vehicle in which this intrusive involvement occurs, but it is not the reason for issuing those orders in the first place. As has been emphasized in sections on the structure of the law and the morality inherent in its code, order, discipline, and the appearance of both order and discipline take high priority. Providing medical treatment, offering options for legal services, and holding units to identical standards, drive at the professionalization discussed earlier, and serve to create a uniform service. As it is true that the issuance of orders is more about leadership than shoring up power through obedience, it is also true that the obedience of those orders is less about compliance for fear of punishment than it is about compliance due to cultural expectation.

Beyond compliance tied to the threat of punishment and prosecution, Tyler offers an alternative means to understand obedience. Consent and cooperation serve as the mechanism for compliance in Tyler's panel study of the residents of Chicago. The study, which was trifurcated, first demonstrated that legitimacy shapes compliance with the law. Second, the study showed that legitimacy was not rooted in experiences, in Tyler's parlance, "instrumental judgments," but was rather grounded in "procedural justice judgments." Finally, the understanding and meaning of "procedural justice" was examined, clarifying that respondents understood procedural justice in reference to noninstrumental issues. These stages, taken together, form the conclusion that people comply with legal authorities as a function of social relationships and ethical judgments, and not out of fear of punishments or to gain rewards (Tyler 1990).

Military culture aligns well with Tyler's conclusions concerning compliance. While it is true that there are legal underpinnings that criminalize certain action or inaction, law, in the military, is a tool, and not the end result. This tool helps to ensure discipline and order, but combined with leadership that attempts to understand people both in and out of uniform, camaraderie of the people within units, and the implicit truth that, due to the military being an all-volunteer force, the servicemembers *want* to be in the military, the nature of obedience turns from fear of punishment or reward toward social relationships that were (and continue to be) developed and a sense of purpose.

THE MEETING OF MILITARY AND CIVILIAN STRUCTURES

Thus far, the uniqueness of the military has been analyzed from the structure of military law, its chivalric morality, and at a micro-level, the involvement of the service on individual members. And, the rationale provided for the uniqueness has been an argument for unity and similarity as part of professionalization. However, there is another substantial reason for the military's uniqueness, which is most evident in observing the interaction between the civilian legal system and the military.

There is a unique relationship that the military enjoys with the Bill of Rights and civilian, judicial scrutiny that must be unpacked for its significance, but will not be extensively discussed. The military deference doctrine sits as an abnormality to the normal application of rules and doctrine, and evidences the uniqueness of the mission and role of the military.

Over time, the United States Supreme Court has evidenced wide deference towards the military on certain issues. "The military is, by necessity, a specialized society separate from civilian society" (O'Connor 2007: 672, quoting *Parker v. Levy* (1974)). In that same case, Justice Rehnquist, writing for the majority, succinctly described the difference between civilian application of the constitution and military application. He stated:

> While the members of the military are not excluded from the protection granted by the First Amendment, the different character of the military community and

> of the military mission requires a different application of those protections. The fundamental necessity for obedience, and the consequent necessity for imposition of discipline, may render permissible within the military that which would be constitutionally impermissible outside it (Parker 1974: 758).

That the treatment is affirmatively discussed is advancement from decades past. Formerly, the military was granted such deference that the Supreme Court would not hear cases relating to military matters (Lichtman 2006: 915). "Dealing with areas of law peculiar to the military branches, the Court of Military Appeals' judgments are normally entitled to great deference" (Middendorf 1976: 43). Moreover, "judicial deference . . . is at its apogee when legislative action under the congressional authority to raise and support armies and make rules and regulations for their governance is challenged" (Rostker 1981: 70). The Supreme Court for decades was so deferential that it "refused to conduct a substantive review, no matter how lenient, of military practices (O'Connor 2000: 170). The Court subsequently began to take cases, and treated them with the deference described, *supra* (Lichtman 2006: 915). That deference was so pronounced that Earl Warren, the then-sitting Chief Justice of the United States, said in remarks given to New York University that:

> So far as the relationship of the military to its own personnel is concerned, the basic attitude of the Court has been that the latter's jurisdiction is most limited. Thus, the Supreme Court has adhered consistently to the 1863 holding of *Ex parte Vallandigham* that it lacks jurisdiction to review by certiorari the decisions of military courts. (Warren 1972: 186—187).

The absence of the Supreme Court's interpretation of law as it relates to the military create a space for the military's interpretation and application of authority and order. The deep roots that military culture has in its members, and that exist within the organization cause it to be unique, distinct, and wholly separate in structure and form from its civilian counterparts. This uniqueness is, as was argued, not just limited to isolated parts of the military, but is true with the whole of the organization. The military's legal and moral structures, down to the everyday practice of leadership, are flooded with examples of its unique culture and purpose, ultimately leading to its distinct treatment by civilian courts and entities.

THE INFLUENCE OF MAX WEBER

Within the body of examples, and specifically the case study of Army basic training, as well as the history provided here, there has been a wealth of scholarly research into the legal, the moral, and the everyday life of servicemembers.[8] This work unifies the distinctions drawn in each of those pieces of the whole under a larger umbrella.

In the course of his study of law, sociology, and religion, Weber argued that there were three forms of authority, and that these forms of domination legitimate power, leadership, and authority (Weber 1958). This was important due to his definition of state as claiming a monopoly on the legitimate use of violence (Weber 1919). That is, for a state to use violence, that violence must be legitimated, which forces examination on the legitimacy of the state itself. The three forms of legitimate rule according to Weber are charismatic, traditional, and legal-rational (Weber 1958). These forms of authority can be loosely thought of as existing on a continuum, with each subsequent one generally succeeding the last.

Charismatic authority is so termed because it draws from the charisma of the leader. The leader evidences that he possesses the right to lead by virtue of magical powers, prophecies, heroism, etc. His followers, or as Weber defines them, "disciples" (Whimster 2004: 139), respect his right to lead because of his unique qualities (his charisma), not because of any tradition or legal rules (Bendix 1977: 295). The leader's followers consist of those who have shown personal devotion to the ruler, and of those who possess their own charisma (Whimster 2004: 139). Weber defined the authority as "resting on devotion to the exceptional sanctity, heroism or exemplary character of an individual person, and of the normative patterns or order revealed or ordained by him" (Ritzer 2010: 132).

Traditional authority is based on a belief of the sanctity of orders and the power of rule (Whimster 2004:135), in which authority is legitimate because it "has always existed." People in power usually enjoy it because they have inherited it. Officials consist either of personal retainers (in a patrimonial regime) or of personal loyal allies, and their decisions are usually similar to those of the ruler above them, just reduced in scale, and they too are often selected based on inheritance (Bendix 1977: 295). On a smaller scale, and to serve as a demonstrative example, traditional authority is similar to the authority of a patriarchal household. In such households, patriarchs set the rules of the home, but have no staff to ensure compliance with those rules. Therefore, compliance is left to the willingness of the members of the family to respect his authority. Taking this small-scale example to Weber's ideation of traditional authority in a state, the power of the ruler is ancient, drawing on tradition, and as with the patriarchal household, the subject's belief in the system perpetuates such a power dynamic.

The third, and final form of authority that Weber contemplated on his quasi-continuum, was legal-rational authority, which is the most evolved form of authority of the three authorities. Legal-rational authority is based on a system of rules that is applied administratively and judicially in accordance with known principles. The persons who administer those rules are appointed or elected by legal procedures. Superiors are also subject to rules that limit their powers, separate their private lives from official duties, and require written documentation. This sense that the law is separate from, but yet still governing, the institution is central to Weber's focus and analysis on bureaucracy. Within bureaucracy, Weber sought to answer the question of how societies bureaucratize and gain (and maintain) legitimacy. For Weber, rationalization and order were key to the emergence of bureaucratization, and he argued that an ideal bureaucracy was characterized by: hierarchical organization, delineated lines of authority in a fixed area of activity, action taken on the basis of and recorded in written rules, bureaucratic officials needing (and receiving) expert training, rules being implemented by neutral officials, and career advancement depending on technical qualifications judged by organization, not individuals (Swedburg 2005).

ANALYSIS

In this chapter, an examination of the structure of the military and its differences from civilian society has been presented. Each of these differences and unique characteristics have well-informed scholarship analyzing them, but the argument is that each of these differences, unique characteristics, and causes for special analysis are not endogenous, but, they are affected, influenced, and governed by a systemic difference in the authority and legitimacy of the institution itself as against the structure and legitimizing authority of civilian society. And, this systemic difference inextricably permeates itself in the lives of its members. In that vein, this section will examine those military structures and analyze those same structures and the differences between them and civilian society using a Weberian lens focused on legitimacy and authority.

Certainly, the military reflects a traditional form of domination, but that to exist as it does, it must also reflect a legal-rational form of domination. That is, the military, due to its history, tradition, and specialized purpose, receives a unique legal analysis from civilian courts with different or watered-down constitutional scrutiny, resulting in a high degree of deference to its policies. However, this unique treatment is only possible because of the resemblance of those legal-rational policies and procedures within the traditional form of authority that the military projects.

As discussed earlier, traditional authority is based on a system in which authority is legitimate because it "has always existed." The United States military has existed since the inception of the nation, but more importantly, it was modeled after medieval knights which provided centuries of structure and form to the military, and brought into the United States Armed Forces a sense of tradition and power, through procedures and policies that existed for centuries.

In the traditional form of authority, people in power usually enjoy it because they have inherited it. In the earlier example of the traditional patriarchal household, the patriarch inherits that position both by gender, but also by the institution of marriage. In the example of the United States military, a commander does not inherit that position by birth. While there are various requirements, including time in service, and importantly, aptitude, the position is not entirely legal-rational, as the authority of that position is conferred by the military. In the example provided in the legal structure section of disrespect crimes, the mere disrespect of someone of higher rank is codified as a criminal action. That is, the institution of the military creates authority for those who are higher ranking. In the example of the patriarch, there is no set of formal requirements to hold that position—once the position is earned, the compliance of the household is dependent on the legitimacy that they perceive the patriarch to possess. Similarly, the authority of the commander is dependent not on formal aptitude tests, but by rank, and the legitimacy that such rank confers within the institution of the armed forces.

Moving beyond the base definition provided in the introduction, traditional authority is, at its core, the belief in the continuity of sacred tradition; the imbued ideas and traditions of centuries past incorporate into its ethos and membership today. Unpacking that includes both specific analysis of definitions and terms, but also something beyond that direct analysis. Understanding the military through the lens of traditional authority means immersing oneself in that mentality. The introduction to the military was meant to create a level of knowledge and to break that knowledge down into academic boxes, but to understand the military and its form of authority and legitimacy means going beyond those boxes and piecing all of that information—illumination of the military from an inside perspective will be fruitful in forming valuable conclusions.

The military culture is immense. Earlier in this piece, that complex culture was dissected, and examined from several different structural viewpoints. However, to comprehend the ubiquitous presence of military culture in the eyes of those that are in the military and subject to its rules and regulations, is to understand its authority on a different, elevated level, and to see the unseen, become aware of the omnipresent, and feel how the combination of the institutions of law and the military materially affect the lives of those who are governed by them.

Military Culture as Ubiquitous and Omnipresent

Thus far, this work has argued that the military uses traditional authority vice legal-rational authority. To succeed in this end, the members of the Armed

Forces must be indoctrinated into the sanctity of the orders that they follow, and, will eventually, issue. To accomplish this indoctrination, recruit training locations were established in each of the military services. These basic training camps serve several purposes, both to mold the recruit physically and vocationally, but also to mentally and culturally shape the recruit.

A fine example of recruit training from the standpoint of physically and vocationally adapting to the military can be found within the United States Army. Army basic training is broken into two parts, Basic Combat Training and Advanced Individual Training.

Basic Combat Training (BCT) consists of the first ten weeks of the total Basic Training period (Soldier Life 2016), and is identical for all Army, Army Reserve, and Army National Guard recruits, ensuring that every Soldier, regardless of their component (active or reserve), or their future position receives standardized training.[9] This is where individuals learn about the fundamentals of being a soldier, from combat techniques to the proper way to address a superior. So involved is this transformation that recruits must relearn how to tell time, identify the date, and even write.

While the notion of a 24-hour clock is not exclusively used by the armed forces, its more common name, "military time," certainly describes it as an alternative means of telling time. This method of telling time supplants common clock nomenclature, "6 a.m." or "4 o'clock," with more specific nomenclature. With military time, "6 a.m." converts to "0600," reducing the potential for miscommunication of "a.m." or "p.m." More drastic, "4 o'clock" might refer to 4 a.m. or 4 p.m. Military time clarifies the intent and meaning, presenting the information as "0400" or "1600," with the times pronounced as "oh-four-hundred" (instead of four-hundred) or "sixteen-hundred."

In addition to the time, the telling of the date is also alternatively presented from normal understanding in the United States. While a majority of citizens of the United States would write the date as "April 1," the recruit is trained to understand, interpret, and write the date as "1 Apr." Should that recruit want to take "leave"—the military nomenclature for "vacation"—they would request off from "24 Jun—10 Jul."

Compounding the re-education of recruits in telling time and identifying dates, new recruits are also provided instruction on the "Army Writing Style." This part of the same manual, Army Regulation (AR) 25—50, that provides instruction on how to tell the time and how to identify the date and provides instruction on how to write a sentence in the Army-style, creating generation after generation of literature, memoranda, and publications that are similar in style (Preparing and Managing Correspondence 2013), creating a larger sense of continuity and durational power, lending credence to a Weberian analysis.

Beyond the immersion experience of learning how to tell time, identify the date, and write in the military style, BCT is also where individuals undergo rigorous physical training to prepare their bodies and their minds for the eventual physical and mental strain of combat. One of the most difficult and lessons learned in BCT is self-discipline, as it introduces prospective soldiers to a strict daily schedule that entails many duties and high expectations for which most civilians are not immediately ready.

Advanced Individual Training (AIT*)* consists of the remainder of the total Basic Training period, and is where recruits train in the specifics of their chosen field. As such, AIT is different for each available Army career path, or Military Occupational Specialty (MOS). AIT courses can last anywhere from 6 to 52 weeks. Although many AIT schools don't center around combat the way BCT does, individuals are still continually tested for physical fitness and weapons proficiency, and upon MOS, may be subject to the same duties, strict daily schedule, and disciplinary rules as in BCT.

There is value to both portions of training, but toward the point of evidencing the power of rule and respect for authority, it is the first portion of training that is most relevant. BCT is the first exposure of the new recruits to the military, and the structure of the training combined with the first few days and hours are most telling.

The structure and purpose of Basic Training reveal much with regard to the intent of such training. The Marine Corps instruction for basic training presents a unity of the concepts above in its attempt to instill tradition and timeliness. This instillation begins with the Commander's Intent for the training program:

> Transforming civilians into basically trained Marines, who are imbued with our core values of honor, courage, and commitment, is the primary focus of recruit training [. . .] As the Nation's premier Expeditionary "Total Force in Readiness" we will continue to instill stamina and toughness in each individual Marine while simultaneously reinforcing character that values honor, integrity, and taking care of our fellow Marines; including treating each other with dignity and respect. (Marine Corps Order (MCO) 1510.32D 2003)

Prior to new military recruits ever showing up at their duty station, the program that they are being thrust into has the primary mission to transform those recruits from whatever and whoever they were prior, into warriors—even, beyond warriors, "Marines" with all of the identity that goes with that title. These Marines have instilled into them honor, courage, and commitment, the core values of the service that are the bedrock on which all else is built.

From its intent to the language that is used during the Basic Training period, recruits are exposed to concepts designed to instill in them the vestiges of tradition and honor. A prime example of this is the time following the initial processing period, but preceding the commencement of the regular training schedule. This time period, known as "forming," is where processed recruits are formed into platoons. Forming varies in duration, depending upon how long it takes to amass a full recruit series or company to begin training. Initial housekeeping tasks, elementary training, and the actions listed in the processing phase will be accomplished (MCO 1510.32D 2003). Beyond the tasks set forth to be accomplished during this period, the name given to this evolution conjures images of clay being molded into defined shapes.

Further into the instruction, the military's degree of control over their recruits—and by extension, all of their members—becomes evident. Earlier, this chapter discussed the involvement of the military into the lives of its members, addressing medical, physical fitness, and legal necessities. The argument then was that each of those were essential to the good order and discipline of the unit, preparations to make it—and its members—deployable if circumstances necessitated. On top of those work-related intrusions into the lives of its members, the service extends itself further. Again using the Marine Corps basic training instruction as a means of evidencing the indoctrination into military culture and the establishment and imbuing of tradition and values into its members, a recruit's training day is broken up into academic hours and non-academic hours. Academic hours are used to learn and master knowledge essential to the being a Marine. Non-academic hours include administrative time dedicated to completing tasks which include:

> haircuts, exchange calls, storage of personal effects, yearbook/photos, blood donations, inoculations, preparation of military identification cards, rifle and equipment issue, clothing appointments, movement time, dental recall, preparation of hometown news releases, pay, issuance of orders, and making travel arrangements.

We see that the involvement of the military—its rules, requirements, and presence—extends beyond the academic day and into the uniform shop, the public affairs office, and even the barber shop, turning regular hair cutting appointments into a means to create compliance with appearance and uniform rules. The above activities are normally associated with errands, and the normal time to run errands is in one's free time. However, the instruction delineates what free time is for the recruits. While free time is time away from Drill Instructors and other officials, the purpose of free time is to "allow recruits to read, write letters, [and] watch instructional television (ITV)," suggesting that "free time" is time without formal instruction, but is far from "free."

Finally, but certainly worthy of note is the recruit's rights. Thus far, the conversation has been centered on indoctrinating recruits into the tradition of the military, changing the way that they think and act through the military's expectations of recruits and its structure. What purpose could recruit rights serve to reinforce such structure and tradition? This section begins by stating that the rights listed in the section are fundamental to the welfare of recruits and will not be denied, and then proceeds to state that included in these rights are the right to eight hours of uninterrupted sleep and one hour of free time daily, and to receive mail on the day that it arrives. However, each of those rights is caveated. Recruits have a right to "Eight hours of uninterrupted sleep, except under the conditions described in paragraph 4c(5)(f)," "One hour of free time daily, except under the conditions described in paragraph 4c(5)(g), and during processing, forming, and weapons and field/combat training, and the Crucible Event," and "Receive mail on the day it is received by the parent company except for Sundays, holidays, and during the Crucible Event."[10] Each of these "rights" is subject to limitation or cancellation due to military requirements or exigencies, reinforcing both the power of the entity that is giving these rights and the mentality that these rights can be amended, abridged, or cancelled due to military need.

The notion of the recruit's rights serves to open the discussion concerning the mental and cultural shaping of the recruit. What creates the expectation that a recruit can be given a right subject to the need of the military? What forms the basis of these cultural notions of subordinate rights, but more to the point, the adoption of the military culture to the ideological exclusion of options that they would possess as a civilian?

Returning to the example of the haircut, what creates the expectation that the recruit will *want* a compliant haircut, such that they no longer ask for an alternative style, such as one that they would get had they not been in the military? Certainly the first thought is that the regulation is in place, criminalizing non-compliance. Beyond the legal consequence, there are also administrative options available. For example, in the Navy, a Sailor can be adversely marked on an annual evaluation for such non-compliance. These evaluations are a contributing factor in selection for training, career advancement, and ultimately, promotion. One of the seven scored traits is "Military Bearing/Character," with the specific guidance stating:

> Strict adherence of every Sailor to the highest personal and professional standards of conduct is paramount in assessing military bearing and character. This performance trait also encompasses standards of physical appearance, fitness, and readiness. To merit high marks, a Sailor must meet and model the highest standards of professionalism in demeanor, deportment, and interaction with, and treatment of, superiors, peers, and subordinates (Bureau of Personnel Instruction. (BUPERSINST) 1610.10D, Enclosure (2) 2015)

More subtle than affirmatively enacting adverse legal action is marking an individual down on a performance evaluation, thus tying compliance to both positive and negative consequences. However, while the reason for such willing compliance with exacting rules, regulations, and customs is somewhat tied to the positive or negative consequences that create the "good order and discipline" that is specifically codified into military law, the reason for such willing compliance is much more simple.

While there are positive and negative incentives for the fringe servicemember who needs them, there are three considerations which are offered to explain willing compliance. First, as discussed in this chapter, law is used as a tool to enforce traditional authority. It is, therefore, the traditional authority that desires compliance with these specific appearance rules, and not the law, *per se*. Second, the fact that rules such as wearing the uniform properly or having the haircut that meets the appropriate regulations help to underscore and understand their importance. The wear of the uniform and the physical appearance of the servicemember are the most visible aspects of that servicemember, to both the military and civilian communities. Visible cracks in discipline undermine the public confidence in the military generally. Finally, and addressing the cultural expectation of people entering the military that they will have uniform and appearance standards is that civilians understand that current members will have to adhere to these regulations. Whether it is by familial connection, the recruiting process, or even through television and/or movies, it is generally known that membership in the military requires a specified appearance as part of a sacrifice of individual rights, and if such a sacrifice is known, it becomes part of a social contract that recruits acknowledge when they sign their name to enter the military.

While each of these three reasons are interrelated, they present different answers to the same question. For the individuals wielding the traditional authority conferred to them, they need compliance with all orders, regardless of how small, to ensure compliance with "large" orders, such as putting oneself in physical jeopardy to complete a mission. Concerning public confidence, the military enjoys a high confidence rating. A Gallup poll in 2016 asked respondents how much confidence they, themselves had in a number of institutions. 73% replied that they either had a "great deal" or "quite a lot" of trust in the military. By contrast, that figure was 36% for the Presidency, 36% for the Supreme Court, and 6% for Congress. More to the point, historical surveys asking the same question found that the percentage of people who either had a "great deal" of confidence in the military or "quite a lot" are consistent over time. Since 1990, the combined percent has not been lower than 68%, nor has it been higher than 85% (Confidence in Institutions 2016). Public disobedience by servicemembers can certainly erode confidence in the institution by the public. Finally, concerning the public's expectation of the military culture, movies such as *A Few Good Men* (1992), *G.I. Jane* (1997), or *American Sniper* (2014) highlight the expectation of military discipline and conduct. Even movies that involve paramilitary forces, such as *Police Academy* (1984) acknowledge the cultural expectation of the military discipline system.[11] The unwavering compliance to these rules on the part of the institution a) reinforces the importance of the rules and the institutional commitment to them, b) creates the expectation that recruits will comply with them, and c) can create a self-selecting effect, with people who want such regulation or discipline volunteering to join the military.

LAW AS SERVING TWO ROLES

Every aspect of the military, from its training, to its daily routine, to its morality, and certainly to its law reflects traditional authority, and the ancient power of time immemorial. However, this form of ancient, traditional domination and legitimacy maintains its power and strength within—and adjacent to—civilian, legal-rational forms of authority by mimicking those same legal-rational constructs within the military's traditional structure. This then requires two analyses—first, that the law is used to internally legitimatize the traditional authority of the military, and second, that the law is used to satiate civilian judges who are viewing law through a legal-rational lens.

Refreshing the discussion of Marine Corps Basic Training, it was argued that it is focused on transforming civilians into members of the military, and that this is accomplished through a series of actions, rules, and behavior that reinforce such a transformation. Law, however, is not absent from this transformation. Rather, it plays a prominent role in reinforcing the mindset and behavior of the recruits. The first duty area that the recruits study as part of their academic curriculum is "Military Justice and the Law of War." This block of study includes explanation of the military's justice system, the identification of offenses that are punishable under the UCMJ, explanation of problem solving mechanisms available to Marines should they feel aggrieved, the rights of the accused, and the forums in which a case could be heard in, with the consequences possible in each of those forums. The presentation and absorption of this material is of such emphasis and import that it is presented chronologically in advance of the organization, history, and courtesies of the Marine Corps (Marine Corps Recruit Training Matrix 2016). From this juxtaposition, it can be inferred that the rules and laws serve as a primer for interpreting the tradition of the military. That is, while it is known from earlier discussion that chivalry and battle-readiness run throughout all actions of the military, and that the authority of the military is introduced in basic training and repeatedly reinforced. It is law internal to the military that provides a mechanism for enforcing these traditions, and providing evidence to external observers that the power of superiors is not unchecked, and appears to be based on law and rationality.

Related to affirmatively legitimating the traditional model of authority that the military represents is using the law to mimic legal-rational structures, having them subordinate to military rules and requirements, and having those mimetic structures treated as providing recourse consistent with legal-rational courts and adjudicative hearings, further externally legitimating the military model that such mimetic courts and hearings reside in. To standardize the separate services' rules and laws, the UCMJ was created. The UCMJ established one system for the administration of military justice, and it superseded the Articles of War that were applicable to the Army and the Air Force, the Articles for the Government of the Navy, and the Disciplinary Laws of the Coast Guard (Background of the UCMJ 1959: 11). The United States Judge Advocate General's School, examined the history of the UCMJ, both in terms of substantive alterations, but also the chronological happenings that either coincided or preceded amendments and/or revisions.

The various services' Articles of War, or articles of similar nomenclature, have a long history that, when traced, draws directly to the uniformity of the UCMJ across the Armed Forces. Prior to the Constitution's enacting, there were two iterations of the Articles of War. The 1775 version of the Articles was the first military justice code applicable to all of the colonies, and each subsequent iteration added procedural rules and protections. In 1776, rules were added that affected the constitution of courts-martial, which provided a more uniform means of trying cases that gave a greater sense of procedural fairness. Revisions in 1806 and 1874 were in response to the constitutional status of the country and the immediate necessity to amend after the Civil War. Reflecting the need to modify the code and both respond to the realities of war and add procedural protection, the Articles were completely rewritten in 1916. Most importantly, jurisdiction was clarified and requirements were put in place to modify the statutes of limitations and to raise the percentage of jury members required to convict from a bare majority to two-thirds. The 1920 version of the Articles included requirements to consult military lawyers before preferring charges and to establish of appellate tribunals and rehearings. The final revision to the Articles of War prior to the passage of the UCMJ was in 1948, and it advanced many procedural points. The Articles now notably require that both the trial lawyer and the defense lawyer in a court case must be judge advocates (attorneys) while enhancing the protections against compulsory self-incrimination (Background of the UCMJ 1959: 7).

The evolution of procedural protections and the eventual uniformity of service regulations within the UCMJ evidence a progression of norms that externally legitimate the military to civilian judges. As Weberian rationalization occurred, and procedures were instilled on paper, and expected to be obeyed by those subject to them, a rational understanding was that there was a reason for any particular rule or regulation. The argument inherent in the military's position is that there is a procedure for everything, whether it is training soldiers, limiting free speech, or determining survivor benefits, and that these procedures are part and parcel to the military's unique purpose. These procedures are deferred to for reasons that have been articulated, but the refusal by military officials to abide by those military procedures—in essence, not following their own rules—provides cause for civilian judges to argue against deference. However, short of the inability of military officials to follow the military's procedures, the deference doctrine states that the military should normally, and does in fact, win in cases against it. The evolution of, and adherence to, procedures is then the signal to civilian judges that, despite the difference in purpose and mission between the military and civilian realms, the case merits deference, permitting that same adherence to procedure to legitimate the traditional authority that the military relies on.

CONCLUSION

This chapter argued that the military, while using law and legal rationality, does not draw its power from that law. Rather, drawing from ancient notions of power and authority, the military utilizes traditional authority, drawing its power from the law and its chivalric tradition, reinforcing that power through everyday military culture, and subsumes the understanding of military law and culture from the eyes of the street-level servicemember. The military's relationship with the law is not just limited to buttressing its traditional authority. This relationship also acts as an intermediary with regard to the military's relationship with civilian courts and judges, serving to allow those civilian judges to acquiesce to the military's unique rules and authority due to the familiar presence of rules and procedures. These rules and procedures, when followed, equate to deference, which substantiates and externally legitimates the military and its traditional authority. The net result, therefore, for those who wear the military's cloth is that they are simultaneously affected by an omnipresent force that is unchecked by civilian counterparts, nearly unseen in that the law which is taught to them on day one of their training doesn't stand on its own but supports military authority, and materially affects their lives in that, for example, their very "free" time is spent obeying orders and acting in a manner consistent with their training.

NOTES

1. At present, the Affordable Care Act could serve as an example of this idea.

2. Examples of this might include laws designed at food or building safety. To the consumer, there is almost no thought given to them, but they govern the safety of what is eaten and constructed.

3. Taxes could be construed as an example of this. They are taken out of every paycheck that a person receives, but are often hidden in the eyes of people until tax forms begin to arrive by mail and email. They, however, deduct what would ordinarily be control over money from the individual to the federal and state government every pay period.

4. In fact, there have been recent examples where persons subjected to orders questioned their lawfulness, and uniformly, courts have held that the order that was given was valid (Murdough 2010). Two such examples include Army Captain (CPT) Yolanda Huet-Vaughn and Army First Lieutenant (1LT) Ehren Watada. Notable because both cases were cases of officers refusing to obey orders, both CPT Huet-Vaughn and 1LT Watada refused to deploy to Iraq to fight what CPT Huet-Vaughn termed a "morally objectionable" war (Murdough 2010:7, citing Huet-Vaughn 1995:109). Feeling that it was her obligation to as a military person . . . to expose what [she] saw at that point as–as a move to a catastrophic consequence," CPT Vaughn argued the invalidity of the order before the Court of Appeals of the Armed Forces. Nonetheless, the Court convicted her of desertion with intent to avoid hazardous duty, noting that "to the extent that CPT Huet-Vaughn intended to contest the legality of the decision to employ military forces in the Persian Gulf, the evidence was irrelevant, because it pertained to a non-justiciable political question" (Murdough 2010:7, citing Huet-Vaughn 1995:115).

5. 10 U.S.C. §802 (Article 2 of the UCMJ) lists the people subject to the UCMJ. Included in the list, in the tenth and eleventh subsections, respectively, are "persons serving with or accompanying an armed force in the field" and "persons serving with, employed by, or accompanying the armed forces outside the United States," potentially opening the door for personal jurisdiction of civilians attached to, or working with military units.

6. One of the most telling statements was by the Chairman of the Joint Chiefs of Staff, General Martin Dempsey who was quoted as saying "We're losing the confidence of the women who serve that we can solve this problem . . . . That's a crisis" (Garamone 2013).

7. In response to the series of events, and with the sequence of events in 2013 acting as a straw that broke the camel's back, Sen Gillibrand (D-NY) and Sen. Collins (R-ME) introduced (and co-sponsored) the Military Justice Improvement Act (MJIA). The MJIA, as drafted, would amend the Uniform Code of Military Justice (UCMJ), to require decisions to court-martial where charges amount to more than one-year confinement to be made by a senior commissioned officer with significant experience in such trials and who is outside the chain of command of the accused. The MJIA would also require a convening authority (the official acting on the sentence of a court-martial), when taking any action other than approving a sentence, to prepare a written justification of such action which shall be made part of the record of the court-martial and prohibits a convening authority from: (1) dismissing or setting aside a finding of guilty, or (2) reducing a finding of guilty to a finding of guilty to a lesser included offense (MJIA, 2013).

8. Here, and throughout this chapter, I use the term "servicemembers." The rationale for this is threefold. First, while the phrase "service men" is more common during previous eras, "servicemembers" presents a gender-neutral term that recognizes the status of all members of the military. Second, the choice to use "servicemember"

vice "service member" is a stylistic one. Finally, the use of "servicemember" is service-neutral, encompassing Soldiers in the Army, Sailors in the Navy, Airmen in the Air Force, and Marines in the Marine Corps. References to a gendered term of "servicemember" or a different stylistic choice, or a specific service, when used, will be left as they were used, for authenticity of the cited source.

9. It is generally accepted that cultural immersion causes a foreign language to be learned faster. Paralleling that argument to the current thought, there are three arguments that are believed, but not expressly made. First, proximity to the immersion—boot camp—will cause higher degrees of acceptance and adoption of its training. Second, those who plan to continue to serve on active duty (vice reservists) will continue to be immersed in the military mindset, actively experiencing intrusive leadership and all the stated military norms, and will have a greater adherence to those norms based on that immersion. Third, those who have the longest exposure to the military culture will increase the likelihoods of acceptance and transformation by it.

10. The Crucible Event is the final challenge of Marine Corps recruit training. From the Marine Corps website, "It is a 54-hour training exercise that validates the physical, mental and moral training they've endured throughout recruit training" (http://www.mcrdpi.marines.mil/Recruit-Training/Crucible/).

11. For instance, in the haircut scene, two bombastic recruits walk into the barber shop as another recruit is preparing to have his hair cut. The recruit already waiting permits the two recruits to go in front of him, with one requesting that the barber "take it all off." After both recruits had their hair shaved off, as one expects at basic training, the original recruit who was preparing to have his hair cut re-assumes his position in the barber's chair, asking for "a little off the side" of his wavy locks. When one of the recently-shaved recruits asks the barber if such a request can be accommodated, the barber states "Sure, this ain't the Army, you know."

REFERENCES

"A Few Good Men." 1997.
"American Sniper." 2014.
Art. 105. Misconduct as Prisoner. 1956.
Art. 115. Malingering. 1956.
Art. 133. Conduct Unbecoming an Officer and a Gentleman. 1956.
Art. 134. General Article. 1956.
Art. 86. Absence Without Leave. 1956.
Art. 88. Contempt Toward Officials. 1956.
Art. 89. Disrespect Toward Superior Commissioned Officer. 1956.
Art. 90. Assaulting or Willfully Disobeying Superior Commissioned Officer. 1956.
Art. 92. Failure to Obey Order or Regulation. 1956.
Art. 94. Mutiny or Sedition. 1956.
"The Background of the Uniform Code of Military Justice." 1959. ed. United States Army: Judge Advocate General's School.

Bendix, Reinhard. 1977. *Max Weber: An Intellectual Portrait*. University of California Press.
Bureau of Personnel Instruction (BUPERSINST) 1610.10D. 2015. ed. Department of the Navy Bureau of Personnel.
"Confidence in Institutions." Gallup.
deVolo, Lorraine Bayard, and Edward Schatz. 2004. "From the Inside Out: Ethnographic Methods in Political Research." *Political Science and Politics* 37: 267–71.
Dunivin, Karen O. 1994. "Military Culture: Change and Continuity." *Armed Forces and Society* 20: 531–47.
Dynes v. Hoover, 61 20 Howard 65 (1858).
Ex Parte Mason, 105 U.S. 696 (1881).
Executive Order 10631. 1955. "Code of Conduct for Members of the Armed Forces of the United States."
Executive Order 12017. 1977. "Amending the Code of Conduct for Members of the Armed Forces of the United States."
Executive Order 12633. 1988. "Amending the Code of Conduct for Members of the Armed Forces of the United States."
Executive Order 13643. 2013. "2013 Amendments to the Manual for Courts-Martial, United States." ed.
Executive Order 13669. 2014. "2014 Amendments to the Manual for Courts-Martial."
Executive Order 13696. 2015. "2015 Amendments to the Manual for Courts-Martial."
Gautier, Leon. 1891. *Chivalry*. Translated by Henry Firth.
Geertz, Clifford. 1983. "Common Sense as a Cultural System." In *Local Knowledge: Further Essays in Interpretative Anthropology*, ed. Clifford Geertz: Basic Books.
"G. I. Jane." 1992.
Grafton v. United States 206 U.S. 333 (1907).
Herbert, Melissa S. 1998. *Camouflage Isn't Only for Combat: Gender, Sexuality, and Women in the Military*. New York: New York University Press.
Lichtman, Steven B. 2006. "The Justices and the Generals: A Critical Examination of the U.S. Supreme Court's Tradition of Deference to the Military, 1918–2004." *Maryland Law Review* 65: 907–64.
"Manual for Courts-Martial." 1984.
"Manual for Courts-Martial." 1994.
"Manual for Courts-Martial." 1995.
"Manual for Courts-Martial." 1998.
"Manual for Courts-Martial." 2000.
"Manual for Courts-Martial." 2002.
"Manual for Courts-Martial." 2005.
"Manual for Courts-Martial." 2008.
"Manual for Courts-Martial." 2012.
"Marine Corps Order (MCO) 1510.32D—Recruit Training." 2003. ed. United States Marine Corps.
"Marine Corps Recruit Training Matrix." http://www.mcrdpi.marines.mil/Portals/76/Docs/MCRDPITrainingMatrix101001.pdf.
Middendorf v. Henry, 425 U.S. 25 (1976).

O'Connor, John. 2000. "The Origins and Application of the Military Defense Doctrine." *Georgia Law Review* 35: 161.

———. 2007. "Statistics and the Military Deference Doctrine: A Response to Professor Lichtman." *Maryland Law Review* 66: 668–706.

Parker v. Levy, 417 U.S. 733 (1974).

"Police Academy." 1984.

"Preparing and Managing Correspondence." 2013. In *AR 25-50*. Department of the Army.

Ritzer, George. 2010. *Sociological Theory*. 3rd ed. New York: McGraw-Hill.

Rostker v. Goldberg, 453 U.S. 57 (1981).

"Soldier Life." http://www.goarmy.com/soldier-life/becoming-a-soldier/basic-combat-training.html.

Swedburg, Richard. 2005. *The Max Weber Dictionary: Key Words and Central Concepts*: Stanford University Press.

Sweeney, James Ross. 1983. "Chivalry." In *Dictionary of the Middle Ages*. Vol. 3.

Trim, D. J. B. 2003. *The Chivalric Ethos and the Development of Military Professionalism.* History of Warfare. Leiden: Brill Academic Publishers.

Tyler, Tom. 1990. *Why People Obey the Law*. New Haven: Yale University Press.

Weber, Max. 1921. *Economy and Society*. Edited by C. Wittich G. Roth. New York: Bedminster Press.

———. 1919. "Politics as a Vocation." *Essays in Sociology*: 77–128.

———. 1958. "The Three Types of Legitimate Rule." *Berkeley Publications in Society and Institutions* 4: 1–11.

United States v. Franz, 2 U.S.C.M.A. 48 (1953).

United States v. Keenan, 18 U.S.C.M.A. 108 (1969).

United States v. Marsh, 3 U.S.C.M.A. 48 (1953).

United States v. Schultz, 18 U.S.C.M.A. 133 (1969).

Warren, Earl. 1972. "The Bill of Rights and the Military." *New York University Law Review* 37: 181.

Whimster, Sam. 2004. *The Essential Weber*: Routledge Press.

Chapter 7

Images of Access to Law in the Age of Body Scanners

John Brigham

Travelers encounter body scanners in airports.[1] And, many travelers think of them in terms of the airport hassles. Most of us, therefore, do not associate scanners with freedom, but in terms of intrusion and limited access. They may signify hassles. I don't want to focus on the hassles as indicative of the meaning we should attach to the scanners but rather the deeper significance of current security procedures, most of which are constructed with at least some reference to perceived implications for the public. Thus, although body scanners are a formidable presence in airports, glowing, often in the distance, and they constitute control over the space through which one aims to pass, in terms of this chapter, scanners serve a social function slightly different. And, in this, they represent access and freedom of movement; both access through the differently regulated departure gates and into the airport shopping malls that have appeared on the other side of the security check points. In this understanding, the scanner transforms the meaning of access that has governed social control in democratic societies since the 19th century.[2]

The idea for seeing the significance of the scanner for law in a different way emerged from a political rally where far more people were given access than would have been possible by means of a more conventional screening process involving identification and background checks. It was a rally for Senator "Bernie"[3] Sanders who was running for the president of the United States in the winter of 2015–16 that turned my understanding of the scanners 180 degrees, if not on its head. The "Bernie" Rally at UMass, Amherst, led me to rethink the meaning of scanners.

As thousands from the university community filed into our substantial basketball arena, on a weekday afternoon in early March, we were confronted with Secret Service agents monitoring the doors. These were not the natty agents with dark glasses and coiled wires running from their ears so they could communicate with the base. These were not the guys who would take a bullet for the candidate from appearances and presidential motorcades past. These were technician agents; impressive in a different way. They had scanners to detect contraband. And, they kept the crowd flowing into the building with no appreciable line. I was happy for this relatively quick and easy access. It seemed to me these security machines were highly efficient. They allowed 9,000 people to enter the building in a few hours. They enabled access rather than precluding it. Presumably they kept out weapons without obvious profiling or intrusive interrogation.

In exploring the meaning of the scanner and the controls it is part of, this chapter shifts from the idea of law as normative to law as constituting social life. The shift will be depicted in the focus on the mechanisms constituting social order as a shift from the alienated conception of law that, while evident in the Charles Dickens novel *Bleak House*, is developed for critical legal scholarship in the United States, the United Kingdom, Canada, and Australia through attention to Franz Kafka's *The Trial*. In comparison with Dickens and Kafka, I call attention to a constitutive framework that is an aspect of the sociology of law. In order to do this, I will consider Charles Baudelaire's flâneur and the widespread attention paid to Walter Benjamin's characterization of the sophisticated wanderer making his way through the arcades of commercial plenty. Some of those arcades are now on the other side of the scanners where they seek to recreate an unencumbered shopping experience now constituted by the protection afforded by the scanners. While the line with the scanner at the end has become the new reality for flyers in and through the United States today it is a throwback that has less to do with the scanner and is rather a function of security policies that have not kept up with technology.

ACCESS TO LAW

In my association with Critical Legal Studies, which began in the 1970s, I was often frustrated by the image of law that was the purported object of our struggle. I don't mean here the injustices of racism, sexism, and economic inequality as things the law was responsible for. But rather the image of the law that was associated with those substantive struggles. The image of what was bad about law. The image of access to law that was presented to me was represented by Franz Kafka's "stranger" waiting his whole life to be able to use "the law." There were antecedents. In *Bleak House*, Dickens offered a mid-19th-century critique of the bureaucratic madness of law in England. His portrayal is richly detailed and full of all sorts of forms and process that amount to a maddening maze of legal form. But it was Kafka's ominous and relatively abstract Eastern European image that became the object of scorn for critics in the 1960s and 1970s.

In Kafka's "Before the Law,"[4] an open door that a petitioner dare not enter signifies the nature of the law. The image of law is of an institution that is mysterious, unknowable, and inaccessible. Lack of access to law along these lines came to be symbolized as lack of access to justice. In this image, there is an ominous kind of control. A doorkeeper, who discourages entry, manages access to the law. The result is that law seems dark and unknowable. For the most part, the power of law is not reachable and its agents are there to keep people out. The law can't be questioned yet it is exceedingly arbitrary. It is an authority that is unreachable. This is an Eastern European vision from the time between the world wars. In the United States, we have law like this but it is not most law.[5]

Today we have scanners at the courthouse doors, inner city schools, athletic contests, and at airports. We don't usually have them in malls, or bridges, or in our national parks. They are in places where authorities perceive a threat. The placement is based on perception of risk. It is socially constructed. We don't usually have scanners in laundromats or supermarkets. We might have them at concerts and arena sized sporting events. We would expect them where there are crowds and authorities, like political rallies. Most of the time, the placement is not a surprise.

Scanning technology has a big brother quality. In the United States, that is what we see first and that impression governs reaction to the technology. This matters because although the scanner definitely regulate, they also promise, indeed they function, as an opening . . . a grant of access as much as an impediment. Scanning technology opens passages, according to certain conditions. Clearly they are thought of as keeping dangerous objects "out." And, to the extent that they represent a constraint on people doing bad things they do regulate people as well as the capacity to do those things. But, a more contemporary metaphor in which scanning technology in general and the full body security scanner, developed in the last decade of the 20th century and widely deployed in the first decade of the 21st century, facilitate access rather than precluding it.

Doors and Social Control

Franz Kafka was born in 1883 in Prague to German speaking Ashkenazi Jewish parents. He studied law and worked at an insurance company. He lived in Berlin and in Bohemia, the mountainous region of the Czech Republic that is closest to Germany and that has been contested for hundreds of years. Kafka's life in urban central Europe was influenced by the First World War, anti-Semitism, and the politics of the period, which swirled around nationalism and communism. His various jobs supported his life, which was consumed with writing. He suffered from TB and had many and complex relationships with women. The most important included Felice Bauer and Dora Diamant. He died in 1924 at 40 years old.

The parable "Before the Law," the short version of the story of failing to get access to the law, was written before the novel, *The Trial*. The story was first printed in 1915 in *Selbstwehr*, a weekly newspaper published in Prague from 1907–1938. The title of the newspaper means "self-help" or "self-defense" and it was associated with the Zionist response to growing anti-Semitism in Europe.[6] *The Trial* is the English translation of the German *Der Process*. It was first published in 1925, the year after Kafka died. The translation was by Willa and Edwin Muir in 1937. Written in the malaise at the end of the First World War, it appeared in English on the eve of the Second World War.

In the parable, "a man from the country" sits by a door for his entire life hoping for access to the law. In this he confronts a kind of ominous arbitrariness in which his belief that people should have access to the law is tested. The other figure is "the gatekeeper" who appears to know the rules about access to the law but who is not very forthcoming. In the story, the door to the law is open but the man from the country dare not enter until he is given permission. Throughout his life, permission to cross the threshold is denied. At the end of his life he is told the door was only for him and that now that he is dying it will be closed.

The images from the parable have a distinctly Eastern European sensibility and are hard to separate from the migration of Jews and the rising anti-Semitism that was engulfing Europe as Kafka wrote. My colleague Larry Zacharias describes the parable as "about the Jews from the shtetl (country) who were flocking into the big cities like Prague and Vienna where they confronted an ever-growing anti-Semitism that excluded them from jobs, etc. The Lueger laws (Vienna, 1905) did just that, shortly after Kafka came of age."[7] But, the image of law as Kafka described it became more generic and then, central to the critique of law in the West in the 1960s. As a consequence of appropriation, Kafka's picture of frustration with law, Bohemian in the original sense, came to symbolize an arbitrary and incomprehensible power. Orson Welles made *The Trial* into a movie in 1962. It starred Anthony Perkins as Joseph K. to whom the story of the alienated man from the country, is told. Harold Pinter wrote the screenplay for a 1993 adaptation of *The Trial*.

Thus, Kafka's image, with its emphasis on the door or doorway became the vision for the positive legal order as well as for the dominant critiques. Law should be accessible but it is not. This is not a story of particular injustices but of law itself being unjustly inaccessible. Little of Kafka's work was widely published during his life but its influence on subsequent generations has been widespread. Beginning with support for his work by his friend Max Brod who was instructed to burn Kafka's manuscripts. Instead, Brod published them beginning in the decade after Kafka's death before fleeing to Palestine with more of Kafka's work. Brod lived until 1968, providing a link between Kafka and the 60s.

The Influence of *The Trial*

The publishing house Schocken Verlag, was a key to the popularization of the work in the 1960s. Schocken was a Berlin company set up by the department store owner Salman Schocken. It would have an office in Prague at its height in Europe but its founder also fled to Palestine in 1933 and moved the company in 1939, first to Palestine and then to New York City where it began publishing in 1945 and in 1987, it became an imprint of Random House, publishing Kafka, Benjamin, and Arendt. Influential early fans of Kafka and *The Trial* include W. H. Auden, Vladimir Nabokov, and Gabriel Garcia Marquez. As has been noted by Gilles Deleuze and Felix Guattari,[8] the themes of alienation and persecution may have been over emphasized but it is Kafka's contribution to these themes, which makes his image of modernity so compelling.

To me, one of the largest influences was a textbook that borrowed the title *Before the Law*. Originally conceived by Legal Studies professor John Bonsignore and carried on by professors Ethan Katsch, Stephen Aarons, Peter d'Errico, Ron Pipkin and Janet Rifkin, colleagues at the University of Massachusetts, Amherst, Department of Legal Studies. *Before the Law* was a course reader in Legal Studies and, like the Department, it enabled critical engagement with law outside of law schools. This Legal Studies perspective was very successful. The Kafka parable set off an entire book focused on alternative and critical views of the law, mostly in the United States. Thus the doorway that could not be penetrated and the shadow of doubt and mystery that surrounded it came to characterize a critical take on law.

The intellectual and political foundations for linking Kafka to the critique of law in the 1960s include other mid-century sources. Writing about Kafka, on the 10th anniversary of his death, Walter Benjamin drew attention to Kafka's focus on the conduct of an aide to Potemkin, the Russian Chancellor and namesake of the battleship that we know from the Russian film by Sergei Eisenstein. Kafka portrayed the Chancellor as a bureaucrat whose work piled up due to depression. Seeking to move the work along, an aide attempted to gain the Chancellor's signature by passing papers to him while he was indisposed and in bed only to have them signed but with the name of the aide rather than the Chancellor. Benjamin points out, as a conventional observation to an entirely unconventional treatment, that "In Kafka the written law is contained in books, but these are secret."[9] But Benjamin's focus, and his critique of a more traditional society, is on the wandering that was threatened by the imagined world that Kafka makes the center of his critical image of law—a world of bureaucracy and arbitrariness that is more ominous than liberating. The official institutions of the state seemed to interest Benjamin more for their absurd forms than for their actual power. He seemed to look to other places for the nature of power.

THE *FLÂNEUR* AND FREEDOM

In Hannah Arendt's Introduction to Benjamin's essays, which she published in 1968, Arendt examines his interest in Kafka and argues that it helps him connect with his present, when it appears he might prefer things at least a little more "old fashioned."[10] Here, the focus on Benjamin's *flâneur* shifts to the constitution of an odd kind of freedom in the 21st century that coexists with discipline and repressive tolerance.[11] He looked, as did Michel Foucault, to more ordinary and more pervasive forms of power.

Baudelaire,[12] in 1863, wrote favorably of the *flâneur*. This was a remarkable conceptual tool for anticipating and articulating the nature of modernity. It would reappear in Benjamin almost 100 years later, in a form more easily digested by social scientists. The *flâneur* was a man of the world who was comfortable in a crowd or the multitude. He was as comfortable traveling as at home. He is, in Baudelaire's conception, "a passionate spectator," "an observer," "a philosopher." In the words of Jeanne S. M. Willette, writing in 2012,[13] the *flâneur* is "the outsider" and Baudelaire's conception of him is a remarkably prescient idea of what modernity is.

The capacity to capture the passing moment, in art and philosophy, had become more important than solidifying something and fixing it for a time, helping it to endure. The outsider as artist, as poet, perhaps even as politician, took on an unlikely capacity in modernity. He came to stand out and, ultimately, to lead. And, here the male pronoun is revealing. Initially, the edges of society were not spaces occupied by women of position. From prostitutes to the homeless the subjects were marginal and their individual hold on society tenuous just as their collective identity was central.

Here, the art of Constantin Guys, for Baudelaire and, one might imagine, of Édouard Manet and J. M. W. Turner,[14] challenged the painting of reality with emotion and made feelings as real as form. For Baudelaire, the feelings are often of the city, but they are the edge of the city and they can be of the garden, or of nature reconceived as a place of emotions. What they are not is of the rack or the guillotine. They are exuberant and difficult to regulate. They capture limits in forms of mobility rather than the limits imposed by bars and barricades.

Benjamin brings the 19th-century symbol of modernity, the flâneur, into the contemporary academy. The vehicle for French insights about the modern condition is an older sensibility that ultimately clashes with the Eastern European sensibilities that had emerged in the 20th century. It is a way of understanding and of feeling that links Kafka and Baudelaire. Where Kafka's bureaucracy, however real, is dark and static, Baudelaire's earlier vision suggests something else entirely. Benjamin's not altogether optimistic vision is embedded even more fully in the tensions of modernity and its abject failures in the period from the end of the First World War to the outbreak of the Second World War.

This vision of freedom of movement in a rich and complex social environment is as much a function of European thinking as it is a function of challenges faced by the man from the country. And the *flâneur*, along with the idea of freedom, survives as ideology that is linked to law less directly. Yet, Kafka and Benjamin, the representation of a desperate inability to move on the one hand and the embrace of movement with its own pathetic side are both useful and instructive for developing a different understanding of the contemporary characteristics of social control.

Foucault's conception of where punishment and force fit into the system of authority that is state power remains compelling in spite of the fact that every other dissertation in political theory a few years ago seemed to reference it. Foucault got to be very important, but as HE grew into legendary status, his ideas faded. For Foucault, the absence of the public spectacle of punishment is indicative of the rise of other forms, which he calls disciplinary. The modern prison was one of those forms.

But, in a disciplinary framework, the focus was not simply on punishment in the traditional sense. Even more important than the prison, less imposing forms, ones we associate with social control rather than punishment, like drugs, therapy, and scanners, epitomize the disciplinary in society.[15]

Thus, while Foucault told about the birth of the prison and might seem to have foretold its rise, it would be wrong to understand the focus on discipline as heralding the carceral state[16] with its exponential increase in the prison population, particularly the incarceration of Hispanic and African American men in large numbers.

The less often referenced "carceral archipelago" which "transported" the penal techniques "to the entire social body."[17] Here it is not the physical prison that enters the social body but the techniques of regulation and self-control whereby movement outside the prison is regulated by social discipline. The ability to enter spaces that might be otherwise regulated with a simple "scan" to assure conformity is more modern than the bouncer and the velvet rope with its list of approved entrants. Schools, often seen as opposites to the prison in a model where they are critical and free, are in Foucault's framework, extensions of the prison and part of the archipelago.

IMAGING AND THE LAW

Images of naked bodies, projected in airports, are associated with body scanners. But so too is the image of travelers zigzaging through airport security lines toward a clerk who will begin the scanning process. The first calls to mind issues of privacy, civil liberties, and the integrity of the person. The ominous wait for security, is a matter of public policy, the collective inconvenience we tolerate if we believe it is necessary. Another image, less vivid to date, is the preferred line, in the United States. "TSA Pre-check." This is the line for people who have paid extra to get special treatment. These are all images of law associated with scanners and scanning technology. How we understand them has a great deal to do with how we understand law.

The Full Body Scanner

What we call a "full body scanner" reveals objects on the person scanned. It is used for security in order to keep certain objects out of a secure space. The person operating the machine may see what is called "an alternate-wavelength image" which looks like it is revealing the naked body. The scanner can also be programmed to show only a representation that looks like a cartoon but with suspicious items standing out. These scanners began replacing metal detectors in the first decade of the 21st century. Some of these scanners used electromagnetic waves. Others used x-rays. These x-ray devices sometimes appeared to show the naked body.

This chapter is not about how the machines work but rather their place among the mechanisms, which, in the United States, we call "police powers." The government in the United States, like most modern governments, is understood to have the obligation to keep its citizens safe. Increasingly this is done with machines: machines that wage war, machines that police the streets, machines that surveil, and machines that control access. Before discussing challenges to the use of mechanical screening devises that have been raised in the courts of the United States and which, for the most part, constitute the public policy discussions we have about the technology, let me mention the alternative idea that I suggest helps us understand what the metal detectors and body scanners do.

The example of the "Bernie for President" rally in 2016 in Amherst, Massachusetts, in the United States, that I began with, suggested that the scanners allowed access for many, many people. They provided access to a relatively safe space in a relatively short period of time. People were not frisked, nor were they questioned or even run through a database. They just slowed down a bit and walked through a machine. They didn't have to take their shoes or belts off. They could carry liquids. They were simply precluded from bringing in weapons or explosives.

There were consequences. Those with no place other than their book bag to carry a pistol were not likely to try and get through the line. In this sense, the crowd was not as diverse as it might have been. But, it was less dangerous and, at least in this case, the sacrifices seemed minor and relatively easily accommodated to the nature of the event. With flying, the situation is different but I think not different enough to change the point being raised here. This is, that the scanners increase social freedom rather than restricting it, or more than they restrict it.

Recent Challenges

The Court of Appeals for the District of Columbia Circuit, in the United States approved body scanners in 2011 for airports. This was in an opinion written by Judge Douglas Ginsburg[18] with Judge Karen Henderson and Judge David Tatel. The opinion was in response to a challenge to scanners by EPIC, the Electronic Privacy Information Center.[19] It addresses the issue of whether the initial use of scanners by TSA was adequately vetted before it became accepted practice.

Judge Ginsburg emphasized in his opinion that it is up to Congress and the Transportation Safety Administration (TSA) to decide on how to screen for terrorist threats on commercial airlines. In response to congressionally mandated objectives, TSA developed the AIT (advanced imaging technology) scanners, which it began to deploy in 2007. Initially a secondary screening device, the scanners began to be used as a primary tool in 2009.

EPIC celebrated Ginsburg's assurance, in 2011, that, "No passenger is ever required to submit to an AIT scan."[20] In its place, they could always request a pat down. The opinion considers Fourth Amendment concerns and addresses EPIC's argument that searches should be the least intrusive as possible. It finds that this has never been a requirement for an administrative search. With regard to the promise that AIT scans will never be primary, the 2011 opinion has come to appear quaint not yet five years later.

In 2012, as a result of the FAA Modernization and Reform Act, full body scanners must use "Automated Target Recognition" software. This technology produces a cartoon like representation instead of an image of the naked body. There are still issues involving safety but, for the most part, the scanning process is not particularly revealing.

On March 2, 2016, the U.S. Transportation Security Administration ruled that passengers could no longer opt out of full body scans. In response to that ruling, a second lawsuit, *EPIC v. TSA* was filed May 2, 2016, in the U.S. Court of Appeals for the District of Columbia.[21] It asks the court to review the final rule that denies passengers the right to opt out of screening using body scanners and asks the court to review alternative means of screening passengers. EPIC also asks to see the data on safety from radiation collected by TSA. We await the outcome of this lawsuit.

Constitutive Processes

A rigid conception of law called positive is the dominant understanding of law in the West. It focuses on the expression of norms emanating from a governing institutional structure. It is positive because those structures, rather than morality or religion are readily identifiable. Kafka's position is a critique of positive law. Appellate court judges in the United States represent positive law. Their concern for civil liberties is the antithesis of the "man from the country" dying while waiting for the law. But the focus on civil liberties may miss, or deny, the point of the scanner, which is to move people through while separating them from contraband. In this sense, the traditional arbiters and images of positive law may not understand the processes we live under. To capture the meaning of the scanner and our instruments of social control in the United States it seems preferable to look at law from a constitutive or process perspective. This is the perspective of the social sciences.

Sally Falk Moore, writing in the late 1970s, was one of the early practitioners. She describes the way behavior is contained by social and physical mechanisms, mechanisms of control.[22] Moore studied law and anthropology at Columbia and taught anthropology at Harvard. Her career predated the Law and Society movement often associated with the United States, but with roots in Europe. Her most influential book, to me, was Law as Process, which was a collection of essays published in 1978. In his highly critical review for the *British Journal of Law and Society*,[23] Francis Snyder emphasized Moore's contribution to seeing law in or as social practices. And he pointed out that it was a perspective with links to legal realism, the idea that law is really just a kind of politics. One might, using Moore's framework, call the processes she identifies "regularizing."

The problem of the prison as emblem of the disciplinary society that Foucault decried and Moore calls up is that it not only disciplines, it controls and constrains with its walls. The more characteristic dimension of the processes that discipline in contemporary society are evident in psychology, in the use of drugs and conceptual modification to control behavior. In this sense, the body scanners, which allow movement following a scan may be more characteristic of the control that is most pervasive than the prison.

With the scanner, technological devices control the space. They may allow access but they may also preclude it. The devices shift the focus from who can enter, to what can be taken in to the next space. They are part of a larger authoritative apparatus that has transformed social control. The initial result, signified by the scanner, is an extension of the democratic principle of access, perhaps a response to the closed door. There is also a shift in focus from persons to things and a perceived absence of agency. In the United States we make a civil liberties argument where we might instead be taking a policy focus to the problem of airport security. We could be examining these processes in terms of their effectiveness, with fairness being a consideration, at the same time that we are asking whether this is the best way for a government or a people to proceed. Because, rights and liberties may be effective ways to advocate for positions but they have costs in terms of policy. In all of this, and with regard to contemporary developments in the United States, it is not the scanner so much as the willingness of the subject populations to stand in line to be scanned that is the disciplinary foundation for the role of the scanner in society. That is being challenged in the United States at this moment.

THE SCANNER AND THE CITIZEN

While civil liberties lawyers focus on the unclothed body exposed to the view of technocrats and occasional passengers, the public experiences new challenges in order to travel. These include controls and hurdles in processing that reach new levels of inconvenience. But the legacy of Benjamin, drawing on Baudelaire and Marx, helps us to see the scanner in a different light. Though it can be an annoyance, it is not as simple as that. Benjamin illuminates the present and allows us to update the legacy of the *flâneur*, which with its emphasis on freedom and autonomy may have wider implications.

The Aesthetic of Process

For me, the route to Benjamin was through Susan Buck-Morss, the author of The Dialectics of Seeing, published in 1989, but the product of years of scholarship.[24] Buck-Morss describes her work on Benjamin's fragmented writings as "unorthodox" because the work is, "a picture book of philosophy."[25] At the center of the book is Benjamin's "Arcades Project" or *Passagen-Werk*. In a review published in *New German Critique* in 1991, Shierry Nicholsen draws on Buck-Morss's reliance on Benjamin's own words to characterize his project as spanning "the spirit of contemporary France." But she is concerned that in focusing on the images, Buck-Morss may have short-changed the linguistic dimensions of the *Passagen-Werk*.[26]

These two undertakings, Benjamin's and Buck-Morss's, are ostensibly about the same thing. They are both reflections on the 20th century.

Benjamin's initial reflections were made as the Second World War loomed. Buck-Morss's were composed as the cultural radicalism of the '60s and '70s ebbed. The attention to the Arcades Project allowed Buck-Morss to consider constructs that were about an older and more circumscribed hedonism than had recently dominated the academy. Yet, the arcades, in Benjamin's treatment, linked commerce and consciousness and the complex approach served as a treatment worthy of the late 20th-century academy. Thus, disrupted by the Second World War, the later treatment of the arcades reappear after hostilities in the postwar period of excess from which Buck-Morss writes.[27] Here, image has philosophical importance and movement is both encouraged and constrained by the arcades.[28]

This legacy of the arcades includes the access provided by new arrangements of space for commerce. In the present it is technologies, including the scanners, that regulate our arcades. Security would be very different, with increased surveillance if scanners were not available. Just as the arcades proved more "modern" than the bazaar, the scanner is more appropriately seen as connected to the arcades than to Kafka's doors. With the scanner, we have traded mobility for social knowledge. By turning the regulation of mobility over to machines, we may lose track of the ways in which we are sacrificing our identity for anonymity. The contexts in which we are negotiating those values today are of terror and our efforts to avoid its ravages.

Process and Politics

Today the processes that apply to everyone, like the scanners, generally get more attention than their alternative, screening based on knowledge of people and attention to their individual circumstances. Thus, a person associated with radical political groups would get more attention in the alternative to scanners than one whose retirement community hosts bridge tournaments. The social divisions that constitute alternatives are concerning when practiced by government at the same time that they are widely practiced in society.

The scanner stands vividly at the end of the passenger line. As those lines become intolerable the social alternatives with their reliance on discernment and discrimination creep in. While the management of goods that are taken to the other side of the line is completely outside of our view, the alternative lines are becoming more obvious. Presently they are off to the side, offering speed for a price. But they have become central to policy debates.

The current processing at airports in the United States is generally different from the stasis that characterized Kafka's image of the mid-19th-century bailiff who refuses to grant access or the fluidity of the *flâneur's* movement through the arcades that was Benjamin's. After the initial shock upon entering an American airport (or awe, if the line is short) one is swept into a slow journey to the scanner. In this line, the scanner becomes a goal. It is more like the finish line than it is a gate. Like the Ferris wheel at the end of a carnival line, the scanner is the ultimate objective. And, the evidence of that is the frustration of not passing successfully so that the moments waiting to be scanned again, after one has failed, loom far more significant than the much longer period in line. At least that has been in my experience.

The regulation of things by the scanners has allowed people to pass with very little knowledge of who they are. They are the autonomous individual of consumer society and modern citizenship. While they maintain the illusion of freedom, they impose a very precise and focused level of surveillance. Both the image on the scanner and the image of policing that now constitutes flying are constitutive of our current condition. They constitute authority around the world in ways that vary slightly from country to country.

In the United States, the many levels of citizenship (or threat), while obvious, get far less attention than the machines for screening, particularly those that screen people rather than packages. The levels of comfort that one passes through on the way to a seat in most American airlines constitute classes and different statuses that are rarely subject to debate or even notice. In the case of the scanner, suspicion is generalized and probable cause is unnecessary. But the exceptions are increasing and the special lines capable of purchase tend to elevate the selective processes that constitute class or at least access via wealth.

Recently, a debate erupted in the U.S. Congress over whether airport security is operating effectively. In this, the American budget process is coinciding with the summer travel season. It is a volatile mix. On May 25, 2016, the United States House of Representatives held hearings on the long security lines at airports.[29] There was some attention to how well the scanners were functioning but to some extent the machines were beside the point. One of the main features of better processes, as proposed by the Congress, was expansion of "Pre-Check" provisions for supplementing scanners with inquiry into the social dimensions of flyers. The answer to cumbersome scanners was, to some extent, to go around them.

The technologies of surveillance, whether public and contested, as the body scanner is, or secret and often unknown processes like background checks, constitute significant elements of our current condition. They build on respect and disrespect, individual and state, new forms of power and places denying or subsuming resistance. Buck-Morss concluded her remarkable study of a theory of society that emerged from the Paris arcades with a shift to modern electronic culture. "In the United States, particularly, the format of television news programs approaches the distracted, impressionistic, physiognomic viewing of the flâneur."[30] The distraction is not only a function of electronic processes it inhibits our ability to engage in other areas.

Insecurity and Identity

This chapter has been about the current meaning of social control and one of the most prominent technical aspects of it. It has explored body scanners and linked their sort of security with modern consumer culture to which it is much more akin than the culture of gates and gatekeepers. I have also suggested that the critical perspective built on a critique of law as mysterious and static seems wrong. The view developed out of a discussion of scanners, proposed a more familiar, more modern alternative that featured movement and access rather than forbidden passages. It proposed that the scanners symbolize an alternative view both in the movement they allow and in the generic treatment of individuals that is characteristic of the way they function. But the modern, civil liberties governed generic individual is also linked to other aspects of electronic culture.

In the end, there is a relationship between the ways Americans have managed security at airports and the curious phenomenon of a reality TV show celebrity president of the United States. In the United States, a culture of autonomy and anonymity exercises significant influence as an ideal. It stands in opposition to a culture based on social standing where background and accomplishment are featured. Or, in the case of airport security, the machine screening focuses on what you are carrying rather than who you are. The electronic screening devices don't much care about background, only what you are trying to bring on the plane. They are indeed, very different, perhaps the opposite of, a system of security based on profiling, questioning and surveillance.

The kind of abstract security tool symbolized by the scanner mirrors the process used in 2016 in the United States for the selection of its nominee from the Republican Party and, ultimately, the successful candidate for president. It does not ask who you are or whether you are "qualified" in order to let you pass. In U.S. primary system that chose the nominee, experience in office and a relevant resume mattered little. Donald Trump became a "frontrunner" in an electoral process that moved about the country over months celebrating Americana while winnowing a pack of generally less well-known candidates and elevating the more familiar personality. Just as the traveler with a too large tube of sunscreen revealed in the scanner gets immediate attention, the celebrity won contest after contest. The paradox, or mirror, has celebrity feeding on itself. Though it appears without significant social meaning other than the recognition, unlike the offending sunscreen celebrity, can't be confiscated. Instead, celebrity feeds on itself.

After Trump happened, one might wonder why it was such a surprise. With no background in elected office but a celebrity identity, his candidacy emerged in a televised selection process. The candidate Donald Trump did not really rise to political prominence so much as shift his celebrity prominence to the electoral arena. And he did that, it seemed, with remarkable ease. Thus, social and cultural phenomenon like relevant experience, sophistication, and character were transcended by the new reality of celebrity and entertainment. But it remained hard to absorb even as it was happening.

On a Sunday morning in the spring of 2016, on the influential American television show "Meet the Press,"[31] hosted by Chuck Todd, internet journalist Matt Bai, former chief political correspondent of the *New York Times* and at the time listed as from *Yahoo News*, observed about Donald Trump: "One thing we learned in this primary process . . . he is not judged by the standards of a politician. He is judged by the standards of an entertainer. And entertainers, by the way, reinvent themselves constantly. Read any gossip magazine, they're constantly changing who they are, what they say." Then, commenting on coverage by Jim Rutenberg, from the *New York Times*, who led the coverage of the 2012 election, Bai argued that Rutenberg had created a false dichotomy between politician and entertainer. Bai concluded with "I think the real mistake is the media not understanding that there is no line between politics and entertainment in this environment." And *Meet the Press* ended with a clip from its long running, topical, comedy show, *Saturday Night Live* which had aired the night before, in which a character paying Donald Trump, whose celebrity personality was honed on celebrity infused shows, is given "the nuclear codes." And, the segue is to the end of the show and the Mother's Day suggestion, that CVS, a national pharmacy chain, was still open that Sunday for the purchase of celebratory cards.

Of course, it is also possible to conclude that Hillary Clinton's campaign was impacted by a circumscribed political discourse. As the presumptive nominee for at least two and as many as eight years, the discussion about whether she should be the candidate of the Democratic Party was less vibrant than it might have been at least in the area of who would be the party's first serious female nominee. And, while the Sanders campaign challenged Mrs. Clinton in a substantive way, her candidacy was always about the milestone of being the first female president of the United States. Since few women seemed to want to challenge her claim to that status, celebrity trumped destiny.

CONCLUSION

I have said that the idea for seeing the significance of the scanner, and by extension the way law operates in the United States in a different way. I began with a view of law that has been around for a while. With antecedents in Dickens, Kafka made the view popular for critics in the second half of the

20th century. I think there is a view that better represents the way law works in the United States, and it came from a political rally.

In the end, the way we see law and the reasons we see it that way may help us to understand American politics. The law of the scanner is driven by a desire to be fair and not to be guided by prejudice. Almost everyone gets scanned and with the machine there is less room for bias or stereotypes.

Finally, in the chapter I have suggested that the meaning of scanners is linked to a perspective on law that focuses on the way law constitutes social life rather than the way social life makes law. Law that matters in the United States is about power that penetrates the social fabric. Law is all around. Law as machines and those who back them up makes us wait to get to our departure gate, unless we have special status, but it is not unknown or unknowable. It is, in fact, all around us. And, ultimately, it is linked to important dimensions in the nature of state power.

NOTES

1. Millimeter wave scanner use the non-ionizing electromagnetic radiation similar to that used by wireless data transmitters. Backscatter x-ray machines use ionizing electromagnetic radiation.

2. An early version of this chapter was prepared for the conference on "Technologies of Law and Religion: Representation, Objects and Agency," June 13–15, 2016, Monash University, Prato Centre, Italy.

3. The informality of the campaign with its cult like enthusiasm for its leader appeared to be driven by a generational shift in style associated with the Silicon Valley culture of Apple, Google, and Facebook.

4. The parable, "Before the Law," is a segment of *The Trial*, "Der Process," in German.

5. When challenging a powerful institution as having violated the law, the system is very much like this but this is not the image of law in the ordinary sense.

6. On March 23, 2017, a popular web based encyclopedia called it Zionist.

7. Zacharias is professor emeritus at the University of Massachusetts, Amherst. He concludes, "My interpretation of the parable is the version of someone whose own self-perception, based on prevailing social prejudices and stereotypes, precludes him/herself from going through the door or scanner, even though something s/he may desire lies on the other side."

8. Gilles Deleuze and Felix Gauttari, "Kafka: Toward a Minor Literature," *Theory and History of Literature*, Vol. 30, University of Minnesota Press (1986).

9. Illuminations, p. 115.

10. Arendt reports that Brecht told Benjamin "that his essay on Kafka gave aid and comfort to Jewish Fascism" (Introduction, p. 53).

11. Wolf, Moore, Marcuse. *A Critique of Pure Tolerance*.

12. "The Painter of Modern Life," *Le Figaro* (1863).

13. http://www.arthistoryunstuffed.com/baudelaire-the-painter-of-modern-life/.

14. I am assisted I this understanding by Alison Hokanson's exhibition *The Whale* (and its catalogue) at the Metropolitan Museum of Art, New York City in 2016.

15. Foucault, 1977.

16. Simon, 2007.

17. p. 298.

18. Ginsburg is the federal judge who President Ronald Reagan attempted to elevate to the Supreme Court in 1987. His nomination was withdrawn when he admitted to having smoked marijuana.

19. EPIC describes itself as a public information research center that was established in Washington, D.C. in 1994. The president is Marc Rotenberg has written widely on privacy and testifies often before Congress. The center's focus is on privacy in the digital age. It monitors the practices of internet companies as well as government agencies. EPIC.org.

20. p. 3.

21. EPIC is located in Washington, DC at 1718 Connecticut Avenue, NW. Marc Rotenberg, Alan Butler, Khaliah Barnes, and Jeramie Scott were of counsel.

22. She also uses the term or framework "semi-autonomous social field," by which she means a social practice with its own conventions.

23. Vol. 6, No. 1 (Summer 1979), p. 135–139.

24. She began publishing on Walter Benjamin in the early 1980s.

25. (1989: ix).

26. She goes on to emphasize the important and complicated relationship in Benjamin between language and photography.

27. In the *Journal of Visual Culture*, Buck-Morss speaks of the place of image in our philosophical world.

28. On the eve of this conference, I attended a lecture at The Bruce Museum in Connecticut, by Sarah Kennel of the Peabody Essex Museum on the Paris photography of Charles Marville with its attention to the Paris Arcades.

29. https://homeland.house.gov/hearing/long-lines-short-patience-tsa-airport-screening-experience/.

30. p. 343.

31. May 8, 2016, NBC News. See also Kellyanne Conway, conservative media strategist, "I don't think Donald Trump could have run as effectively four or eight years ago. He's got this multilevel media platform now. If he's not tweeting, he's rallying. If he's not rallying, he's giving interviews to folks like you, Chuck."

REFERENCES

Adelman, Rebecca A. *Beyond the Checkpoint: Visual Practices in America's Global War on Terror,* Amherst and Boston: University of Massachusetts Press, 2014.

Arendt, Hannah. *Introduction to Illuminations,* New York: Schocken Books, 1968.

Benjamin, Walter. *Illuminations: Essays and Reflections,* New York: Schocken Books, 1968.

Bloom, Harold, ed. Charles Dickens's *Bleak House*, New York: Chelsea, 1987.
Bonsignore, John et al. *Before the Law: An Introduction to the Legal Process*, 8th Edition, Boston: Houghton Mifflin, 2005.
Brigham, John. *Material Law,* Philadelphia: Temple University Press, 2009.
Brown, Wendy. *States of Injury: Power and Freedom in Late Modernity,* Princeton: Princeton University Press, 1995.
Buck-Morss, Susan. *The Dialectics of Seeing: Walter Benjamin and the Arcades Project,* Cambridge: MIT Press, 1989.
———. "Interview," *Journal of Visual Culture*, posted March 11, 2013.
Electronic Privacy Information Center v. Transportation Security Administration, United States Court of Appeals for the District of Columbia, May 2, 2016.
Electronic Privacy Information Center v. Department of Homeland Security, 653 F.3rd 1 (D.C. Circuit 2011).
Foucault, Michel. *Discipline and Punish,* New York: Random House, 1977 (Paris, 1975).
H.R. 2843 TSA PreCheck Expansion Act, "To require certain improvements in the Transportation Security Administrations PreCheck expedited screening program, and for other purposes," 6-19-15.
Kafka, Franz. *The Trial,* New York: Modern Library, 1956 (1937).
Marx, Karl. "Der 18th Brumaire des Louis Napoleon," *Die Revolution* (1852) Karl Marx and Friedrich Engels, Werke, vol.8. Berlin: Dietz Verlag, 1960.
MacNeil, William P. Novel *Judgements: Legal Theory as Fiction,* New York: Routledge, 2011.
Meet the Press. *NBC News*, May 8, 2016.
Moore, Sally Falk. *Law as Process: An Anthropological Approach,* London: Routledge, 1978.
Mitchell, W. J. T. "Picturing Terror: Derrida's Autoimmunity," 33 *Critical Inquiry* (Winter 2007), 277–90.
Nicoholsen, Shierry Weber. "Review," *New German Critique* 51:1990, 179–188.
Scarry, Elaine. *The Body in Pain,* New York: Oxford University Press, 1985.
Simon, Jonathan. "The Rise of the Carceral State," 74 *Social Research* (2007), 471–508.
Valverde, Mariana. *Law and Order: Images, Meanings, Myths,* New Brunswick: Rutgers University Press, 2006.
Wolf, Robert Paul, et al. *A Critique of Pure Tolerance,* Boston: Beacon Press, 1965.

Chapter 8

Laughing Matters

Critical Race Theory and Comedy

Aaron Lorenz

American society is increasingly turning to comedy for serious and cogent analysis of important contemporary issues like racism, gun control, and health care. It is certainly not the only place one can go for social criticism but scholars have been incorporating humor into the classroom for generations, often to the dismay of the students. Today, the internet and accessibility to virtually anything via YouTube has meant that comedians like George Carlin and Jon Stewart can quickly reinforce a scholarly point in terms that undergraduates and laypeople can easily digest.[1] Three comedians in particular provide social criticism on race that sociolegal scholars are unable to emulate. Whether it is Richard Pryor: "There's a lot more hypocrisy than before. Racism has gone back underground . . . What I am for is justice for everyone, just like it says in the Constitution," Chris Rock: "Yeah, I love being famous. It's almost like being white, y'know?" or Dave Chappelle: "Oh my god, open and shut case, Johnson. I saw this once when I was a rookie. Apparently this nigger broke in and put up pictures of his family everywhere," it is clear that comedy and race are ripe for overlapping analysis.

EVOLUTION OF CRITICAL RACE THEORY

One of the most important developments in law regarding race in the past twenty five years is Critical Race Theory (CRT). Described by Kimberle Crenshaw, CRT provided analysis on race while simultaneously critiquing the faults of the civil rights movement and providing insight on the Critical Legal Studies movement. CRT proposes that race and racism are endemic to the American normative order and a pillar of American institutional and community life.[2] Law is not a mediator of social conflicts but rather a part of the social fabric and one that constitutes, constructs, and produces race relations in ways that support white supremacy.[3] CRT presents law and race in the context that legal scholars and those who study race cannot be complicit in the reconstruction of racial stereotypes. The contemporary political and social arguments often presented that we now live in a "post-racial" America only further entrenches the theorist to mobilize against this kind of complacency. CRT is both a movement and a theory and one that can be seen as influential in scholarly circles but as we will see, is also clearly present in the work of various nontraditional "legal actors" like the comedians I mentioned earlier.

Crenshaw, in addition to coining the phrase, has helped explain why CRT emerged as an intellectual movement. She writes, "CRT was not, however, simply a product of a philosophical critique of the dominant forces on racial power. It was also a product of activists' engagement with the material manifestations of liberal reform."[4] CRT provided a post-civil rights oppositionalism toward racial power. The demand by activists that the notion of race-neutrality and color-blind constitutionalism be more clearly critiqued has been at the forefront of the CRT movement. Essentially, this meant that that institutionalized racial dominance became a more common discussion inside legal circles as well as outside them. As CRT influenced law and society, its power and importance grew. But more importantly, critiques of race neutrality became more commonplace and accessible for the layperson.

The attraction of CRT resides in its basic tenets, which were established by the founders of CRT in the late 1980s and include: Holds that racism is pervasive and endemic to, rather than a deviation from, American norms; Rejects dominant claims of meritocracy, neutrality, objectivity and color-blindness; Rejects ahistoricism, and insists on contextual, historical analysis of law; Challenges the presumptive legitimacy of social institutions; Insists on recognition of both the experiential knowledge and critical consciousness of people of color in understanding law and society; Is interdisciplinary and eclectic (drawing upon, inter alia, liberalism, poststructuralist, feminism, Marxism, critical legal theory, postmodernism, and pragmatism) with the claim that the intersection of race and the law overruns disciplinary boundaries; and Works toward the liberation of people of color as it embraces the larger project of liberating all oppressed people.[5] The interdisciplinary nature of CRT is clear in the presentation of its main tenets. However, for the purposes of this project, while its interdisciplinarity is important, more important is the societal palatability of the theory.

Since comedy provides commentary and critique, it is a medium to present the tenets of CRT to those outside the field of the law. Redd Foxx, the groundbreaking comedian who began performing in the 1940s, was a critical race theorist before the theory came about, once saying, "I carry a knife now because I read in a white magazine that all black people carry knives. So I rushed out and bought me one."[6] Foxx was using humor to critique the social norms, in this instance one presented from the perspective that racism is the dominant norm.

CRT emanated from the early construction of race by law. American law has been historically race conscious. Judges defined race through case law and used that precedent to reinforce racism. Subsequently, institutional racism developed and became more engrained. Slave law, black codes, and Jim Crow all exploited black labor and maintained black subordination for the purposes of white wealth accumulation and white racial class consolidation.[7] Race was constructed for the purposes of defining who could vote; who could work in a professional field; where people could live; who they could marry; what schools they could attend; what trains, restaurants, or theaters they could attend. CR theorists saw all of these as sanctions by the law.

White, wealthy property owners continued to present racism as society's burden and not one manifesting from doctrines or codes. The laws were neutral on their face, or so the plantation owners argued. This race neutrality or color-blindness led to the reinforcement of the law as the protector of white supremacy. The Civil War, Emancipation Proclamation, 13th, 14th, and 15th amendments, all seemed like disruptions to the construction of race. But ultimately, that was not the case. Rather, the promise of Reconstruction was fleeting. Legal actors, including judges, enacted laws and interpreted legal doctrine to narrow the rewards of citizenship and strengthen Jim Crow segregation.[8]

Color-blindness gained momentum in juridical and social circles. Courts began to narrow laws during the middle part of the 20th century which legitimized white privilege and nonwhite disadvantage. Examples were common of the courts retreating from the promise after Reconstruction and through the 1960s. Though the desegregation (integration) of secondary schools in the United States began (in earnest) in 1964, the Supreme Court's hesitancy and massive white resistance brought withdrawal from the cause. The Court had already signaled its retreat from desegregation by 1973 by allowing a school board to escape the imposition of desegregation orders if it could show that segregation occurred in the district without intention from the board.[9]

Antisubordination

A cornerstone of CRT entails transforming the relationship between law and racial power through an approach utilizing antisubordination efforts. This goal of racial emancipation overlaps nicely with the work of Pryor, Rock, and Chappelle. CRT scholars critiqued the attention given to color-blindness and intentional discrimination and focused their attention on the broader conditions of racial inequality. Like the Pryor, Rock, and Chappelle, racism and racial inequality are more complex and best considered with the proper critical lens.

The debate between the antisubordination and antidiscrimination principles of equal protection has a long history. The antisubordination scholars use a race-conscious approach to understanding equality.[10] While I do not argue here that Pryor, Rock, and Chappelle are reading the work of Owen Fiss and incorporating it into their stand-up routines, the overlap of antisubordination scholarship and the aforementioned comedians reinforces the accessibility of CRT to laypeople.

After The Civil War and Reconstruction, the Court's opinions in *The Slaughterhouse Cases* (1873), and *Strauder v. West Virginia* (1880), the expansion of the reach of the Equal Protection Clause in regards to race became quite clear. The idea was to secure to subordinated races, as a class, a formal equality of "all the civil rights that the superior race enjoy" under the notion of equal protection.[11] The de jure discrimination that followed has been reinforced by law, seen in both *Plessy v. Ferguson* (1896) and *Brown v. Board of Education* (1954). In *Plessy*, the pronouncement of "separate by equal" claimed to secure racial minorities formal equality but rather continued to permit the enforcement of racial subordination. In *Brown*, the Court "struck down" the notion of "separate but equal" and ordered desegregation on the basis that the separation of the races tends to "denote the inferiority of the negro group."[12] Of course, the court's opinion in *Brown* failed to address the important components of racial discrimination either initiated under the guise of the law or supported by the silence of the law.

Scholars and citizens responded to *Brown* with begrudging support. I categorize it that way because the impact of *Brown* was understood by many but not because of the language used in the unanimous decision. Civil rights activists like Malcolm X were publically discussing the language, noting that the Court seemed to essentially state that when "whites and blacks must go to school together, it is the whites that are so much superior that just their presence in a black classroom balances it out."[13] That was the pronouncement of *Brown*. If an all-white school did not have their academic diet affected by a lack of racial diversity, why would all-black classroom be affected by a lack of white children? The answer was never given by the Court and after *Brown,* it was not a likely conversation for many to have given the political and racial climate in the United States. However, the impact of that avoidance can be seen not only in the cases and laws that followed but in the social criticism, in this setting in the form of comedy.

Unconscious Racism

The socially constructed nature of race and ethnicity is a target throughout *The Dave Chappelle Show*. In his scripts, Chappelle uses humor to connect racial and ethnic and stereotypes that exist in society, while commenting on the very nature of social constructs like race and ethnicity. Throughout the *Show*, Chappelle investigates one of the most common social problems, racial and ethnic stereotyping. Chappelle reveals these images in an exaggerated way to highlight the way these stereotypical images about race are socially constructed.

Scholar Donileen Loseke states, "humans categorize conditions and people and this is important because it encourages us to react to these conditions and people in predictable ways." She describes how humans classify without having any experience in a particular category, making grouping easier. In forming classifications, Loseke claims the meanings drawn from these categories are "typifications."[14] Since we cannot individually experience everything, we often find it comforting to use other people's experiences and draw conclusions, or create stereotypes from those experiences (e.g., all black people eat chicken). Another example of typification is presented in Horton's (1993) article, in which he writes about the television and radio series *Amos and Andy*, noting that African Americans were constructed as "ignorant human beings." The person who creates a social construct, for Loseke, is a "claim-maker."

According to Loseke, "a claim is any verbal, visual, or behavioral statement that seeks to persuade audience members to define a condition as a social problem."[15] A verbal claim creates meaning through words.

For example, using particular slang or derogatory terms to describe a minority group (e.g., people have described white people as "crackers" and black people as "niggas"). A visual claim constructs images to persuade an opinion. A visual claim can be very influential because it leaves an image in our head of what we are supposed to think about that particular subject. For example, always showing particular minority group members engaged in activities (e.g., blacks smoking marijuana) is a visual claim. Behavioral claims are claims "where the social problems work involves doing something rather than saying something or creating a visual picture of something."[16]

Comedy may engage the social problem of racism. Chappelle, in particular, uses skits to draw attention to racism. Chappelle and *The Chappelle Show* are sociolegally provocative because the skits, and show as a whole, address race in ways that drama and even classic journalism cannot. Chappelle introduces racial stereotypes while simultaneously undermining them as social constructs. For example, in Episode One, Chappelle creates a white family called the "Niggar Family." Through this family, Chappelle demonstrates how African Americans are stereotypically constructed in white culture. Chappelle uses this family's last name, "Niggar," to show how this word is degrading. Phrases that would normally be used negatively, even hatefully, toward blacks are comedically constructed in the skit with a positive message. "Damn Niggars," "Your dating a Niggar," and "Niggar lover" are some examples of phrases that Chappelle twists to show how differently a phrase feels when directed at a different racial group. Each time the word "Niggar" is used in this episode, Chappelle is presenting it as a positive attribute for the whites, while simultaneously critiquing its negativity toward blacks.

In Episode Two, Chappelle re-creates a season of the popular MTV reality show *The Real World.* Chappelle "constructs" an episode of *The Real World* with an all-black cast except for one white character, informing the viewer how it feels to be the minority in a group. Chappelle demonstrates stereotypical perceptions of particular races in their "real world" by overexaggerating stereotypes about blacks.[17] For instance, in the skit, blacks are categorized as lazy, jobless, and as people who choose to engage in harmful activities such as participate in crimes and use drugs. In this episode, all of the characters are given a job. The only character that faithfully does their work is the white character. The black characters are seen taking breaks, smoking marijuana or cigarettes, and leaving their work for the white character to finish. From baggy jeans (black character) to tight khakis of the white character, Chappelle is critiquing the stereotypes associated in these particular races.[18]

In Episode Three, Chappelle plays a black man who is also the member of a white supremacist group. Born blind, the character Clayton Bigsby, was raised in a society where he was socialized to be white. Throughout this episode, Chappelle demonstrates that "acting white," even acting racist is socially constructed. Chappelle clearly is commenting on the socially constructed nature of "whiteness" by creating a Black character who "acts white," and thus exemplifies the stereotypical views of African Americans.[19] Being a strong white supremacist, the character Clayton stated many reasons why he did not like black people. For example, they are "lazy, no good, big lipped . . . niggers." These are all stereotypes that were placed upon blacks by society, and become fodder for Chappelle's comedy.

Perhaps the episode with the deepest critique on how race is socially constructed was the "racial draft" episode. Here, Chappelle is clearly questioning what is really meant by "race?" And, who decides what racial category any individual belongs to? For instance, in the "racial draft," the famous golfer Tiger Woods was drafted to the Black race. When drafted by the black contingency, Tiger Woods yelled, "so long fried rice, hello fried chicken." Woods is of mixed racial background, black and Japanese. Chappelle plays on the stereotype that the Japanese eat fried rice, while blacks eat fried chicken. Yet the very fact that Tiger can strip away his ethnic identities, also demonstrates the constructed nature of race.[20] In the same episode, Colin Powell and Condoleezza Rice are drafted by the whites. The black musical group, The Woo-Tang-Clan, is drafted by the Asians. Each "draft" reveals the socially constructed nature of race.

The Chappelle Show is portraying how American society has adopted stereotypical perceptions about race and ethnicity. Through comedy, Chappelle is critiquing racial stereotypes with exaggerated portrayals. In *The Chappelle Show*, verbal, visual, and behavioral claims were made about blacks and whites.[21] Chappelle draws upon stereotypes that have been repeated throughout society, but he does so through exaggeration to make the stereotypes comical, and therefore unbelievable. Chappelle is doing more than social commentary on race relations. Chappelle's comedic motivation is about forcing society to see the transformative ways that law and society has played in creating racial inequity.

Chappelle uses comedic skits to construct a behavioral claim that draws attention to the social problem of racism. In Episode Two, Chappelle creates a black man who is the leader of a white supremacist group. Clayton Bigsby, the blind black white supremacist may have grown up in a world without a clear perception of race, but the culture socializes one to "see" race. While Chappelle may be critiques for feeding into racial stereotypes in these skits, much the same way Archie Bunker from the 1970s TV series *All in the Family* was viewed as reinforcing bigoted views, Chappelle is trying to use humor to undermine racist stereotypes that exist in American society.

Distinctions in Humor

Humor occurs in most aspects of human life and thus, in legal contexts. Of course, what is funny to one person may not be to another. Nonetheless, attempting to define humor helps explain why comedy is such a poignant critical component of intellectual life. In defining humor in this context, one will inevitably receive countless forwards from the internet, scenes from movies and TV shows, or old classic jokes, all attempting to show that *that* is precisely what is funny. This research seeks not only to provide criteria for what is funny but also explain the effect of that humor on the listener. Part of the dilemma of studying humor is that funny comes in various forms—words, intonations, accents, appearances, characters, actions, situations—all of which are designed to be funny and enhance the totality of the joke.[22] Ultimately we find ourselves laughing and commenting, "I'm not sure why I find that funny but I just do." Laughter, I argue, is evolutionary.

Laughter is both innate and learned behavior. The slapstick comedy of The Three Stooges is funny to many (most) people because it touches a visceral part of what we find funny: being bonked on the head with sound effects. But comedy, particularly of the three mentioned in this research, is both innate and learned: it requires thought and consideration, especially when dealing with complex issues of race. Philosopher and evolutionist Daniel Dennett explored, "Why do we enjoy laughter so much? Why do we especially enjoy laughter *together*?"[23] Humor theorists attempt to explain these complexities. While these theories are not exhaustive, they help shed light on how the overlap between humor, law, and race all converge for Pryor, Rock, and Chappelle. There is general consensus among humor theorists that these three theories help explain, with some overlap, why something is funny.

Superiority Theory

This theory is identified with Aristotle, Plato, Socrates, and Cicero who associated humor with aggression. They viewed humor as an opportunity to disparage others to increase one's own self-worth. Plato believed that weak individuals engaged in humorous tactics only when it was unlikely that they would encounter a counterattack. Pryor's humor applies here in his 1975 *Saturday Night Live* appearance where he hosted the show and was involved in one of the most famous skits in the show's history. Pryor had already wreaked havoc on CBS in 1973 after he adlibbed obscenities, in cornrows no less. In 1974, ABC executives were infuriated when he showed up drunk to emcee a Redd Foxx roast. However, NBC executives Lorne Michaels and Dick Ebersol were not scared off by Pryor's antics when they asked him to host in 1975. Pryor required a few conditions for committing to the show: Paul Mooney must write and Gil Scott-Heron would need to be the musical guest.[24] NBC obliged.

The evening was filled with memorable sketches but none more quintessentially Pryor than the one in which he plays Mr. Wilson, a man being interviewed by Chevy Chase's character to determine word association, ostensibly used for employment.

Interviewer: I'll throw out a few words—anything that comes to your mind, just throw back at me, okay? It's kind of an arbitrary thing. Like if I say "dog," you'd say?
Mr. Wilson: Tree.
Interviewer: Tree. (Chase then nods, as if to prepare himself for the next set of odd answers from Pryor.)
Interviewer: Fast.
Mr. Wilson: Slow.
Interviewer: Rain.
Mr. Wilson: Snow.
Interviewer: White.

Mr. Wilson: Black.
Interviewer: Bean.
Mr. Wilson: Pod.
Interviewer: Negro.
Mr. Wilson: Whitey.

Pryor's brilliance (and Chase to some degree) is on display here in presenting a strong black man to counter the weak, frightened, and cowardly interviewer played by Chase.

Interviewer: Tarbaby.
Mr. Wilson: (He leans in, unsure that he heard what the interviewer said.) What'd you say?
Interviewer: Tarbaby.
Mr. Wilson: Ofay.
Interviewer: Colored.
Mr. Wilson: Redneck.
Interviewer: Jungle Bunny!

Pryor is now beginning to get angry. It is clear that Chase's character was hoping to get Pryor's character angry, but assumed he would be submissive.

Mr. Wilson: Peckerwood!
Interviewer: Burrhead.
Mr. Wilson: Cracker! (Pryor's character is aggressive and the audience is now laughing, even if it is nervous laughter.)
Interviewer: Spearchucker.
Mr. Wilson: White trash!
Interviewer: Jungle Bunny!
Mr. Wilson: (now upset) Honky!
Interviewer: Spade!
Mr. Wilson: (very upset) Honky honky!
Interviewer: Nigger!
Mr. Wilson: (immediate response) Dead honky![25]

The skit ends as Chase's character awkwardly agrees that Pryor is qualified for the job and offers him $5,000, then $7,500, and then $15,000. He states, "don't hurt me, please" Pryor uses superiority theory through the lens of a critical race theorist.

Some time ago, the political theorist Thomas Hobbes also saw the power of humor, particularly when inferiority was involved. Hobbes stated, "Sudden Glory, is the passion which maketh those Grimaces called LAUGHTER; and is caused either by some sudden act of their own, that pleaseth them;

or by the apprehension of some deformed thing in another, by comparison whereof they suddenly applaud themselves."[26] In other words, laughter for Hobbes is no more than basking in one's victory or superiority over another. This kind of superiority connects with humor on race because it is used by critical race comedians to invert the superiority. Rock attempts to invert superiority and this can be seen in his 2008 joke regarding his house and neighbors.

Rock prefaces the joke to explain that he is rich; he readily admits to this. As an aside, he does explain in 2004 that there is a difference between being rich (black NBA star) and being wealthy (white NBA team owner). I digress. Rock's joke about his house and neighbors presents the notion that Rock is surrounded by many wealthy people, only a few of which are black. Rock:

> In my neighborhood, there are four Black people. Hundreds of houses, four Black people. Who are these Black people? Well, there's me, Mary J. Blige, Jay-Z, and Eddie Murphy. Only Black people in the whole neighborhood. So let's break it down, let's break it down: me, I'm a decent comedian. I'm a'ight. Mary J. Blige, one of the greatest R&B singers to ever walk the Earth. Jay-Z, one of the greatest rappers to ever live. Eddie Murphy, one of the funniest actors to ever, ever do it. Do you know what the White man who lives next door to me does for a living? He's a fucking dentist. He ain't the best dentist in the world. . . he ain't going to the Dental Hall of Fame . . . he don't get plaques for getting rid of plaque. He's just a yank-your-tooth-out dentist. See, the Black man gotta fly to get to somethin' the White man can walk to![27]

Rock exaggerates to show that there is humor in the traditionally weakened person inverting superiority over the traditionally powerful person for the sake of humor. This kind of humor allows the audience to have some ownership over the joke, regardless of whether they are the traditionally weakened or traditionally powerful.

Superiority theory helps explain why the context of the joke is so important, reinforcing why critical race comedians use history to shed light on racial inequity. Lenny Bruce, considered by many to be one of the most influential modern comedians had a routine about his wife wanting to have a child. His response to her, "Why bring strangers into the house?"[28] However, scholars note that superiority theory does little to explain why this Bruce joke is funny.

Incongruity Theory

This second theory of humor attempts to put humor in a more positive light and move away from the negativity of superiority theory. Identified with Immanuel Kant and Arthur Schopenhauer, incongruity theory suggests that humor arises from the juxtaposition of two incongruous or inconsistent phenomena.[29] Like most humor, incongruity theory can work with surprise. It is simply categorized as a good-news/ bad-news joke. An example might be O'Riley was on trial for armed robbery. The jury came out and announced, "Not guilty." "Wonderful," said O'Riley, "does that mean I can keep the money?"[30] The setup leads you to believe that one acquitted of armed robbery would not be likely to admit to the crime. The surprise is where the humor lies. Laughter comes from both expectation and surprise.

The laughter provoked by the surprise and anxiety is not evidence of humor.[31] The anticipation by the audience of the imminent joke can often be where the humor resides. Little notes:

> So far, then, the explanations for why incongruity can produce humor are intellectual provocation, mental exercise, colorful or ear-catching contexts, emotional workouts, and social critique. Coming at the connection between incongruity and humor from another perspective, some psychiatrists and psychologists hypothesize that incongruity must combine with another condition for humor to result.[32]

George Carlin and other comedians have addressed this issue and described it as a connection between comedy and pain. Carlin explains:

> There is an anger that precedes comedy. There's an outrage at the base of it. I guess it's natural to associate that outrage with some sort of ill beginnings or some sort of sadness. You know, crying and laughter are very close because they both produce tearing of the eyes, bearing of the teeth, and a kind of rhythmic expulsion of air that's involuntary. They're very, very close. "I laughed until I cried." And all of the words associated with comedy have violence attached to them: gag, slapstick, punchline, I killed them, I slaughtered them, I died out there. There is something there that serious scholars should take a look at someday.[33]

There is something there. Comedy provides us a set of norms, values, rules, and regulations through humor.

Chappelle's 2004, *For What It's Worth*, stand-up act looks to connect some of that inconsistent phenomena. Chappelle explains why he has decided that he will only smoke weed around white people:

> I've stopped smoking weed with black people. You didn't let me finish, motherfuckers. Goddamn. I'm sorry black people to break the news so publicly, but I can't smoke with you anymore.
>
> Every time I smoke weed with my black friends all you talk about is your trials and tribulations. I'm sick of that shit. I got my own problems. They're going to waste the weed. I'm smoking weed to run away from my problems, not take away yours. From now on, I smoke weed exclusively with white people. Calm

> down, motherfuckers, you win by default. You got good weed conversation. All white people talk about when they get high is other times that they got high. I could listen to that shit all night. "Dude, remember at Frank's last week, I was fucking smashed, man." And catalogs everything they drink. "I had two shots of Jäger, tequila, four bong hits, man, beer, cheeseburger." That shit is great.

Chappelle is underscoring the idea that marijuana is a convenience for white folk while it is more of a release from the obstacles for the Black man in America.

Release Theory

The last theory of humor argues that humor taps into repressed sources of pleasure, pressure, or anxiety.[34] Release theory is most often associated with Sigmund Freud and English philosophers Alexander Bain and Herbert Spencer. Some see this as the notion that the joke lies within our "inner censor." It is funny because it is taboo. The idea is that we prepare ourselves for a flood of emotions and release those emotions through laughter.[35] Release theory also provides both a psychology and sociolegal perspective. It points out that "laughter is a kind of release from social sanction physically and psychologically."[36] Scholars note that Freud, a champion of release theory, posited that "people long for getting rid of restraint set by morality, law, and some other aspects of human life, back to the stage of being relaxed, free, and pleased, not to worry about anything.[37] Humor allows this very possibility. The critical race comedians provide humor to both release the burden of the listener and to force that listener to ponder his/her place in society.

Rock's comedy helps society contemplating where racial conversations take place. Rock wailed about the difference between "niggas and black people":

> I love black people but I hate niggas. Boy I wish they'd let me join the Ku Klux Klan. Shit, I'd do a drive-by from here to Brooklyn . . . You know the worst thing about niggas? Niggas always want some credit for some shit they supposed to do. A nigga will brag about some shit a normal man just does. A nigga will say some shit like, "I take care of my kids." You're supposed to, you dumb motherfucker. What are you talking about? What kind of ignorant shit is that? "I ain't never been to jail!" What do you want, a cookie? You're not supposed to go to jail, you low-expectation-having motherfucker.[38]

Rock was using humor, I would argue various theories discussed above, to demonstrate the way in which society differentiates race to suit their political (and legal) mores. As CRT scholar Derrick Bell has noted in his research, race was a social construct post-Civil War in the United States and was presented as an option for poor white folks to have property value in their whiteness. Being asked if you'd rather be a poor white or a poor black allowed whites to differentiate themselves from blacks and reinforce racial inequity. Rock's bit here shows how racial conversations in the United States have been constructed to provide this kind of racial juxtaposition. It allows the listener to release the burden of their thoughts on racial discrimination, yet uncomfortably ponder the continued inequity that persists in society.

Provoking Laughter

The success of the Chappelle Show led Dave Chappelle to receive national and international attention for his ability to deal with race in ways that provided much-needed humor on an incredibly important issue in the United States. With this attention and success, Chappelle found himself wondering if some of the sketches that he was creating for the show were misunderstood by the viewers. Chappelle explained in interviews after he abruptly left the show in 2004 that he recalled in one taping where a spectator, a white man, appeared to be laughing extremely long and loud. The laughter struck Chappelle as odd and he wondered if the show had moved from critiquing stereotypes to simply reinforcing them. There is a complexity here in what is funny and acceptable as funny to not only the comedian but the viewer as well.

Discussions on race are often complex and emblematic of racism being an enduring social problem. Studies suggesting the level at which racism is "taken for granted" shows prevalence that criticism of policies on race are often cursory and not given the attention they require.[39] In the Walton et al. (2013) study, the researchers revealed that racializing an issue may not always constitute racism. Essentially, that logic can be presented that some aspects of race, even jokes, are acceptable discussion points if they simply present some of the stereotypes in society. This is a fine line that leads back to the earlier discussion on color-blindness and antisubordination. I look to further consider how critical race comedians examine the interplay between racializing and racism.

The argument that popular humor confirms damaging stereotypes more than subverting them is popular among some scholars.[40] I would argue that such an approach fails to recognize the importance of understanding context and history. As noted earlier, CRT rejects ahistoricism, and insists on contextual, historical analysis of law. Critical race comedians do the same and while the audience may not digest the material as social criticism but rather a way to feed into their own prejudices, the comedian must be concerned with the crafting of the joke and not the interpretation of it. To view it otherwise, at least in the context of critical race comedy, is to essentially present the argument that talking about race is equal to racism. Society's understanding of race is often conceptualized through the various tropes of comedic intent and familiarity with the subject matter. The listener may not be consciously aware of the mere *possibility* that the conversation borders on what some might deem racist. However, the comedian is conscious and that is what makes the act of constructing that joke, using the foundation of CRT, an act that creates, molds, manipulates, informs, and emboldens discussions about race and CRT. Thus, comedy is both accommodation and reconciliation.

Humor in a Time of Political Divergence

As each of us considers the Mt. Rushmore of comedians, we individually balance criteria: length of career, innovative style, cultural impact, and other criteria important to each audience member. While there are comedic characteristics that differ among audience members, the impact of the humor, particularly when it becomes a part of society, is impactful across socioeconomic circles. Given that race is such a constant conversation in American political discourse and part of street level conversations as well, it is no surprise that the reach of Pryor, Rock, and Chappelle extends beyond the stage and onto the streets.

Humor can be a universal experience and one that allows for connections through puns, jokes, and wit, all designed to show intelligence, injustice, and to simply laugh at the intensity of the moment. For most comedians, no topic is off limits and every topic, in fact, is ripe for the perfect joke. Comedians can say what politicians cannot. Like music, comedy speaks to the people on the streets and those in the penthouses. Humor, distinctly, is both for the bourgeoisie and proletariat, and may even be one of the most effective ways for those two (and everyone in between) to communicate.

American humor over the past thirty years has not just been enjoyable but relaxing and distracting.[41] The critical race comedians that I have mentioned have dedicated their art to inhabiting anxieties and wallowing in them. The best comedians recognize problems and find solutions and provide the audience with the knowledge that the humor lies in the complacency of those in power. Humor can be insidious and morph into political speech. The critical race comedian wants their joke to be a verbal tranquilizer. It is progressive, constructive, and healing.

After 9/11, *The Daily Show* went off the air for 9 days. *Saturday Night Live* began its season with producer Lorne Michaels asking New York Mayor Rudy Giuliani, "Can we be funny?" The question was not unlike what philosophers have been asking for thousands of years: what is comedy's role in society? Is there an evolutionary purpose?[42] After 9/11, America was waiting for various leaders to provide some explanation of the horrific acts of that day. For some, their religious leaders provided comfort, while for others it was politicians. Yet for many across the country, it was humor that could best allay our fears, even if for a moment. That is the power of humor.

How can we laugh in the face of racism? Are we complicit in perpetuating stereotypes if we laugh at the discussion of inequity? Are we accepting this unequal treatment? Critical race comedians—and one could argue *all* comedians—use their comedy to not simply shine light on the tribulations of the human race but to point out the lunacy. This awareness actually provides a sense of relief as the listener knows he/she is not alone. Scholar Robert Storey addresses this and writes, "When faced with polar opposites, the problem of comedy is always how to resolve conflict without destroying the participants. Comedy is the art of accommodation and reconciliation."[43] As noted earlier in this piece from George Carlin, the comedian often looks to get the listener to "laugh until they cry." There is a catharsis for all those involved in the entire process.

Richard Pryor performed his work using humor as mechanism for enlightenment. If read, Pryor's work could often be seen as drafts of what critical race theorists might have been writing in the 1970s and 1980s. Pryor quipped, "yeah, he was alright for a white man."[44] It is those kinds of comments which elicited laughter across the auditorium in 1975 that seem almost innocuous today. Yet, somehow they are funny. Not in some kind of slapstick way and certainly not in a way that allows for the joke's stereotypical premise to be socially acceptable. Nonetheless, it is funny because the humor reminds us that unless we laugh at the inequity, we just might cry.

Humor is, simply, a tool. Critical race comedians use that tool to communicate in ways that provide the layperson context, information, and knowledge mixed with exaggeration to "prove" a point. Humor provides a new way of viewing a problem. Humor seeks to reinforce beliefs or dismiss them through a guttural laugh. Mark Twain once wrote, "the human race has only one really effective weapon and that is laughter." A good joke unites us and reminds us that our differences, whether they are race, gender, sexuality, or ethnicity, can all be celebrated.

I write this on the heels of yet another police shooting of an unarmed black man in America. Richard Pryor already had the conversation on Trayvon Martin, even though he didn't mention the young boy's name. Chris Rock and Dave Chappelle already opined about Eric Garner or Alton Sterling or Philando Castile. Critical race theorists have been talking about these legal lynchings for generations. None of this is funny. None of it. But critical race comedians provide us healing in a time of fear and turmoil. They help calm the streets and oftentimes that is more than any judge, jury, or politician can do.

NOTES

1. I thank Fralvin Munoz, my student research assistant, for his work compiling the comedy of Pryor, Rock, and Chappelle. And special thanks to my wife, Jessica,

who really is the funniest person I know—she could make any seasoned comedian laugh.

2. Athena D. Mutua, (2006), "The Rise, Development and Future Directions of Critical Race Theory and Related Scholarship," *Denver University Law Review*, Vol. 84, 333.

3. Ibid.

4. Kimberle Williams Crenshaw, (2011), "Twenty Years of Critical Race Theory: Looking Back to Move Forward," *Connecticut Law Review*, Vol. 43, 1260.

5. Mutua, 353–354.

6. http://www.dead-frog.com/comedians/comic/redd_foxx

7. Mutua, 359.

8. Ibid., 361–362.

9. See *Keyes v. School Dist. No. 1*, (1973).

10. Stacy Hawkins, "Diversity, Democracy, and Pluralism: Confronting the Reality of Our Inequality," *Mercer Law Review*, Vol. 66, 581.

11. *Strauder v. West Virginia* (1880) at 306.

12. *Brown v. Board of Education* (1954) at 394.

13. Malcolm X in 1963.

14. Loseke, 15–16.

15. Ibid., 26–27.

16. Ibid., 26.

17. Abatiello, 6.

18. Ibid.

19. Ibid.

20. Ibid.

21. Ibid.

22. Brian Boyd, (2004), "Laughter and Literature: A Play Theory of Humor," *Philosophy and Literature*, Vol. 28, 2.

23. Ibid., 3.

24. Scott Saul, (2014). "*Saturday Night Live's* Edgiest Night: The Inside Story of Richard Pryor's Brilliant Evening." *Salon*, December 14.

25. Richard Pryor, (1975), *SNL*.

26. R. E. Ewin, (2003), "Hobbes on Laughter," *The Philosophical Quarterly*, Vol 51, 29–30.

27. Chris Rock, (2004),

28. Boyd, 1.

29. Little, 1246.

30. Ibid.

31. Robert R. Provine, (2000), *Laughter: A Scientific Investigation*, (Viking Adult), 11.

32. Little, 1248.

33. George Carlin, (2002), *On Comedy* (Laugh.com).

34. John Limon, (2000), *Stand-up Comedy in Theory, or, Abjection in America*, (Duke University Press), 42.

35. Boyd, 4.

36. Shuqin Hu, (2012), "An Analysis of Humor in *The Big Bang Theory* from Pragmatic Perspectives," *Theory and Practice in Language Studies*, Vol. 2, No. 6, 1185.

37. Ibid.

38. Chris Rock, (1997), *Roll with the New*.

39. See Julie McLeod and Lyn Yates, (2003), "Who Is 'Us' Students? Negotiating Discourses of Racism and National Identification in Australia," *Race, Ethnicity, and Education*, Vol. 6, No. 1, 29–49; Jessica Walton, Naomi Priest, and Yin Paradies, (2013), "'It Depends How Your Saying It': The Complexities of Everyday Racism," *International Journal of Conflict and Violence*, Vol. 7, No. 1, 74–90.

40. See Ji Hoon Park, Nadine G. Gabbadon, and Ariel R. Chermin, (2006), "Naturalizing Racial Differences Through Comedy: Asian, Black, and Whites Views on Racial Stereotypes in *Rush Hour 2*," *Journal of Communication*, Vol. 56, No. 1, 157–177.

41. Lewis, 205.

42. Olga Khazan, (2014), "The Dark Psychology of Being a Good Comedian," *The Atlantic*, February 27, 2014.

43. Robert Storey, (1996), "Comedy, Its Theorists and the Evolutionary Perspective," *Criticism*, Vol. 38, 436.

44. Richard Pryor, (1975), "Is It Something I Said?" *LIVE at the Latin Casino*.

REFERENCES

Abbatiello, Jasmin. (2005). In Black and White: A Content Analysis of Racial Humor in *The Chappelle Show*. Unpublished dissertation: St. Mary's College.

Boyd, Brian. (2004). "Laughter and Literature: A Play Theory of Humor." *Philosophy and Literature*, 28, 1–22.

Carlin, George. (2002). *On Comedy*. Laugh.com.

Chapman, Antony J., & Hugh C. Foot. (1976). *Humor and Laughter: Theory, Research, and Applications*. NY: Wiley and Sons.

Crenshaw, Kimberle Williams. (2011). "Twenty Years of Critical Race Theory: Looking Back to Move Forward." *Connecticut Law Review*, 43, 1253–1352.

Ewin, R. E. (2003). "Hobbes on Laughter." *The Philosophical Quarterly*, 51, 29–40.

Foxx, Redd. http://www.dead-frog.com/comedians/comic/redd_foxx. Retrieved on April 11, 2013.

Hawkins, Stacy. (2015). Diversity, Democracy, and Pluralism: Confronting the Reality of Our Inequality. *Mercer Law Review*, 66, 577–649.

Horton, James. (1993). "Humor and the American Racial Imagination." *American Quarterly*, 45, 166–170.

Hu, Shuqin. (2012). "An Analysis of Humor in *The Big Bang Theory* from Pragmatic Perspectives." *Theory and Practice in Language Studies*, 2(6), 1185–1190.

Keyes v. School Dist. No. 1, Denver, Colorado, 413 U.S. 189 (1973).

Khazan, Olga. (2014). "The Dark Psychology of Being a Good Comedian." *The Atlantic*, February 27, 2014.

Lewis, Paul. (2006). *Cracking Up: American Humor in a Time of Conflict*. The University of Chicago Press.

Little, Laura. (2009). "Regulating Funny: Humor and the Law." *Cornell Law Review*, 94, 1235–1292.

Limon, John. (2000). *Stand-up Comedy in Theory, or, Abjection in America*. Duke University Press.

Loseke, Donileen. (1999). "Language, Interaction, and Social Problems." *Social Problems*, June, 10–55.

Martin, Rod A. (2006). *The Psychology of Humor: An Integrative Approach*. Academic Press.

Mutua, Athena D. (2006). "The Rise, Development and Future Directions of Critical Race Theory and Related Scholarship." *Denver University Law Review*, 84, 329–394.

Provine, Robert R. (2000). *Laughter: A Scientific Investigation*. Viking Adult.

Pryor, Richard. (1975). *Is It Something I Said?* Recorded live at the Latin Casino, Atlantic City.

Rock, Chris. (1997). *Roll With The New*, Dreamworks Records, Los Angeles.

Roeckelein, Jon. (2002). *The Psychology of Humor: A Reference Guide and Annotated Bibliography*. Greenwood Press.

Saul, Scott. (2014). "*Saturday Night Live's* Edgiest Night: The Inside Story of Richard Pryor's Brilliant Evening." *Salon*, December 14.

Storey, Robert. (1996). "Comedy, Its Theorists, and the Evolutionary Perspective." *Criticism*, 38(3), 407–441.

Strauder v. West Virginia, 100 U.S. 303 (1880).

Walton, Jessica, et al. (2013). "'It Depends How Your Saying It': The Complexities of Everyday Racism." *International Journal of Conflict and Violence*, 7(1), 74–90.

Chapter 9

Ears on the Street

Coqui Frog Patrols and the Guarding of Silence in One Hawaiian Village

Marilyn Brown and Sarah Marusek

The State of Hawai'i, as both a tourist destination and importer of all manner of goods, is also a destination for many unwanted, invasive species. In many places on the Island of Hawai'i, the evenings ring with the chirping of tiny, yet noisy coqui frogs. Few residents are enchanted by these sounds. They can be quite deafening and, to some, spoil the ambience in this largely rural paradise. The arrival of these noisy amphibians was initially ignored. But when it seemed to be too late, the County government declared defeat in the face of the frog's rapid proliferation. But in one small community, the challenge has been taken up by individuals who object to this aural environmental pollution. Our study focuses on one socially and culturally distinct community made up of nominal outsiders whose environmental sensitivities depart from those of most local residents of Hawai'i Islands. In contrast, these Volcano residents refuse to accept the foreign frog invasion of their construction of paradise and have taken to the streets to fight.

The residents of Volcano, a community on the slope of the Kilauea Volcano, decided to promote their notion of what the night should sound like. In this chapter, we explore the socio-legal reaction to the noise generated by the coqui frog and how the community of Volcano created and enforced their own neighborhood-based response to the frogs. They sought the sanctity of silence, both out of environmental concerns and to protect their own property values. In absence of effective environmental actions by the State and County to suppress the frog, citizens of Volcano have engaged in a vigorous program of policing the night's "natural" silence and asserting their sovereignty rights relative to the little, invasive amphibians.

In this analysis, Volcano's coqui project provides insight into the cultural aspects of law,[1] the regulability of space,[2] and the legal frameworks of offensive noise.[3] On Hawai'i Island, the Big Island in the State of Hawai'i, a host of sounds can be heard. They range from native and non-native birds, airplanes, the tsunami siren (which is tested monthly), and the occasional streetcar race in the middle of the night. But with a decibel level seemingly off the scale, there's the call of the coqui frog. Sounding like "ko-kee," the coqui frog (*Eleutherodactylus coqui*) sounds like beautiful night music to some (and is celebrated in its native Puerto Rico). But to residents of Volcano, it is a high-pitched, pervasive and offensive noise. Emitting chirps up to 80–90 decibels, the tiny frog when alone or in great numbers is loud and it drowns out other available sounds. Arriving in Hawai'i from Puerto Rico in about 1988,[4] the tiny coqui, which is roughly the size of a dime, has thrived in its new habitat where populations of the frog have exploded throughout the island. With no known enemies except the human being, the coqui comes out at night to mate and "ko-kee" with abandon.

The frog is considered an invasive species by the state and numerous state agencies, which initially thought to eradicate the frog, now attempt merely to contain it to Hawai'i Island. Currently, under state law, "any person or organization who intentionally transports, harbors, or imports with the intent to propagate, sell, or release the coqui may be charged with a class C felony and is subject to a minimum fine of $50,000 and maximum fine of $200,000, plus three years in prison."[5] In addition to the Hawai'i Department of Agriculture, the Hawai'i Department of Land and Natural Resources, nonprofit environmental groups, schools, realtors, and even neighborhood patrols, have joined the crusade against the noisy coqui. But, the coqui even have their advocates, making nocturnal soundscapes contested spaces.

SOUNDSCAPES AND ECOLOGY

Sounds that emerge from landscapes may be produced by biological processes, called biophony, or geophysical processes, called geophony, as well as by human activity, whose sound is called anthrophony.[6] Biological or geophysical sounds (such as the wind blowing through trees) may be construed by some as being natural and therefore preferable to anthrophonically produced sounds. For example, urban nocturnal soundscapes are filled with the blare of sirens, roaring motors, and the intrusive noise of road traffic. Indeed, residents of rural communities may well prefer the ambience of "natural" nocturnal sounds and choose such areas for the relative tranquility of their soundscapes. But what of biophonic sounds that some argue don't belong to a particular soundscape, despite their natural origins? The meaning of what we hear is premised not only on audible sounds, but also on who we are as listeners.

In his article "Hearing and Belonging: On Sounds, Faiths, and Laws," Massimo Leone[7] describes the impact of Islamic and Christian-based sound on social space and characterizations of belonging based upon the presence or absence of certain sounds. Leone speaks of these sounds as the creation of socially expected frameworks of noise as a soundscape, which is that "space in which sounds can be produced, perceived and potentially correlated with meaning."[8] As Leone asserts, the creation and reception of sound is a reflection of culturally based parameters of what should be heard. While the coqui's nocturnal calling is beloved in rural Puerto Rico,[9] some residents of Hawai'i Island argue that these sounds are out of place and should not be heard in nighttime surrounds. They are frustrated by the lack of effective official responses to the coqui infestation in Hawai'i. And, they are discouraged that eradication is no longer considered by scientists to be possible there, although some hope is held out for the state's remaining islands.[10]

LAW'S INATTENTION AND COMMUNITY ACTION

Since the arrival of the Puerto Rican frogs as stowaways in imported nursery plants, multiple statutes have resulted in various forms of coqui management under what Mariana Valverde[11] calls a commonsensical approach to legal remedy. From prizes awarded by the Hawai'i Department of Education to schoolchildren for killing coqui to mandatory real estate disclosures regarding noise to state-sanctioned citric acid pesticides, the cultural embeddedness of anti-coqui sentiment pits law against frog.[12] However, community-level responses to the frog infestation have devolved into resignation in all but a very few cases.

The village of Volcano, situated on the rainy, upper slopes of Kilauea Volcano, has initiated the Coqui Control Hotline for the purpose of coqui eradication. It takes calls day or night. In this eradication program, the ears on the street are just as important as the eyes on the street for stopping these alien species and their noise.[13] The soundscape of silence,[14] threatened by the invasive frog, is the foundation for a neighborhood-based ecological justice. However, in Volcano, justice is not for the frog, but instead for those who fight for maintaining property values in this community of mainland haole,[15] middle-class professionals, scientists, academics, and artists. These residents set themselves apart from other Hawai'i Island communities infested with coqui by their proactive efforts to keep the frog out.

THE POLITICAL ECONOMY OF INVASIVE SPECIES

Coqui are everywhere in on the Big Island, with possibly the highest concentration on the wetter eastern side of the island, in the Hilo and Puna Districts.

In Lava Tree State Park, in Puna, for example, coqui are estimated to "exceed 20,000 individuals an acre."[16] According to Robert Sugawarda of the U.S. Department of Agriculture's Hilo Field Station on Hawai'i, speaking about the numbers of coqui, "It is almost [*sic*] undescribable. They're pretty much out of control."[17] "The coqui invasion is of economic concern to the State of Hawai'i because it threatens multimillion dollar floriculture and nursery industries . . . private property values and tourism."[18] While the coqui is purported by some to be a danger to the island ecosystem, the noise generated by the coqui is to many a far more detrimental impact. The chirp of the coqui at 80–90 decibels threatens the "enjoyment of life" framework in excess of the human health and welfare limits above the 70dBA level determined by the Hawai'i Department of Health, Hawai'i Revised Statutes Section 324F-1.[19] Effectively, the coqui's chirp is a violation of state noise ordinances.

In Hilo, children have been contemplated as playing a role in frog control efforts. In 2007, the Hawai'i Island Economic Development Board and the Coqui Frog Working Group proposed a "Coqui Bounty Hunter" program for East Hawai'i schoolchildren. The plan rewarded school kids for turning in coqui in zippered plastic bags over a two-week period. The students with the most coqui kills could win Xbox 360s, PlayStation 3s, iPods, and cash awards for their schools. For various reasons, this "frog-killing binge" did not prevail. A variety of school principals objected to the killing, the collection, or the lack of school officials' involvement in the proposal. According to an Associated Press report, Hilo High School Vice Principal Chad Farias stated, "As for actual eradication, I don't see a way of the school being involved in that. It's not part of our standards to be involved in eradication."[20]

While the frog is now safe from bounty-hunting schoolchildren, the noisy coqui nonetheless creates a stir in the real estate market. According to Hawai'i Revised Statutes Chapter 487A "Language of Consumer Transactions," the Hawai'i Association of Realtors must make both seller and buyer aware of the presence of coqui in all private real estate sales. In Hawai'i Island Property Disclosures, buyers are warned about aircraft noise, wastewater disposal, insurance, volcanoes, and the presence of the coqui. "Because tree frogs are nocturnal, Buyers and their Realtors will not hear any chirping sounds that are associated with the frogs during the daytime hours of the subject property . . . [and are] advised to visit the subject property in the evening to determine the level of frog infestation and frog chirping and whether it is acceptable to Buyer" (Hawai'i Island Property Disclosure). Despite the legal warnings, some buyers still may not be fully aware of the noise created by the coqui. Three days before the finalizing of $1.9 million sale of a vacant lot in the Wainaku area of Hilo, the buyers sued on the grounds that the property has been misrepresented as "all one could hear is the sound of dying and tortured animal (which is the sound of the frogs occupying the area)." The property was also in an area frequented by drug dealers and prostitutes.[21] The case was dismissed by Hawai'i Third Circuit Judge Glenn Hara in January 2010. Judge Hara cited the buyers' signature of the Hawai'i Island Property Disclosure, in which the audibility of the coqui could have been heard prior to signing. Apparently, the presence of drug dealers and prostitutes was an acceptable neighborhood phenomena.

At night, the sound of the coqui can be deafening in some areas. Brooks A. Kaiser and Kimberly Burnett[22] assert "the primary economic effect of the frog is noise pollution." The noise generated by the tiny coqui goes further than just annoyance or ecological damage to create an economic harm to the island. "Economic theory suggests that property values for locations with noise pollution should be lower than comparable properties without."[23] The two authors focus on property values in Puna. They assert that "the presence of frogs, however, does have a significant negative impact on property values."[24] With such evidence, homeowners in Volcano who are experiencing a slower increase of coqui when compared to lower Puna, are nonetheless concerned about their property values. Additionally, the endemic noises of the rain forest where Volcano is located on Hawai'i Island may be just as valuable for purposes of property valuation.

PATERNAL CARE AND THE SCIENCE OF COQUI

As objects of scientific study, the coqui frog garners a good deal of interest on Hawai'i Island. Usually it is with community members wanting an applied solution to the pest.[25] Research at the University of Hawai'i College of Pharmacy aims to examine unique neurotransmitter systems in these frogs and trace their early development. Drugs like antidepressants can be tested on coqui since their neurochemical systems are similar to those of other vertebrates. Another line of research here tests the role of prolactin in making coqui frogs "good dads."[26] Indeed, male coqui zealously guard their eggs, keeping them moist while the female goes on to seek new reproductive opportunities.[27] As interesting, and even admirable, as these paternal activities may seem to scientists, most coqui connoisseurs bemoan the frogs' reproductive success.

The translation of coqui research from the lab to the public is being shaped by community demands for ways to control the frogs. One University of Hawai'i researcher[28] specializing in behavioral neuroscience and developmental biology, is in demand as a speaker for community groups such as Rotary. His finding that stimulation of the serotonin subsystem could quiet the frogs was greeted with great interest as a potential new weapon in the anti-frog arsenal.

Figure 9.1 Anti-Coqui Signs Posted in Volcano

Science has, in fact, provided effective techniques to control coqui. There are a range of agricultural, chemical, and mechanical means to kill the frogs or prevent them from invading an area.[29] Those Volcano residents fearful of infestation are encouraged to wash decorative or other plants prior to transporting them home. Warnings about frogs "hitchhiking" to Volcano appear on a coqui control web site built by anti-coqui activists. Readers can find instructions to wash vehicles that have been parked in infested areas. A range of chemical agents are sprayed or applied to coqui habitat, many of which can be easily used by the homeowner.[30] Lastly, capturing the coqui by hand is a preferred method among experienced coqui patrollers. The "coqui-stadores," alerted by vigilant property owners, arrive after sundown with illuminating headgear to keep hands free for catching frogs. One, two, or more of them attempt to triangulate on the frog's chirp—a difficult task since the frogs are said to throw their voices among the tree ferns like amphibious ventriloquists.

COQUI: ADVOCACY AND RESIGNATION

While the scientific discourse about coqui has been appropriated by many residents with an eye toward strategies of eradication, coqui do have their advocates on Hawai'i Island. Syd Singer[31] maintains that Hawai'i doesn't have a frog problem; it has an attitude problem. This coqui advocate appears on a video advertising his coqui sanctuary featuring the "Coqui Cottage" where visitors can listen to what he maintains are the mellifluous tones of tree frogs, in his words, an "enchanted night of coqui song." Singer and a few volunteers plan to set up a program of deportation of the coqui back to Puerto Rico, where they are celebrated, not hunted.[32]

The fact is that, having no natural enemies in Hawai'i, the coqui isn't leaving the island anytime soon.[33] At a community meeting aimed at addressing a beachhead of coqui in the southern part of the Island of Kaua'i, some residents voiced strong opposition to using County funds to control coqui, noting that they were here and people might as well learn to live with them.[34] And it does appear that Hawai'i Island residents who may have no love for the frogs manifest a passive resignation in the face of the overwhelming "invasion." By contrast, communities like Volcano have mounted aggressive and well-organized campaigns to control coqui despite the fact that eradication is no longer possible on Hawai'i Island.[35] Hawaii's coqui problem and responses to it exemplify diverse approaches to environmental threats, the way these dangers are constructed, and the role of citizenry when government is no longer perceived as being effective.

Even in Volcano, however, resignation is beginning to set in given the incursions made by the frogs into more and more of the subdivisions. Leadership in the effort is shifting as long-time participants become burned out. Discourses of fighting the battle against frogs are sprinkled with talk of global warming and the inevitability of defeat as the formerly cool, wet winters of Volcano become friendlier to the amphibians. Lately, volunteers have begun to triage sections of Volcano into those areas ranging from the least infested to almost complete saturation. Volunteers or property owners can catch frogs by hand in the lightly infested lots where frogs have "hitchhiked" as singletons on material deliveries or vehicles and can be found along the road. In more heavily infested areas that contain breeding populations, volunteers or individual homeowners spray foliage with citric acid to remove frogs and eggs. The most heavily infested lots are considered saturated and are written off as unsalvageable. The volunteers fear that Volcano, once distinctive for its cool, quiet nights, will succumb to the frogs just as the rest of the Island has.

VOLCANO VILLAGE: COQUI CONTROL AND PRIVILEGE

Volcano Village is situated at an elevation of about 3500 to 4000 feet. Its 2,646 residents live in one of Hawaii's increasingly rare upland rainforests, characterized by cool temperatures and abundant rainfall. In contrast with more developed areas of the state, house lots are comparatively large, ranging from a half to three acres. Many of the roads are unpaved and a significant number of households are off of the electrical grid. Volcano boasts a strong community association which encourages new and old residents to preserve as much as possible the 'ohia trees and hapu'u ferns that are the primary habitats of rare and endangered native birds. The more radical rainforest advocates are entirely prepared to confront transgressors. Homeowners who have violated this community compact by clear-cutting house lots have been targeted by these angry citizens who sometimes tag their errant neighbors by spray-painting "shame" in large letters on the adjoining road.[36] Conformists comply with community constructs of nature and wilderness by hand-clearing just enough trees to accommodate a new house's footprint. This is a far more expensive proposition than clearing land with heavy equipment and earth-movers, so preservation comes with a price. But environmentally minded newcomers appear quite willing to pay it.

This preservation of natural and wild spaces, even in the midst of human incursion into a formerly pristine rainforest, is reflective of a certain tradition in American environmentalism going back to the 19th century. As Taylor[37] describes in her analysis of social characteristics associated with environmentalist movements, race, class, and gender have always shaped environmental frameworks, goals, and strategies of implementation. She notes that white, middle-class males have long dominated environmentalist movements associated with the goals of conservation and preservation of the wild spaces, as well as how notions of nature and wilderness are framed. Individuals from white, middle-class backgrounds have also dominated urban environmentalist efforts to address issues such as establishing open spaces and parks, pollution, workplace safety, and sanitation. In contrast, Taylor points out that people of working class backgrounds, native peoples, and communities of color most often mobilize around aspects of ecology related to social justice. These groups are primarily concerned with self-determination, loss of native lands, and environmental hazards sited disproportionately among the poor and powerless.

It would be unfair to write off Volcano Village as merely a white enclave whose residents are unconcerned about all of the issues above except for preservation of the wild. Saving the rainforest and its native species are legitimate environmental goals but their hegemonic prioritization tends to suggest a certain privilege. An analysis of the community's social characteristics suggests that race, class, and other related factors distinguish Volcano from other East Hawai'i communities, most of which have not mobilized against coqui to such a great extent. The town of Hilo, hardly an urban metropolis at 46,165 people, is far larger than Volcano's 2,646 souls. Volcano residents are slightly more likely to be employed in professional, scientific, and management services industries than Hilo residents (7.9% vs. 7.4%). The annual per capita income in Volcano ($25,897) somewhat exceeds that of Hilo ($25,116). Differences in educational attainment are more apparent with 36.6% of the Village's residents having a Bachelors or graduate degree compared with 29.7% of Hilo residents having such credentials. But the most striking differences are those having to do with place of birth and race. While recent census data for Hilo show that 17.4% of residents were born in another state, that figure for Volcano is 43.2%. Finally, of those Hilo residents endorsing single race membership in the 2010 census, 18.5% report being white. In contrast, 51.8% of Volcano residents report being white, nearly a three-fold difference.[38]

These data on race and place of birth suggest that Volcano is a residential destination for whites and other newcomers to Hawai'i. (Fewer than 10% are Native Hawaiians, who make up approximately 22% of the State's population.) Framed in terms of American environmentalist movements, Volcano residents may be more likely than others to conceptualize the natural environment in romantic or poetic terms, embedded within a framework of freedom and wild spaces.[39] Residents active in the coqui control initiative tend to be highly educated white males of nonlocal birth. Nevertheless, invasive plants and animals along with the loss of native birds and plants to extinction trouble Volcano environmentalists and regular citizens alike. Nor are these concerns overblown; the Hawaiian Islands have one of the very highest extinction rates of avian species on earth with a loss of 36 taxa since the beginning of the 20th century.[40] The preservation of the audible nightscape from coqui chirping, signals comparative privilege, especially when compared to Native Hawaiian people who view the loss of indigenous lands and their traditional gathering rights to be far more critical environmental issues.

In Volcano, the coqui is hunted by local resident volunteers as part of the neighborhood watch group responsible for the Coqui Control Hotline. If a coqui is heard, a simple phone call to the hotline results in trained community volunteers arriving at the house to hunt and capture the coqui (which are usually frozen as a humane method of eradication).[41] Called "coqui-stadores," these volunteers are coqui bounty hunters who receive a bounty of $25 per frog, paid for from the Coqui Control Hotline's Association. This activity is the social response to the state's inability to contain, much less eradicate the frog. As Volcano Village is nestled within a native tropical rain forest, sounds of endemic wildlife can be heard. The cultural framework of what Volcano sounds like can be transmogrified through the actions of the Coqui Control Hotline to engender a frontier response to law.[42] Frontier law in this case refers to enforcement efforts considered to be the responsibility of those who are self-selected as agents of the community consciousness. If legal culture is "everything that makes a difference besides rules and structures,"[43] then this regulation is inherent in the worldview of these outsiders, one where environmental ideas are informed by claims grounded in scientific imperatives. The actions of these privileged settlers in a local community invert the dynamics of social control between empowered insiders and marginalized outsiders as described by Engels[44] in his study of legal consciousness in a rural mid-western town.[45]

Because the coqui have not yet entirely saturated in this part of Hawai'i Island, Village residents demonstrate that social control is a mobilization of law.[46] By taking measures to control the coqui through the coqui-stadore program, this type of neighborhood watch group has taken law into their own hands. These volunteers have become the informal actors of legal mandate in order to keep the peace (and the ko-kee out) in Volcano and eliminate the obnoxious nocturnal cacophony.

CONCLUSION

Formal law can only go so far. Efforts at the state level to eradicate the coqui have not worked, while efforts to contain the coqui have shifted away from the Big Island to keeping the coqui off from the other islands. Meanwhile, coqui-generated noise challenges the cultural expectations of what Hawai'i is supposed to sound like. When human-generated, noise can be protected speech,[47] regulated speech, or sanctioned speech[48] as it is heard in public spaces. However, animal-generated noise, particularly by tiny, nocturnal, invasive frogs, is much more difficult to control, much less regulate. Social responses to coqui-based noise pollution reveal a source of law that despite legal sanction, might be characterized as "frontier" law.

Social characteristics shape the mobilization of groups such as the coqui-stadores against an incursion into the nightscape that these residents find objectionable. Law and action are situated within white, middle-class experiences and knowledge (backed up by science) of what constitutes the natural environment. In a sense, coqui disturbance comes to symbolize the social structure[49] and helps heighten the distinctiveness of Volcano as a community made up largely of white outsiders. Volcano citizens police the nightscapes of the rainforest, melding environmental boundaries with the social, marking off what is acceptable and what is pollution, establishing order in the face of nocturnal disorder. Yet, the irony that a large proportion of Volcano residents are themselves non-native outsiders like the coqui remains, for the most part, largely unarticulated.

NOTES

1. Macaulay, Stewart, "Law and the Behavioral Sciences: Is There Any There There?" *Law & Policy*, 6 (1984): 149–187, accessed September 12, 2016, doi:10.1111/j.1467—9930.1984.tb00321.x.

2. Kohn, Margaret, *Brave New Neighborhoods: The Privatization of Public Space* (New York: Routledge, 2004).

3. *Hill* v. *Colorado* 530 U.S. 703 (2000); Loukaitou-Sideris, Anastasia and Renia Ehrenfeucht, *Sidewalks: Conflict and Negotiation over Public Space* (Cambridge, MA: MIT Press, 2009).

4. College of Tropical Agriculture and Human Resources, University of Hawai'i at Manoa. "Control of Coqui Frogs in Hawai'i," accessed April 4, 2013, http://www.ctahr.hawaii.edu/coqui/background.asp.

5. State of Hawai'i Plant Industry Division. "Coqui Information," accessed April 4, 2013, http://hdoa.hawaii.gov/pi/ppc/coqui-information/.

6. Pijanowski, Bryan C, et al., "Soundscape Ecology: The Science of Sound in the Landscape," *Bioscience* 61(3) (2011): 203–216.

7. Leone, Massimo, "Hearing and Belonging: On Sounds, Faiths, and Laws," In *Transparency, Power, and Control: Perspectives on Legal Communication*, ed. Vijay K. Bhatia et al. (Burlington, VT: Ashgate, 2012), 183–195.

8. Leone, "Hearing and Belonging," 184.

9. Kim, Jed, "Invasive Coqui Frogs Starting to Shatter California's Quiet Nights," *89.3 KPCC: Environment & Science*, March 11, 2016, accessed July 12, 2016, http://www.scpr.org/news/2016/03/11/58140/invasive-frogs-starting-to-shatter-california-s-qu/.

10. Beard, Karen H, et al., "Biology and Impacts of Pacific Island Invasive Species. 5. *Eleutherodactylus coqui*, the Coqui Frog (Anura: Leptodactylidae)," *Pacific Science* 63(3) (2009): 297–316.

11. Valverde, Mariana, *Law's Dream of a Common Knowledge* (Princeton, NJ: Princeton University Press, 2003).

12. Bhatia, Vijay K, et al., *Transparency, Power, and Control: Perspectives on Legal Communication* (Burlington, VT: Ashgate, 2012).

13. Jacobs, Jane, *The Death and Life of Great American Cities* (New York: Random House, 1961).

14. Leone, "Hearing and Belonging."

15. "Haole" is the colloquial term in Hawai'i for Caucasians.

16. Booth, William, "Amphibious Invasion," *The Washington Post*, May 5, 2002, accessed September 12, 2016, https://www.washingtonpost.com/archive/politics/2002/05/05/an-amphibious-invasion/9b02f211—8470—4f88-a408-edc0ad37f49a/.

17. Booth, "Amphibious Invasion."

18. Beard, "Biology and Impacts," 427.

19. Beard, "Biology and Impacts."

20. Associated Press, "Coqui plan croaks," *Honolulu Star Bulletin*, October 20, 2007, accessed August 8, 2016, http://archives.starbulletin.com/2007/10/20/news/story07.html.

21. Sur, Peter, "Appeals Court Upholds Ruling in Real Estate Disclosure Case," *West Hawai'i Today*, March 19, 2012, accessed September 12, 2016, http://www.westhawaiitoday.com/sections/news/local-news/appeals-court-upholds-ruling-real-estate-disclosure-case.html.

22. Kaiser, Brooks A. and Burnett, Kimberly, "Economic Impacts of E. coqui Frogs in Hawaii," *Interdisciplinary Environmental Review* 8(2) (2006): 1.

23. Kaiser and Burnett, "Economic Impacts," 1.

24. Kaiser and Burnett, "Economic Impacts," 5.

25. Ten Eyck, Gary, Personal Communication with Authors, April 5, 2013.

26. Ten Eyck, Gary, Personal Communication with Authors, April 5, 2013.

27. Coqui Control in Volcano, "Coqui Control Summary," accessed May 23, 2013, http://volcano-coqui.org/.

28. Ten Eyck, Gary, Personal Communication with Authors, April 5, 2013.

29. Kalnicky, Emily A., "A Coupled Human and Natural Systems Approach to Understanding an Invasive Frog, *Eleutherodactylus coqui*, in Hawaii" (PhD diss., Utah State University, Logan, 2012).

30. Beard, "Biology and Impacts" in Kalnicky "A Coupled Human."

31. Singer, Sydney, "Syd Singer on the Coqui Frog," accessed August 8, 2016, http://www.youtube.com/watch?v=c7XXoCxW_nY.

32. Siler, Julia Flynn, "When It Gets Too Noisy in Paradise, They Call the Frog Whisperer," *Wall Street Journal*, April 3, 2013, accessed May 23, 2013, http://online.wsj.com/article/SB10001424127887324883604578399363445540472.html.

33. Tunison, Tim, Personal Communication with Authors, April 25, 2013.

34. Chang, Lester, "Most Speakers Favor Funding to Fight Coqui Frogs," *Garden Island News*, November 22, 2006.

35. Tunison, Tim, Personal Communication with Authors, April 25, 2013.

36. Harby, William, "Living On Top of a Volcano," accessed August 8, 2016, http://www.trvl.com/hawaii/.

37. Taylor, Dorceta E., "Race, Class, Gender, and American Environmentalism," *United States Department of Agriculture Forest Service Pacific Northwest Research Station General Technical Report PNW-GTR-534*, 2002.

38. United States Bureau of the Census, "Demographic Profile," United States Department of Commerce, 2010, accessed May 27, 2013, http://www.census.gov/popfinder/.

39. Taylor, "Race, Class, Gender."

40. Szabo, Judit K, et al., "Global Patterns and Drivers of Avian Extinctions at the Species and Subspecies Level," *PLOS ONE* 7(10) (2012): e47080, doi:10.1371/journal.pone.0047080.

41. Tunison, Tim, Personal Communication with Authors, April 25, 2013.

42. Macaulay, "Law and the Behavioral Sciences."

43. Macaulay, p. 178.

44. Engel, David M, "The Oven Bird's Song: Insiders, Outsiders, and Personal Injuries in an American Community," *Law & Society Review* 18(4) (1984): 551–582.

45. We extend our thanks to the anonymous reviewer of this manuscript for suggesting the relevance of Engel's work to this discussion.

46. Daniel P. Doyle and David F. Luckenbill, "Mobilizing Law in Response to Collective Problems: A Test of Black's Theory of Law," *Law & Society Review* 25(1) (1991): 103–116.

47. *Hill* v. *Colorado* 530 U.S. 703 (2000).

48. Loukaitou-Sideris, Anastasia and Renia Ehrenfeucht, *Sidewalks: Conflict and Negotiation over Public Space* (Cambridge, MA: MIT Press, 2009).

49. Douglas, Mary, *Purity and Danger: An Analysis of the Concepts of Pollution and Taboo* (London: Ark, 1988).

REFERENCES

Associated Press. "Coqui plan croaks." *Honolulu Star Bulletin*, October 20, 2007. Accessed August 8, 2016, http://archives.starbulletin.com/2007/10/20/news/story07.html.

Beard, Karen H., Emily A. Price, and William C. Pitt. "Biology and Impacts of Pacific Island Invasive Species. 5. *Eleutherodactylus coqui*, the Coqui Frog (Anura: Leptodactylidae)," *Pacific Science* 63(3) (2009): 297–316.

Bhatia, Vijay K., Christoph A. Hafner, Lindsay Miller, and Anne Wagner. *Transparency, Power, and Control: Perspectives on Legal Communication*. Burlington, VT: Ashgate, 2012.

Booth, William. "Amphibious Invasion." *The Washington Post*, May 5, 2002. Accessed September 12, 2016, https://www.washingtonpost.com/archive/politics/2002/05/05/an-amphibious-invasion/9b02f211—8470—4f88-a408-edc0ad37f49a/.

Chang, Lester. "Most Speakers Favor Funding to Fight Coqui Frogs." *Garden Island News*. November 22, 2006.

College of Tropical Agriculture and Human Resources, University of Hawai'i at Manoa. "Control of Coqui Frogs in Hawai'i" Accessed April 4, 2013, http://www.ctahr.hawaii.edu/coqui/background.asp.

Coqui Control in Volcano. "Coqui Control Summary." Accessed May 23, 2013, http://volcano-coqui.org/.

Douglas, Mary. *Purity and Danger: An Analysis of the Concepts of Pollution and Taboo*. London: Ark, 1988.

Doyle, Daniel P. and David F. Luckenbill. "Mobilizing Law in Response to Collective Problems: A Test of Black's Theory of Law." *Law & Society Review* 25(1) (1991): 103–116.

Engel, David M. "The Oven Bird's Song: Insiders, Outsiders, and Personal Injuries in an American Community," *Law & Society Review* 18(4) 1984: 551–582.

Harby, William. "Living On Top of a Volcano." Accessed August 8, 2016, http://www.trvl.com/hawaii/.

Hill v. *Colorado* 530 U.S. 703 (2000).

Jacobs, Jane. *The Death and Life of Great American Cities*. New York: Random House, 1961.

Kaiser, Brooks A. and Burnett, Kimberly. "Economic Impacts of E. coqui Frogs in Hawaii." *Interdisciplinary Environmental Review* 8(2) (2006): 1–11.

Kalnicky, Emily A. "A Coupled Human and Natural Systems Approach to Understanding an Invasive Frog, *Eleutherodactylus coqui*, in Hawaii" (PhD diss., Utah State University, Logan, 2012).

Kim, Jed. "Invasive Coqui Frogs Starting to Shatter California's Quiet Nights." *89.3 KPCC: Environment & Science*, March 11, 2016. Accessed July 12, 2016, http://www.scpr.org/news/2016/03/11/58140/invasive-frogs-starting-to-shatter-california-s-qu/.

Kohn, Margaret. *Brave New Neighborhoods: The Privatization of Public Space*. New York: Routledge, 2004.

Leone, Massimo. "Hearing and Belonging: On Sounds, Faiths, and Laws." In *Transparency, Power, and Control: Perspectives on Legal Communication*, edited by Vijay K. Bhatia, Christoph A. Hafner, Lindsay Miller, and Anne Wagner. 183–195. Burlington, VT: Ashgate, 2012.

Loukaitou-Sideris, Anastasia and Renia Ehrenfeucht. *Sidewalks: Conflict and Negotiation over Public Space*. Cambridge, MA: MIT Press, 2009.

Macaulay, Stewart. "Law and the Behavioral Sciences: Is There Any There There?" *Law & Policy*, 6 (1984): 149–187. Accessed September 12, 2016, doi:10.1111/j.1467—9930.1984.tb00321.x.

Pijanowski, Bryan C., Luis J. Villanueva-Rivera, Sarah L. Dumyahn, Almo Farina, Bernie L. Krause, Brian M. Napoletano, Stuart H. Gage, and Nadia Pieretti. "Soundscape Ecology: The Science of Sound in the Landscape." *Bioscience* 61(3) (2011): 203–216.

Siler, Julia Flynn. "When It Gets Too Noisy in Paradise, They Call the Frog Whisperer." *Wall Street Journal*, April 3, 2013. Accessed May 23, 2013, http://online.wsj.com/article/SB10001424127887324883604578399363445540472.html.

Singer, Sydney. "Syd Singer on the Coqui Frog." Accessed August 8, 2016, http://www.youtube.com/watch?v=c7XXoCxW_nY).

State of Hawai'i Plant Industry Division. "Coqui Information" Accessed April 4, 2013: http://hdoa.hawaii.gov/pi/ppc/coqui-information/.Sur, Peter. "Appeals Court Upholds Ruling in Real Estate Disclosure Case." *West Hawai'i Today*, March 19, 2012. Accessed September 12, 2016, http://www.westhawaiitoday.com/sections/news/local-news/appeals-court-upholds-ruling-real-estate-disclosure-case.html.

Szabo, Judit K., Nyil Khwaja, Stephen T. Garnett, and Stuart H. M. Butchart. "Global Patterns and Drivers of Avian Extinctions at the Species and Subspecies Level." *PLOS ONE* 7(10) (2012): e47080. doi:10.1371/journal.pone.0047080.

Taylor, Dorceta E. "Race, Class, Gender, and American Environmentalism." *United States Department of Agriculture Forest Service Pacific Northwest Research Station General Technical Report PNW-GTR-534*, 2002.

United States Bureau of the Census. "Demographic Profile." United States Department of Commerce, 2010. Accessed May 27, 2013, http://www.census.gov/popfinder/.

Valverde, Mariana. *Law's Dream of a Common Knowledge*. Princeton, NJ: Princeton University Press, 2003.

Chapter 10

Naples' Piazza Cavour or the Playground of the Law

Patrícia Branco

As a parent, there are things one might start noticing and questioning.[1] These are things that one probably took for granted, like playgrounds or parks. These are the sort of places where, in the city, one would like to take the kids out to play and have some fun (and get a bit of vitamin D in the process).

When I was a kid, I didn't question the legal arrangement of the playgrounds I went to play in. I just played. And, mostly I enjoyed the swing. I probably got bored after a while. After all, there was not much to do but "obey" the pattern imposed: swing, slide, swing. I suppose I probably had more fun inventing my own games or playing with friends where I could do different things, like just running around. Even so, I got used to the so-called traditional playgrounds, the ones that generally contain conventional play equipment like the popular "four Ss": swing, slide, sandbox, and seesaw.[2]

And then I had a child. And I went to live in a large city. The city was Naples, Italy. I moved from a medium size city, Coimbra, Portugal. And I started looking for places to take my child to play outside of the home, like my parents had done when I was a child. It proved to be hard, as a parent, but wonderful for social observation, as a researcher.

Naples, as you can read from Wikipedia,[3] is the capital of the Italian region Campania and the third-largest municipality in Italy, after Rome and Milan. It is the ninth most populous urban area in the European Union. It has a long and rich history, and a strange love-hate relationship with Vesuvius, the mountain-volcano. It is a city that can be read as a palimpsest, showing to us the continuous rewriting of its shape and form, layer by layer, era after era. And it has endured many social, political, criminal, and economic crises, being recently known worldwide also because of several garbage crises.

As one of the most populous urban areas in the European Union, the city is mostly covered by buildings, roads, and cars (and, of course, the hundreds of *motorini* that roar over the streets and sidewalks, every day, every hour of the day). This does not leave much space for natural environments, like parks. But it is also difficult to find urban open spaces, like playgrounds. And even if you do, you probably have to consider whether or not you find it appropriate for children to play in it, given its state of maintenance.[4] That is why some reporters have commented that "Naples is not a city for children" (2014) or that "Naples, [is] the city of broken slides" (2013), since almost all city parks and children playgrounds are in a shameful condition, are unsafe and are often vandalized or damaged due to neglect and indifference.[5]

In my quest for playgrounds, I have found one in our neighborhood, located in Piazza Cavour, and another one about a one km walking distance away, near the Basilica of Santa Chiara. Although the latter is better maintained and in a much better condition, my child's preferences go to Piazza Cavour (or, as my child has "baptized" it, to "Santa Bour," his toddler way of mixing the two playgrounds together: Santa [Chiara] plus [Piazza Cav] Bour). And since I have spent there many hours of my life, it has turned out to be a familiar place, as well as a site of observation. The playground "Santa Bour" provides me with a unique set of "motion pictures" on the social order it governs.

Even if it is commonly known as Piazza Cavour, its full name is Piazza Camillo Benso Conte di Cavour. This piazza is one of the old town squares in Naples. It is situated between the districts Stella and San Lorenzo. And it is a very busy place because there are two metro stations where it is located.[6] Nevertheless, it is considered as a periphery within the city's center,[7] where micro-criminality is a frequent occurrence, and where many people have to deal with economic difficulties. Actually, unemployment, poverty, and the widespread presence of Camorra (a Mafia-type organization operating in Campania)[8] have long characterized the quarter.[9] As Ricotta[10] highlights, urban sociology warns us of the critical trends affecting contemporary urban territories. In Piazza Cavour's case: if some areas of the city are able to connect to the global flows of production and consumption, thus beneficiating in terms of development and quality of life, there are other areas which are incapable of connecting to such flows, and so they pay a high price in terms of impoverishment and exclusion. In addition, the attention of public policy toward the needs of this territory is usually activated only in front of serious cases of disorder and violence.

Piazza Cavour's playground, built in 2001, was renovated in 2015, and it was vandalized almost immediately after. When the playground was renovated, a swing for disabled children was put there. This could be read as a sign of justice, accessibility and equality of opportunities for all children, but it was used by (the abled children and teenagers) for everything else but that. The swing for the disabled children was one of the first things to get broken. Now, this broken swing stands as an empty structure, where the disabled sign—like a stigma[11]—is quite visible. Destitute of its primary function, it is revealing yet another: it reproduces the idea of a singular type of abled body and insists on its existence as the norm, excluding what is considered as a deviance.[12]

The playground is also a space of confrontation with the other(s), on so many levels: kids from different nationalities, with diverse backgrounds, languages and cultures playing together in the same spot—sometimes the slide's tower resembles a Babel Tower; or where moms, dads and grandmas argue and fuss about their kids' business and their own lives. It is also a place that teaches adults and kids about safety, as many adults also use it as a gathering place, where they go to drink and smoke, and then leave bottles of beer all over. These, get broken and are potentially harmful. And they use the place to walk dogs—fortunately, it gets cleaned from time to time.

In spite of all this, the playground is a place of fun and learning.

In this paper, I will thus consider Piazza Cavour's playground and some of its many ways of seeing, feeling and sensing the law, in the manner the editors of this collection envisaged: a place where "the framework of the public good is contrasted with the privatization of interest and is manifested in quotidian responses to rules and authority." Hence, I will examine the playground: (1) as jurisdiction, using Brigham's notion of «playing with jurisdiction»;[13] (2) as a place of homogenization and normalization of the bodies, by turning disability invisible through the broken swing; (3) as social structure, where the playground's state of maintenance is framed and frames the way the law, and particularly civil law, still considers children, that is, as minors or weaker citizens;[14] and, finally, (4) as a site of emancipation, where children reclaim the effectiveness of their rights, such as the right to play, to safety, to autonomy, to learning and to participation, as full citizens.

PLAYING WITH JURISDICTION

A playground is much more than a place where kids can go and play. It is more than a mere place. It materializes the spatialization of a network of practices, roles, and rules of conduct, social and legal. It is as well a privileged site where to observe the law playing with us, children and adults, how we respond to that, and how that recursive relationship shapes the way we understand our place in the world in our everyday lives.[15]

In that sense, a playground resembles jurisdiction, because it is about the reach of law, be it formal or informal law, over a defined territory.[16] Within its fences formal law is present in terms of its location in the geography of the city, according to the municipality's regulation over the city's urban design. As Valverde[17] recalls, municipal and quasi-municipal law have for centuries now regulated activities and persons by exercising control over access to and use of spaces, public and private.

Formal law is also present in the type of equipment chosen, the materials and colors that were used, that must comply with the rules regulating playgrounds, in order for safety[18] to be guaranteed (after all, we live in a risk society, as Beck[19] argued), which indicates that the municipality must be covered by some kind of assurance (in case it needs to respond in terms of civil liability).

Formal law is also usually visible in the signs placed on the playground's walls indicating opening hours, that children must be supervised by an adult, that certain behaviors are forbidden or that the equipment should not be used by children over a certain age. This kind of plaque or sign usually lists the kind of activities that can or cannot occur within the boundaries of the playground territory. In Piazza Cavour, however, this type of sign is nowhere to be seen; nevertheless, its absence does not account as an explanation for the kind of behaviors that occur, for, as we are all well aware, the existence of a sign does not stand as a deterrent on its own.

Informal law is present as well. It is present in the way societal rules shape parents/children relationships, showing the gender role differences still present in our societies, were mothers (and, in many situations, other female relatives, like grandmothers too) are still seen as the primary caregivers for the family, especially when children are involved. In Italy, male cooperation inside the family is still scarce, thus Piazza Cavour's playground offers a dynamic vision of the visible asymmetry in the division of gender roles[20] in what concerns the responsibility of both parents in the education and raising of children.[21]

Informal law is as well seen and felt in the different ways children play, either when they are using the equipment and/or when playing with each other, creating among them codes of conduct that can be quite flexible and accommodating, but that can sometimes be exclusive and discriminative. And in this context of playing, informal law is present too when the adults nearby intervene in such play, acting as mediators when small quibbles arise, or as self-interested parties—I will return to this later.

Informal law was also present when a "baby gang" decided to make the playground their own jurisdiction, applying a tax (between 1 and 5 euro) for the use of the equipment and thus deciding over who could and who could not use the playground, overruling municipal (public) laws over the territory and the population served by the playground. That is what happened in 2011, when a group of teenagers, aged between 15 and 17 years, with links to the Camorra (many claimed to be the sons of *camorristi*) started frightening adults and children frequenting Piazza Cavour's playground,[22] arrogating themselves property entitlements over the ground and equipment (private law prerogatives). Inside the precinct of the playground these teenagers imposed their own rules and whoever decided to refuse obeying them was subjected to a penalty (thus creating a parallel set of rules and sanctions analog to what we would term as penal law): interdiction of playing or robbery, depending on the case or the subject. Brigham's notion of jurisdiction finds concretion in this situation: the limits of Piazza Cavour's playground were the boundaries of this baby gang's jurisdiction, its area of actuation, where they defined their own authority and subject matter.[23] Consequently, swings and slides were removed from the playground, and for a while were placed in front of the police station of the Stella district so to make them available for everyone. An intervention that clearly manifests what has been said before regarding policies over the territory, that most times are activated only in front of serious cases of disorder and violence, as was the case.

As claimed by the media reporting the facts, these teenagers were really violent and did not recognize the authority of adults. Adults here account not only for the parents and other relatives that frequented the playground when taking children to play, but particularly police authority. The baby gang's deliberate ignorance of rules and disapproval of adults' authority has a deeper meaning, as adults here represent society as a whole, so it conveys an act of resistance to the state, embodied in formal law (civil and penal norms) and in the enforcement of rules by the police (and possibly, the courts). As Giacca[24] pointed out, the phenomenon of juvenile delinquency in Naples can be better understood starting from the causes or structures that have generated it (along with the forms of organized crime) and that can be divided into environmental, cultural, and economic-political factors. Regarding the environmental causes, the author highlights the Neapolitan metropolitan context, characterized by a gradual and steady increase in social disintegration: poor housing and life conditions, undeclared work, the deterioration of school facilities, the distortions that characterize the Public Administration functioning, or the shortage of employment opportunities.

Playgrounds are thus concrete jurisdictions, defining an area, or ground, where playing can occur, particularly where children can play, and how they should play.[25] This means, in a negative sense, that children should only play within the boundaries established by the municipality, using the existent equipment under the supervision of a responsible adult, and playing should not occur beyond those limits, that is, in the city's streets, or against what is permitted by a city mainly suited to the needs of adults.[26] As a recent report has highlighted, in Italy children's shared space with peers is getting increasingly more circumscribed in terms of time and place.[27] As it reports, 95% of Italian children and teenagers spend much of their spare time in front of a screen (television or computer). It is suggested that the insufficiency of adequate leisure spaces and spare time, as well as the lack of safety in frequenting outdoor venues, press the kids to confine themselves in enclosed spaces, considered safer, in particular in front of the television or video games. There is, thus, an anxiety about children's safety that is profoundly affecting the relationships between children and public space.

The United Nations Convention on the Rights of the Child (1989), ratified by the Italian State in 1991, declares, in article 31, that: 1. States Parties recognize the right of the child to rest and leisure, to engage in play and recreational activities appropriate to the age of the child and to participate freely in cultural life and the arts; 2. States Parties shall respect and promote the right of the child to participate fully in cultural and artistic life and shall encourage the provision of appropriate and equal opportunities for cultural, artistic, recreational and leisure activity. According to Hart,[28] the references to play in the Convention have very different implications for children in different countries: they are very important for children in those countries we call "The South," where many children are engaged in exploitative work for extremely long hours with no opportunity for play. But in the industrial North, most children have opportunities of playing, the problem has to do with what kind of play and in what kind of places. As noted by Stefanelli,[29] we notice the "disappearance" of children from public spaces (since birth rates are decreasing) and the "disappearance" of public spaces from contemporary western cities, where there has been a slow but inexorable decline of public spaces, seen as increasingly insecure environments in which opportunities for socialization become rare.

Then again, we are repeatedly told that playing is not a serious activity, for it is the exclusive domain of children, or a sign of immaturity or frivolity in adults; or because it is worthless or unproductive.[30] And yet, as pedagogy and pediatrics have shown, play is a significant part of child development because it contributes to the cognitive, physical, social, and emotional well-being of children and youth.[31] And "play," Hart claims, often looks more like work, for children define goals for themselves; they plan with one another, and busily carry those plans out.[32] As a result, it is serious and worthy business. Not only because it lays the foundation for individual development, and may serve as a parameter in urban policies,[33] but it also generates monetary value, since there is a whole market specialized in playground equipment, and many experts, from urban designers to architects and city planners, make a living out of playground design.

Therefore, playing is learning; as we are entertained we acquire knowledge of law and its institutions develop meaning for us.[34] And play is a spatial practice.[35] Historically, children's use of streets has been restricted, with many cities enacting regulation banning children's play on the street, and at the same time, with the appearance of different pedagogical and governance theories demanding for the institution of special and separate places for children to play within the city.[36] Many factors were here involved: the development and transformation of the urban design of the cities and city degradation, that results in children spending less time playing outside than they used to; policies concerning child and teen vagrancy and begging, as well as juvenile delinquency; or changes in family law, particularly in what concerns children and risk and the role of family in society throughout time.

Playing in a playground thus helps the child understand that he/she is in a dedicated place where playing is allowed, against what is forbidden, such as playing on the street (acknowledgment of rules and duties). He/she learns that it is necessary to wait in a line to use the slide (rules of conviviality). He/she learns to deal with bullies (power and social relations). He/she learns there are others in the world his/her body occupies and who will fight to occupy a piece of the spot he/she desires: what Philippopoulos-Mihalopoulos[37] defines as spatial justice—the fact that only one body can occupy a specific space at any specific moment. In Piazza Cavour children learn this too. And they learn a lot more within the jurisdiction set by its boundaries: they learn to deal with the risk posed by the garbage and the broken bottles left there by (unconscious?) adults (risk assessment and liability); to assess if the equipment can or cannot be used safely; to know when to escape when criminal teenagers wander the area; that they are part of a community composed of children, and adults, coming from different places and sharing diverse languages and cultures, thus learning about diversity and tolerance, confronting ego with alter. Consequently, children playing in Piazza Cavour's playground notice jurisdiction, and they play with it when and how they can.[38] And, as "residents" of the playground, they tend to assert proprietary rights over the setting too,[39] which entitles all of them the fruition of the good, and may be considered to entitle (some of) them the right to destroy one's own property.

BROKEN SWINGS AND THE HOMOGENIZATION OF THE BODIES

As was said by the president of the municipality in 2015, "Piazza Cavour is central for the neighborhood and the city and it is important to also consider the children who have physical disabilities, providing playing equipment for them."[40] And a swing was provided. While the playground was made more accessible, the municipality has not ensured that the children could play on the equipment, and soon after it got vandalized and broken. All that is left now is the structure and the handicap sign. And if we zoom in the picture, the eyes can see that right next to the playground there is a building that is completely covered in with bad graffiti and in a poorly shape, windows all broken and rubbish all around: it used to house a NGO, called ANIDA (Associazione Nazionale Italiana Diversamente Abili), that used to work with people with disabilities in the area.[41]

The sign—the well-known white (in the case, yellow) wheelchair against a blue background—was intended to be a statement reminding the public of the stated equality of equal access.[42] In this case, of equal access to play and equal opportunities of leisure activity, as consecrated in the aforementioned Convention on the Rights of the Child, by enjoying a ride on the swing. So, how to interpret it now, that the swing is gone?

Perhaps a broken swing is not just about vandalism and disregard of the public good. It reveals a deeper notion, which has endured in society since modernity: the hegemony of normalcy and the elimination of deviance from the public space.[43] It reproduces the idea of a singular type of abled body and insists on its existence as the norm, thus excluding and placing the disabled body outside the parameters of public space.[44] Normalcy thus becomes the project we should all strive for, the only one possible, useful, and desirable in terms of identity. But only to the extent that it makes he/she belong to a collective and social homogeneity.[45]

Figure 10.1 The Handicap Sign on the Broken Swing. Piazza Cavour 2016.

Figure 10.2 The Handicap Sign on the Broken Swing. Piazza Cavour 2016.

A broken swing on which hangs a handicap sign is, in fact, discrimination made visible. It puts forward what is structurally invisible—the implications of the hegemony of normalcy, which are profound and extend into every layer of society.[46] The empty handicap swing, next to the vandalized building where the NGO operated, not only reconfigures the playground's space itself, but the meaning and the public interest in disability get reconfigured too.[47] As such, the broken swing states: this playground is for the abled children only.

Piazza Cavour not only mirrors the correlation between disability and discrimination, but also the correlation between poverty and social exclusion.[48] In one of the poorest quarters of the town, the broken swing looks like a scar, a stigma, confirming that poverty and disability go hand in hand, not in the sense that poverty results from disability, but because the latter is socially constructed and is thus a consequence of all the barriers—physical, social, and cultural—built around handicap and people with disabilities.

In addition, and as Johnston has argued,[49] there are people who consider childhood analog to disability, and vice versa. And it has not just to do with how they behave or should behave in public spaces. It has to with value too. There is a whole set of labels we are taught to associate with the idea of childhood—characterized by concepts such as incompetent, unstable, credulous, unreliable, emotional, or irresponsible[50]—that we are taught to associate with disability as well. As a result, children and people with disabilities are considered as unproductive citizens. They are seen as a burden to society. And so, they may or may not use public space—whether it is the city, the whole playground, or simply the swing—at our indulgence, because public space is not theirs, it is ours. We, the normal. We, the adults. We, the abled children. Hence, a broken swing in a children's playground is the result of a normalization of discrimination and structural exclusion of the "non-abled" body.[51] As Santos has argued,[52] and Piazza Cavour's swing is one such example, this normalization of discrimination translates into a kind of social fascism, produced by society and not by the state, although the latter behaves here as complacent witness, if not indeed as an actual guilty part. The fact it has been more than a year since it has been broken and that the municipality has done nothing to remediate the situation demonstrates that, in the design of public policies, it may not be a priority to address the social causes that create discrimination.

THE MINOR CITIZEN

Italy features a social organization unfriendly of families with children—poorly equipped public playgrounds; or social activities geared mainly to adults; and a city life unsuitable for children—traffic disorder, or paucity of public spaces for families and children to spend leisure time together.[53]

For many decades now, the production of urban space has been ruled by priorities that, in reality, have rendered children "invisible" in towns and cities.[54] According to Tonucci,[55] the city adapted to suit the needs of the adult, male, working, and driving citizen. This is modernity at its best. And law went along, by creating a myriad of subaltern subjects, such as children (and women). Modernity confined children to the private space and to the care of the family (which means the mother or a female substitute); banished the deviant youngster from the streets; and created segregated and dedicated places where they were allowed to play, thus making children and youth invisible to society.[56] Even if, in recent times, infancy and youth have gained prominence and a different social and legal status, children's life is still lived according to the models and definition of infancy the adults have constructed for them.[57] This has led to constantly monitoring children's development and to unprecedented surveillance of children; and in some Western societies children have been virtually excluded as independent actors from public spaces.[58]

Adults, therefore, regulate the place occupied by children in society in many ways. In Piazza Cavour such ruling occurs, first, through municipal regulation concerning location and access to public spaces or playground equipment; second, when chaperoning children, which translates into family rules governing children's protection and parental supervision; and third, via the adults' invasion of the playground, as self-interested parties, claiming possession and usufruct of the playground land. In Piazza Cavour's playground, that invasion is there for everyone to see: broken bottles or empty cans of beer, empty pizza cardboards, cigarette ashes, urine, and dog feces. In a city where playgrounds do not abound, play space ends up being curtailed, and such reduction translates as a delegitimization of the right to play and a minorization of infancy. As Mayall asserts,[59] defining children as inferior—as incompetent and inadequate versions of adults—means we do not take them seriously. And we depersonalize children, which makes them more vulnerable to every kind of violence. Glass, garbage, and ashes hence create lines framing sovereignty. Sovereignty is here understood as designating supreme authority within a precise territory: at a macro scale, that of the city, and at a micro scale, that of the playground; and over a polity consisting of the children playing in Piazza Cavour: a polity whose rights and entitlements are dependent upon those of the governing body, the adults. It simply concretizes a well-established social and legal model: that children are weaker citizens, and thus their right to play can be sacrificed because adults are entitled to fully enjoy their personal rights, even those of trespassing and littering. In other words, children are marginalized by an adult-centric society that tries to maintain its spatial hegemony.[60]

There is, therefore, a distinction to be made here. On the one hand, Piazza Cavour is frequented by parents or other relatives who go there, mostly with younger children, and supervise their activities (generally, mothers and other female relatives). On the other hand, the playground is frequented by (mostly, young male) adults, that are neither parents or relatives to the children there, and who use the playground as their leisure place, drinking beer and smoking. Occasionally, some people take the dogs there. And even more rarely, some homeless people may wander around the playground, but not within its ground. The same can be said about the children: Piazza Cavour is frequented by little children (1–5 years), from both sexes, accompanied by parents or relatives; but is frequented too by older children, that are more autonomous and, living nearby, go play in the playground without an adult present. And, of course, there are teenagers too, mainly male. Although adults and children do not comprise a homogenous group or entity and there is an interplay of various identity categories, for the purposes of this paper it is simpler to operate a division between children and adults.

There is, thus, a split in the playground, that creates blurred boundaries[61] between the children's and the adults' leisure spaces. Probably the drinkers do not consider their practice of drinking alcohol in a children's playground as a transgressive practice, but rather that drinking is about being part of a certain community,[62] about building social relations with peers. Their practice serves to construct an adult space of play, where adults have no obligations or responsibilities.[63] Just like children playing in a playground. The children and the adults do not to engage with one another, but both groups use the same public space in Piazza Cavour. There is, thus, an interpenetration of the bodies of children and adults in their desire to occupy this specific space.[64] However, as Jayne and colleagues assert,[65] the place of drinking in our cities raises some interesting issues, for drinkers can sometimes engage in bad behaviors or may not conform to discourses of polite, civilized, and cosmopolitan urbanity and security. As when they leave bottles that get broken or other types of garbage, that may be potentially harmful to the children playing in the playground.

In addition to this adults' invasion and littering of play space, there is, on the other hand, the (quasi)absence of maintenance of that same space, or adults doing nothing about it (which translates a lack of investment). The maintenance conditions of Piazza Cavour's playground, which have also been frequently reported by the media,[66] serve as a mirror of how (in this case, Italian's) society still considers children: as minors. According to article 2 in *Libro I* of the *Codice Civile Italiano*, a person is a minor until the age of 18, thus determining a person's legal capacity. Until that age, he/she lacks the capacity of acting and knowing as an adult. Thus, we are confronted with the (problematic) legal concept of minority, and that of childhood and youth, as a social and political issue—children are those whom adults have defined as non-adults.[67] Even though the meanings of childhood are culturally constructed and changeable over space and time, as Johnson rightfully claims, this legal minor is an oddly amorphous, genderless, raceless, classless, and ageless sort of thing.[68]

These quotidian acts show how power relations are shaped: adults matter more than children; playing is childish and needs to be controlled. These understandings of childhood underlie the way that adults negotiate and control children's use and experience of public space.[69] Consequently, playgrounds—and especially Piazza Cavour's one—can be seen as disciplinary institutions, where the child's body and behavior are controlled: surveilled, and punished in different ways—for not playing as it should be done; or because they should not play in that location, which serves as a metaphor for society as a whole. As Foucault argued about the prison or the school, the playground too serves as a technology of power, submission, and discrimination.[70] And in Piazza Cavour this reflects a paradoxical situation: adults controlling, making sure kids play orderly and safely; adults invading, exerting their power over the space through unsafe behaviors; adults' disinvestment on children's spaces. Behaviors that later get copied by children, and may account for broken equipment and disrespect for the public good, bullyism and juvenile delinquency, discrimination, and exclusion of other children.

CONTESTING SOVEREIGNTY: RECLAIMING THE SPACE, RECLAIMING THE RIGHTS

But if kids learn by playing, then they can learn of rights enforcement, emancipation, equality, tolerance and freedom, too. Telling children that they have certain rights is not sufficient because they need to have a practical experience of these rights, as well as the notion of the forces that deny them and the ways to fight for them.[71] That is why we need more discussion on the place of play together with that of the play places in children's education and in their development throughout the life cycle.[72]

Children are not only shaped by, but they also have the capacity to shape their (micro and macro) environments. In fact, through their everyday actions children often contest, negotiate and modify their surroundings. There is thus what we could term, using Santos' concepts,[73] a tension between social regulation and social emancipation, or, in Piazza Cavour's terms, a tension between the adult's regulation of the playspace, through their various behaviors, and children's emancipation, through how they exploit the discapacities and hurdles of the playground and then change them into their own advantage. In the process, they reclaim the space and their rights, and contest sovereignty over a place that is conceived, regulated, possessed and enjoyed by the adults.

Such emancipation thus occurs in two different but interconnected forms: contestation of sovereignty and reclamation of the rights. On the one hand, the contestation of sovereignty happens through the spatial practice (as Lefebvre theorized,[74] this consists of the cohesive patterns and places of social activity) of playing in a decadent playground, which indicates (1) their daily presence inside the territory, (2) their inconformity to a set of practices that are meant to dismiss their right to play (serving, here, as an umbrella under which others rights are included), and (3) their refusal to be conceived of as minor citizens, by the law and by society. One such example is linked to the issue of migration, multiculturalism and foreign policies.

Observing Piazza Cavour's playground one perceives how Italian society, and particularly the Neapolitan one, has mutated in recent years in terms of immigration. Actually, it is immigrants who still maintain birth rates in Italy.[75] Nevertheless, according to the law governing the subject of nationality and citizenship, the child of a foreigner is considered a foreigner too (it is a matter of *ius sanguinis*). This means many of the kids playing in Piazza Cavour have to endure a double situation of discrimination: being a child and being a foreigner, and what such status entails in terms of political and social discrimination. Thus, playing becomes much more than a right: it is an act of defiance and resistance against legal, political, economic, social, and cultural obstacles, communicating to all those who care to pay attention that they are citizens—they do exist and occupy a place in the world. Even if it is one as small as a slide or a swing in Piazza Cavour's Playground. They thus reclaim their *ius soli*, or the right to be considered a national citizen of Italy, independently of their parents own nationality, by the sole fact they were born on Italian ground.

On the other hand, this reclamation of the rights exists in a dialectical tension with public law (either as municipal regulation and configuration of recreational areas within the city, as absence of public policies concerning children's playspaces, or as a deficiency of maintenance conditions of the playground), and the adults' quotidian actions of exclusion of children from the playground (which embody a deeper notion, that of minority, still present in the legal system). Both—public law and adults' actions—stand as representations of space in the way theorized by Lefebvre (for Lefebvre, representations of space have to do with how space is conceived by different actors and they consist of a system of signs and codes used to organize and direct spatial relations).[76]

Against this state of affairs, children playing in Piazza Cavour seek to change and appropriate the playground space by transforming it into an alternative space—a representational space[77]—where their imagination is capable of turning a rundown traditional playground into an adventure playground.

Figure 10.3 Reclaiming the Playground's Space. Piazza Cavour 2016.

An adventure playground differs from a traditional one in that it emphasizes the use of recycled or found materials and has a flexible or informal layout, made of moveable playground components, and where cognitive play, including fantasy, constructive and cooperative play, takes place.[78] In Piazza Cavour, children are often seen playing with the many (now) removed floor mats, that covered the ground and served to protect them from injury in case of fall, and which have been transformed into a sort of cross country running path, where children can exercise their dexterity. Other times, the piled mats form a tower that needs to be conquered, jump by jump, or after careful negotiation between rival soldiers, that is, between boys and girls or between older and younger children. Other times, empty fruit boxes serve as poles in improvised football games. Chasing pigeons is also an entertaining activity that triggers velocity and amusement.

And in the process, children actively claim their rights against a set of structural and social inequalities. And they oppose being treated as subaltern subjects of the law. That is what is at stake when municipal law sees them as a group or a category of people that is somewhat removed from personhood.[79] Children are also considered as minor citizens by civil law, which means children are allocated a limited personhood capacity. Immigrant children are considered as foreigners by the law of nationality, in one of the countries with the most stringent rules to acquire citizenship in Europe, thus having a limited legal capacity (although changes have been introduced in 2015 to the law on nationality, enforced since 1992, *Legge N. 91 del 1992*, inserting a moderate *ius soli*). Children oppose as well the adults' conducts of invasion and littering of the playground, a state of degradation that enunciates the society's explicit attitude toward the silencing and outcasting of children from the public sphere.

As a result, and while playing, children demand the recognition of their right to play and leisure activity, of their right to safety and autonomy, of their right to an active participation in the community, and of their right to a full citizenship.

CONCLUDING REMARKS

Like Marusek has argued,[80] politics happens in ordinary, everyday places, such as playgrounds. And playgrounds are particularly interesting places, as they reflect philosophies concerning the role of play and the place of children within society.[81] In Piazza Cavour's playground, where the mother in me asks for safety when taking her kid out to play, the researcher within sees power relations, control over childhood, and discrimination of disability. Hence, it leaves us with the question: what kind of society are we preparing children for?

In Piazza Cavour, the playground frames the place the law, particularly family law (not the one from the books, but the one in action), and society, still assigns to mothers/grandmothers and to fathers, and gender roles division, while spatializing the role of children in society and in the public sphere. It renders their invisibility in the public space visible and reinforces their vulnerability. Piazza Cavour looks like a mini-ghetto, establishing the boundaries where children are confined to play, if their families want them to play (relatively) safe, in a city where the law of cars and motorbikes—and the adults driving these machines—is all over. In the end, a playground will always be a place carved out of the adult world.[82]

The maintenance situation in Piazza Cavour reflects how society regards children and families, and it demonstrates how power relations, hierarchical control, the regulation of behavior and exclusion occur, not only at an institutional level—showing a lack of investment in terms of familial, childhood and disability related policies—but also at a community level—through an abusive use of place, vandalism and degradation. Structural inequalities get thus spatialized and manifest.

Piazza Cavour's playground sets a jurisdiction of its own. And kids are aware of the limits. Those imposed by the city's own municipal regulation, boundaries, limitations, and urban hostility; and those imposed by a hierarchical society of adults, in a country where birth rates are one of the lowest in the world. But children play with those limits, making their own rules and negotiating their own terms. They have their own ways of perceiving and living the playground as a place of development, conviviality, imagination, and identity. As a place of law, identity is realized not only through formal legal norms but also through the informal manipulation of the space where they play and that they occupy, thus creating different sets of norms, that children interpret and recreate daily in order to contest adult sovereignty over their playing space and over their rights.

NOTES

1. I thank the helpful comments made by the anonymous reviewer. I also thank the Luso-American Foundation for Development for the financial support granted me to present this paper at the 2017 Annual Meeting of the Association for the Study of Law, Culture & the Humanities.

2. Shan Sivakumaran, "The Right to Play: Towards an Urban Environment with the Child in Mind," *Edra* 27 (1996): 131; Emma Sheppard-Simms, "The Evolution of Playspaces," Landscape Architecture Australia 135 (2012).

3. Cf. https://en.wikipedia.org/wiki/Naples. Accessed August 16, 2016.

4. Like Emma Sheppard-Simms has noted in her article, this is a twofold problem: on the one hand, children often do not have access to public or private places

where they can go and play; and on the other hand, even when such spaces are available, many parents are reluctant to let their children play in them, for they fear for their safety. In Sheppard-Simms, "The Evolution of Playspaces."

5. See http://www.vesuviolive.it/ultimenotizie/39732-napoli-non-citta-per-bambini-dovremmo-per-migliorarla or http://www.ilmattino.it/inchieste/napoli_no_misura_bambino-200765.html. Accessed August 18, 2016.

6. Cf. https://it.wikipedia.org/wiki/Piazza_Cavour_(Napoli). Accessed August 25, 2016.

7. See Parco di piazza Cavour, i bambini giocano tra cassette di frutta e tombini divelti, published in 2015 in the italian newspaper *La Repubblica*. http://napoli.repubblica.it/cronaca/2015/06/27/news/parco_di_piazza_cavour_i_bambini_giocano_tra_cassette_di_frutta_e_tombini_divelti-117810692/. Accessed August 26, 2016.

8. See https://en.wikipedia.org/wiki/Camorra. Accessed September 20, 2016.

9. Cf. https://en.wikipedia.org/wiki/Rione_Sanit%C3%A0. Accessed August 26, 2016.

10. Giuseppe Ricotta, Prefazione to *Sicurezza in città*.

11. A stigma is usually seen as a mark of disgrace. As Robinson and Thompson have written, a stigma is a powerful social force that may be difficult to eliminate; and it involves an agreement on what is considered normal, a category defining what is not normal and a devaluation of what is not normal. See Julia W. Robinson and Travis Thompson, "Stigma and Architecture," in *Enabling Environments*, edited by Edward Steinfeld and Gary Danford (Dordrecht: Kluwer Academic/Plenum Publishers, 1999).

12. Dea Busk Larsen, "Creating Disability—Invisible Bodies and Public Space," (2015).

13. John Brigham, "Seeing Jurisdiction: Some Jurisprudential Issues Arising from Law Being '. . . All Over,'" *Law and Policy* 31/1 (2009): 395.

14. Francesco Tonucci, "Citizen Child: Play as Welfare Parameter for Urban Life," *Topoi* 24 (2005): 183.

15. Sarah Marusek, "Visual Semiotics of the Spaces We Inhabit: Preface," *International Journal for the Semiotics of Law* 27 (2014): 1.

16. Brigham, "Seeing Jurisdiction," 383.

17. Mariana Valverde, "Taking 'Land Use' Seriously: Toward an Ontology of Municipal Law," *Law Text Culture* 9 (2005): 34.

18. According to Yagod, in "Risk, Danger and the Makings of Enjoyment Playgrounds: Between Safety and Fun," *Design Museum Holon Magazine* 9 (2014), during the 1970s and '80s, when a litigious culture began to emerge in the western world, playground development became a frequent battleground for designers, planners, and legislators, thus resulting in playgrounds that became more uniform, safer and unimaginative.

19. Ulrich Beck, *World Risk Society* (Oxford: Blackwell Publishing, 1999).

20. Karsten has shown, based on observational studies in Amsterdam playgrounds, that playground participation, activities and micro-geographies are structured by gender. See "Children's Use of Public Space. The gendered world of the playground," *Childhood* 10/4 (2003).

21. Osservatorio Nazionale per l'Infanzia e l'Adolescenza [ONIA], *Relazione sulla Condizione dell'Infanzia e dell'Adolescenza in Italia 2010–2011* (Perugia: Del Gallo Editori, 2013).

22. See http://stella.napolitoday.it/stella/pizzo-giostre-piazza-cavour.html or http://www.blitzquotidiano.it/cronaca-italia/napoli-baby-gang-pizzo-giostre-801277/. Accessed August 23, 2016.

23. Brigham, "Seeing Jurisdiction," 386.

24. Francesco Giacca, "I minori e la criminalità organizzata a Napoli, riflessioni sulla dimensione dell'azione criminale e la costruzione del processo di significazione della devianza," *Rassegna dell'Arma dei Carabinieri* 4 (2005).

25. The specific characteristics of the playgrounds promote certain play behaviors, which are different whether the playground's type is traditional (as in Piazza Cavour's case), contemporary (that emphasize novel forms and textures) or adventure (where play materials instead of conventional equipment are supplied and children plan and develop the area themselves). See Sivakumaran, "The Right to Play."

26. Tonucci, "Citizen Child," 185.

27. ONIA, *Relazione*.

28. R. A. Hart, "Creating Playscapes by and for Children," (1994).

29. Antonella Stefanelli, "I bambini nella gestione quotidiana del proprio spazio: quale autonomia?," (PhD diss., Università degli Studi del Molise, 2011).

30. Brigham, "Seeing Jurisdiction"; Tonucci, "Citizen Child"; Sheppard-Simms, "The Evolution of Playspaces."

31. Kenneth R. Ginsburg, "The Importance of Play in Promoting Healthy Child Development and Maintaining Strong Parent-Child Bonds," *Pediatrics* 119/1 (2007).

32. Hart, "Creating Playscapes."

33. Tonucci, "Citizen Child," 185.

34. Brigham, "Seeing Jurisdiction," 396.

35. Fyllio Katsavounidou, "Child, City, Play: A Polyphonic Biography," (2012).

36. Sivakumaran, "The Right to Play;" Tonucci, "Citizen Child."

37. Andreas Philippopoulos-Mihalopoulos, "Spatial Justice: Law and Geography of withdrawal," *International Journal of Law in Context* 6/3 (2010): 2.

38. Brigham, "Seeing Jurisdiction," 396.

39. Karsten, "Children's Use of Public Space," 459.

40. See http://www.ilmattino.it/napoli/cronaca/piazza_cavour_giostre_bambini_degrado-1117757.html. Accessed August 26, 2016.

41. Due to lack of rental paying the NGO was evicted from the place in 2012. http://www.napolivillage.com/Napoli/cronaca-sfratto-coatto-allanida-lassociazione-di-diversamente-moda.html. Accessed August 26, 2016.

42. Sarah Marusek, "Between Disability and Terror: Handicapped Parking Space and Homeland Security at Fenway Park," *International Journal for the Semiotics of Law* 20 (2007): 258.

43. Lennard J. Davis, "Constructing Normalcy: The Bell Curve, the Novel, and the Invention of the Disabled Body in Nineteenth Century," in The Disability Studies Reader, edited by Lennard J. Davis (Abingdon: Routledge, 2013).

44. Larsen, "Creating Disability."

45. Gabriela Maia Rebouças, *Tramas entre Subjetividades e Direito. A constituição do sujeito em Michel Foucault e os Sistemas de Resolução de Conflitos* (Rio de Janeiro: Lumen Juris Editora, 2012).
46. Larsen, "Creating Disability"; Davis, "Constructing Normalcy."
47. Marusek, "Between Disability and Terror," 259.
48. Fernando Fontes, "Pessoas com deficiência e políticas sociais em Portugal: Da caridade à cidadania social," *Revista Crítica de Ciências Sociais* 86 (2009).
49. Angus Johnston, "Childhood, Disability, and Public Space," (2010).
50. Berry Mayall, "The Sociology of Childhood in Relation to Children's Rights," *The International Journal of Children's Rights* 8 (2000): 246.
51. Larsen, "Creating Disability."
52. Boaventura de Sousa Santos, "Poderá o direito ser emancipatório?" *Revista Crítica de Ciências Sociais* 65 (2003).
53. ONIA, *Relazione.*
54. Katsavounidou, "Child, City, Play."
55. Tonucci, "Citizen Child," 185.
56. Tonucci, "Citizen Child"; Manuel Jacinto Sarmento, "Sociologia da Infância: Correntes e Confluências," in *Estudo da Infância: educação e práticas sociais*, edited by Manuel José Sarmento and Maria Cristina Gouvêa (Petropolis: Vozes, 2008).
57. Ana Isabel Sani, "Reflexões sobre infância e os direitos de participação da criança no contexto da justiça," *e-cadernos ces* 20 (2013).
58. Mayall, "The sociology of childhood."
59. Mayall, "The sociology of childhood."
60. Stefanelli, "I bambini nella gestione quotidiana del proprio spazio."
61. Rebecca Johnson, "Blurred Boundaries: A Double-voiced Dialogue on Regulatory Regimes and Embodies Space," *Law Text Culture* 9 (2005).
62. Mark Jayne, Sarah L. Holloway, and Gill Valentine, "Drunk and Disorderly: Alcohol, Urban Life and Public Space," *Progress in Human Geography* 30/4 (2006): 456.
63. Johnson, "Blurred Boundaries."
64. Johnson, "Blurred Boundaries"; Philippopoulos-Mihalopoulos, "Spatial Justice."
65. Jayne, Holloway and Valentine, "Drunk and disorderly."
66. See, for example, Piazza Cavour: tra degrado, rapine e senzatetto (2014), in http://www.roadtvitalia.it/piazza-cavour/, accessed August 29, 2016; Parco di piazza Cavour, I bambini giocano tra cassette di frutta e tombini divelti (2015), in http://napoli.repubblica.it/cronaca/2015/06/27/news/parco_di_piazza_cavour_i_bambini_giocano_tra_cassette_di_frutta_e_tombini_divelti-117810692/. Accessed August 29, 2016.
67. Mayall, "The sociology of childhood."
68. Johnson, "Blurred Boundaries."
69. Gill Valentine, "Children Should Be Seen and Not Heard: The Production and Transgression of Adults' Public Space," *Urban Geography* 17/3 (1996).
70. Michel Foucault, *Surveiller et Punir: naissance de la prison* (Paris: Gallimard, 1975).

71. Sani, "Reflexões sobre infância."

72. Hart, "Creating Playscapes."

73. Boaventura de Sousa Santos, "Beyond Abyssal Thinking. From Global Lines to Ecologies of Knowledges," *Review* xxx/1 (2007).

74. Henri Lefebvre, *The Production of Space*. Trans. Donald Nicholson-Smith (Oxford: Blackwell Publishing, [1974] 1991).

75. ONIA, *Relazione*.

76. Lefebvre, *The Production of Space*.

77. Ibid.

78. Sivakumaran, "The Right to Play"; Sheppard-Simms, "The Evolution of Playspaces."

79. Valverde, "Taking 'land use' seriously," 37.

80. Marusek, "Between Disability and Terror."

81. Sheppard-Simms, "The Evolution of Playspaces."

82. Karsten, "Children's Use of Public Space."

REFERENCES

Beck, Ulrich. *World Risk Society*. Oxford: Blackwell Publishing, 1999.

Brigham, John. "Seeing Jurisdiction: Some Jurisprudential Issues Arising from Law Being '. . . All Over.'" *Law and Policy* 31/1 (2009): 381–404.

Davis, Lennard J. "Constructing Normalcy: The Bell Curve, the Novel, and the Invention of the Disabled Body in Nineteenth Century." In *The Disability Studies Reader*, edited by Lennard J. Davis, 3–16. Abingdon: Routledge, 2013.

Fontes, Fernando. "Pessoas com deficiência e políticas sociais em Portugal: Da caridade à cidadania social." *Revista Crítica de Ciências Sociais* 86 (2009): 73–93.

Foucault, Michel. *Surveiller et Punir: naissance de la prison*. Paris: Gallimard, 1975.

Giacca, Francesco. "I minori e la criminalità organizzata a Napoli, riflessioni sulla dimensione dell'azione criminale e la costruzione del processo di significazione della devianza." *Rassegna dell'Arma dei Carabinieri* 4 (2005): 109–129.

Ginsburg, Kenneth R. "The Importance of Play in Promoting Healthy Child Development and Maintaining Strong Parent-Child Bonds." *Pediatrics* 119/1 (2007): 182–191.

Hart, R. A. "Creating Playscapes by and for Children." 1994. Accessed August 29, 2016, http://www.pps.org/reference/righttoplay-2/.

Jayne, Mark, Sarah L. Holloway, and Gill Valentine. "Drunk and Disorderly: Alcohol, Urban Life and Public Space." *Progress in Human Geography* 30/4 (2006): 451–468.

Johnson, Rebecca. "Blurred Boundaries: A Double-voiced Dialogue on Regulatory Regimes and Embodies Space." *Law Text Culture* 9 (2005): 157–177.

Johnston, Angus. "Childhood, Disability, and Public Space." 2010. Accessed September 9, 2016, https://studentactivism.net/2010/05/15/childhood-disability-and-public-space/.

Karsten, Lia. "Children's Use of Public Space. The Gendered World of the Playground." *Childhood* 10/4 (2003): 457–473.

Katsavounidou, Fyllio. "Child, City, Play: A Polyphonic Biography." 2012. Accessed September 9, 2016, https://www.academia.edu/26622846/Child_city_play_A_Polyphonic_Biography.

Larsen, Dea Busk. "Creating Disability—Invisible Bodies and Public Space." 2015. Accessed September 9, 2016, http://www.hystericalfeminisms.com/creating-disability-invisible-bodies-and-public-space/.

Lefebvre, Henri. *The Production of Space*. Trans. Donald Nicholson-Smith. Oxford: Blackwell Publishing, [1974] 1991.

Marusek, Sarah. "Between Disability and Terror: Handicapped Parking Space and Homeland Security at Fenway Park." *International Journal for the Semiotics of Law* 20 (2007): 251–261.

———. "Visual Semiotics of the Spaces We Inhabit: Preface." *International Journal for the Semiotics of Law* 27 (2014): 1–5.

Mayall, Berry. "The Sociology of Childhood in Relation to Children's Rights." *The International Journal of Children's Rights* 8 (2000): 243–259.

Osservatorio Nazionale per l'Infanzia e l'Adolescenza [ONIA]. *Relazione sulla Condizione dell'Infanzia e dell'Adolescenza in Italia 2010–2011*. Perugia: Del Gallo Editori, 2013. Accessed July 22, 2016, http://www.minori.it/sites/default/files/rel-biennale-2010-11.pdf.

Philippopoulos-Mihalopoulos, Andreas. "Spatial Justice: Law and Geography of Withdrawal." *International Journal of Law in Context* 6/3 (2010): 1–16.

Rebouças, Gabriela Maia. *Tramas entre Subjetividades e Direito. A constituição do sujeito em Michel Foucault e os Sistemas de Resolução de Conflitos*. Rio de Janeiro: Lumen Juris Editora, 2012.

Ricotta, Giuseppe. Prefazione to *Sicurezza in città: pratiche di controllo all'interno dello spazio urbano*, edited by Sebastian Saborio, 7–10. Milan: Ledizione, 2015.

Robinson, Julia W., and Travis Thompson. "Stigma and Architecture." In *Enabling Environments*, edited by Edward Steinfeld and Gary Danford, 251–270. Dordrecht: Kluwer Academic/Plenum Publishers, 1999.

Sani, Ana Isabel. "Reflexões sobre infância e os direitos de participação da criança no contexto da justiça." *e-cadernos ces* 20 (2013): 75–89.

Santos, Boaventura de Sousa. "Poderá o direito ser emancipatório?" *Revista Crítica de Ciências Sociais* 65 (2003): 3–76.

———. "Beyond Abyssal Thinking: From Global Lines to Ecologies of Knowledges." *Review* xxx/1 (2007): 45–89.

Sarmento, Manuel Jacinto. "Sociologia da Infância: Correntes e Confluências." In *Estudo da Infância: educação e práticas sociais*, edited by Manuel José Sarmento and Maria Cristina Gouvêa, 17–39. Petropolis: Vozes, 2008.

Sheppard-Simms, Emma. "The Evolution of Playspaces." *Landscape Architecture Australia* 135 (2012). Accessed August 29, 2016, http://architectureau.com/articles/the-evolution-of-playspaces/.

Sivakumaran, Shan. "The Right to Play: Towards an Urban Environment with the Child in Mind." *Edra* 27 (1996): 130–135.

Stefanelli, Antonella. "I bambini nella gestione quotidiana del proprio spazio: quale autonomia?." PhD diss., Università degli Studi del Molise, 2011. Accessed September 9, 2016. http://road.unimol.it/bitstream/2192/131/1/tesi_Stefanelli.pdf.

Tonucci, Francesco. "Citizen Child: Play as Welfare Parameter for Urban Life." *Topoi* 24 (2005): 183–195.

Valentine, Gill. "Children Should Be Seen and Not Heard: The Production and Transgression of Adults' Public Space." *Urban Geography* 17/3 (1996): 205–220.

Valverde, Mariana. "Taking 'Land Use' Seriously: Toward an Ontology of Municipal Law." *Law Text Culture* 9 (2005): 34–59.

Yagod, Maier. "Risk, Danger and the Makings of Enjoyment Playgrounds: Between Safety and Fun." *Design Museum Holon Magazine* 9 (2014). Accessed August 8, 2016, http://www.dmh.org.il/magazine/magazine.aspx?id=222&IssuesId=12.

Conclusion

How Law Happens

John Brigham and Sarah Marusek

As editors of this collection, we began, in the Introduction, with the idea that "Law Happens." Our chapters have developed how it happens, in our lives and on the street. In the previous chapters, we have collected many stories of the living law and said that it may involve sovereignty. We have argued that when norms are present in social interactions, both the norms and the interaction may be about sovereignty. In the Introduction, we gave the example of stop signs. And in the volume, there have been discussions that bring out the difference between a stop sign sitting alone on a lonely road and one that has an occupied police car parked next to it. It is sometimes hard to know whether behavior that conforms to law is about law. The material published here examines various dimensions of law on the street. These dimensions are examples of street-level sovereignty, whether they are evident in uniformed systems of authority imposed by the military and illuminated by Linken's treatment, the kind imposed on sex at college discussed by Mott, or the violent policing that we see so often in the United States that is described by Henao Castro.

The examples suggested in our Introduction, of a selfie at a high school party with alcohol or the image of an arrest, maybe even after the same party, are activities mixed with issues of law and authority whether or not they every deal with judges or the police. We used to say imbricated for "mixed with" and it gave the idea a little weight, or seemed to. The weight of law is not just the involvement with courts or judges, though that is significant on its own, but rather weight, in the sense of sovereignty can also come from all the cultural meanings and inevitable possibilities that are contained in the notion of sovereignty. In the end, it may be those cultural meanings that constitute limits on uniformed police or robed judges. In American life, an office holder reaching into the culture with "social media" is himself governed by the meaning of that media in the culture. We suggest that the reality of street-level sovereignty is a "A live by the tweet, die by the tweet" sort of thing.

In this sense, the videos that fueled the Black Lives Matter movement are linked to the same extension of authority that both empowered candidate and then ultimately limited the authority of Donald Trump. Going back even further, the gloved fist that was raised by Tommy Smith and Juan Carlos at the Olympics or the national anthem protest of Colin Kaepernick in 2016 have not just political meanings but meanings for sovereignty. Just as Tommy Smith and Juan Carlos influenced Kaepernick, the sit-down protests in the fall of 2016 presented a claim that was answered at the ballot box with the election of Trump to the American presidency. The gloved fist, an act of defiance given meaning by the cameras focused on the Olympic medal stand, the political disrespect, tolerated under law but responded to politically, that was the Kaepernick protest both have meaning more for their social context than for anything in the law. They are widely appreciated contests, which we say are the sort chronicled here.

As our authors have suggested, law will not only govern the social reaction but the reaction that is social constitutes the reach of the law. This is what we called the "understudied" living life of the law. There is study, of course. Over the last 50 years, law IN society has flourished and we have drawn on that tradition. But much of the popular understanding that is the social life of law is thought to be politics or feelings or attitudes. That is, a special needs child playing in Branco's playground, who is unable to use the broken equipment, absorbs socially, as do those around her, the meaning of her condition as truly as the racial consequences recognized by the US Supreme Court as adhering to Linda Brown in her 1954 case against the Board of Education of Topeka Kansas.

For the same half-century that scholars have built on Oliver Wendell Holmes' idea that "the life of the law is experience." While ordinary people have often treated that experience as something other than law, the chapters collected here have suggested otherwise.

THE STREET

We have said that our street draws inspiration from Michael Lipsky's 1969 formulation. Lipsky was a young scholar in the 1960s and he sought to open up the study of power to places traditionally ignored. His scholarship did that and, to some extent, the informalism and dispersed power that followed those years was part of the movement he was on early and at an intellectual level. Although his framework was literally the storefront bureaucratic outposts of the administrative state, our broader concept owes a great deal to this pioneer.

Incorporating our broader collection of situations reflects law's breadth. Law has a range that challenges even that of bureaucracy. There are nuances that add to the study of power when we challenge the notion that authority is dependent on hierarchy. And, by incorporating sovereignty into the framework we suggest that the authoritative structures lead to jurisprudential issues more than the sociological ones. Both formulations are quite abstract and both take those abstract concerns to expand the meaning of bureaucracy and sovereignty to be one of taking it to a form where democratic participation is to be expected, to the streets, as it were.

We said in the Introduction that "governance and power are constituted in the banalities of our daily activities." This is a very different image from the one popularized by the Critical Legal Studies movement. That one relied heavily, as is discussed in Brigham's chapter, on the work of Kafka. It had the protagonist cut off from law, which was mysterious. Here we suggest that law is "all over." And, if it is hidden, it is hidden in plain sight. If law is hiding in our daily activities it becomes easy to miss it. But that is not because we don't see law. It is because we don't know how to understand that what we see is law. The chapter by Broekman is a remarkable investigation of the many philosophical dimensions of the street as a place to focus on law. After our Introduction, we began with this chapter. At one point we want to make it THE Introduction. It is a very serious investigation into the philosophical dimensions of the street. Broekman was serious about the charge, to look at sovereignty from the societal surface. As we have already noted, there is a concept of the person at the heart of Broekman's work. It is a complex personhood that emerges in and from common experiences that we agree is highly evident on, and may even be a function of, the street.

We don't write directly about the Supreme Court here, but of course cases that get to the highest courts start with contests over "street-level sovereignty." Brigham's treatment of body scanners, which are generally in the building and not, literally, in the street, provide a line of demarcation that constitutes a structure of authority, not only by delineating who can get in but in the form by which it is done and what that form is taken to mean. In the case of the scanners we said that they may be more indicative of the nature of modern law than Franz Kafka's doorkeeper.

And, similarly, the "Wise Latina" who gets to the High Court famously, brings her understandings of the street as part of that wisdom. Justice Sonia Sotomayor's Bronx streets were a version of the type made famous on the American late 20th-century children's television show "Sesame Street," whose picturesque urban landscape was no more or less constituted by law (and mutually constituting it) than the middle class streets of the white suburbs popularized in the 1950s on "Leave It to Beaver" or "Ozzie and Harriet." One of the aspects of the street, then, is that it gets carried around. In the volume, the frogs that stowed away to Hawai'i find themselves contending with human neighbors in a Pacific paradise who do not appreciate their noisy, foreign chirps. Then there are the cultures of humor, which come from other places and constitute cultures. The Jewish, often immigrant comedians of the Borscht Belt, become the mainstream on early television in shows like Red Skelton, Jack Benny, and Groucho Marx.

SOVEREIGNTY

We have said that the sovereignties we have been discussing are akin to those addressed by radicals in the 1960s who spoke of putting their bodies on the "cogs of the machine." Sovereignty here is not an abstraction or simply a facet of political theory. It is those things, but it is also something that lives on the street. We have said, with reference to Schattschneider, that authorities generally want to limit the scope of conflict. This means limiting the range where we can see a conflict or even a conventional practice as constituted by fundamental issues over the authority behind the practice or bearing on the conflict.

In the preceding chapters we have cultivated an awareness of aspects of a political and legal structure at their most basic, on the street. At least it is more likely that we would be aware of sovereignty when we see it as something that might be contested. In street-level encounters like those over invasive species or play structures or sex, when we become aware of sovereignty dimensions it not only heightens encounters, it transforms them. Becoming aware transforms the structures of society from unseen patterns or behaviors we take for granted to potentially contested territory. To see a source of authority is often to unmask its power. The signs outside of markets that designate handicap spaces or spaces set aside for pregnant women take on meanings as we understand who puts them up and who stands behind them.

We have said that at the level of the street it is sometimes the case that knowledge of sovereignty, even the concept of sovereign authority itself, is often unequally held. Some may know whether something is private property or how it might be enforced and some may not. As Marusek has pointed out, in the United States, many random bystanders are reading to challenge, or at least challenge in principle, use of a handicapped parking spot. We understand that comedy sometimes works with this principle and have mentioned how in the 1950s and '60s, Lenny Bruce drew crowds to his shows in part over the excitement stimulated by the possibility that they might be raided. Similarly, we saw how the children of Hawaii got a little too engaged in frog killing even for those who despised the invasive *coqui*.

Hobbes' image of the sovereign as Leviathan, a giant made up or constituted by masses of people is familiar in political theory circles. It is on the frontispiece of his book on the subject. All those little people are, in the Hobbesian image, subsumed in the giant's body. And, in the theory of the Leviathan, they are reconstituted and consequently controlled. But we could also see the people in various respect as functioning in their ordinary life "as part of" or "incorporated into" the sovereign. When we skirt land that is patrolled or trespass where we know that no one cares (or is looking) we may be contesting sovereignty. Branco says that as a mother, playgrounds take on new meaning. They not only become places of healthy exercise but also of social learning. The broken equipment made explicitly for the handicapped may teach a little something to the child who has no physical limitations herself, and to the mother. And activity is as normative and consequential as any formal law, and way more vibrant.

We suggested various ways to connect the chapters in this volume and draw out the lessons of street-level sovereignty and we have reviewed some of them in drawing out these conclusions. Here are some other considerations that return to the initial formulations. Pavoni, like Branco, is writing from Europe and, like Broekman, makes an important theoretical contribution. In her urban landscape mixing of sovereignties are the norm because spaces are obviously shared. She outlines a number of aspects that influence the sharing and they in turn become considerations in the story of sovereignty. One of these is mobility, both the mobility that is made possible by rules like those for traffic and the mobility that challenges the authorities behind those rules and reconstitutes the street as with the *woonerf*.

Mohr and Hosen are also interested in how the street is constituted and they focus on dimensions of culture, the cafés, restaurants, and food stores that mean something different about the street than its meaning for cars. Like Pavoni, their streets are urban and they are also interested in the ways streets can be reconstituted as more than places for cars to travel. By focusing on smoking and *halal* meat, the authors call attention to one of the more basic contests over the uses to which property can be put. This is where animals may be killed for their meat. But they also cover nearly universal phenomena such as the ability of one crossing a street to "make the cars stop," with the help of various signs and signals.

Clearly sexual activity is as vitally important as what we eat and how we travel. And sex has always been regulated but in what seems to be very new ways discussed by Mott, sex in the United States is facing new forms of regulation that she sees as tied to a form of political economy. This is the neoliberal framework of consent that has been imposed in the United States, and particularly on college campuses. In this story, a traditional dichotomy between freedom and violence is given heightened significance by a moral panic compounded by a neoliberal regime. It is a fascinating story.

The notion that the use of violence in a regime may be understood politically should not be a surprise but we think that the notion that we see the imposition of force on the street as contestable and not simply a function of right and wrong or benighted "first responders" versus the rabble is both more and less than one might already have thought. For Henao Castro, the concept of biopolitics helps us to interpret sovereignty at the level of public interaction with the police. Using images of life (bio) and death (necro) he encourages us to see the most basic sphere where we live and "writ" larger. Policing itself is a newer formulation of control arising in the 19th century and coming to fruition less than 100 years ago. Yet it attempts to impose the mechanisms of state power down to the level of the street. Where one might easily once have thought of the street as simply an aspect of the natural environment, the policing of the street in the last century displaces that possibility. What we see as a threat to life itself, is, in this piece, the state extending its physical reach and, perhaps, threatening our ability to live on our own.

By covering the military and its differences from civil authority, we think that Linken's chapter challenges us to think of the ways ordinary life is constituted by comparing it with the very different but often nearly overlapping nature of military life. In the military, authority and hierarchy are to the front and in the center. In this sphere, military practices work with otherwise ordinary men and women to make them different. And, a challenge to those practices has different consequences than otherwise similar challenges in ordinary life. In fact, when the "Gold Star" parents of Army Captain Humayun Khan spoke at the Democratic convention in 2016, the power of military culture for the ordinary processes of politics was brought to the forefront. The meaning of a death at work for the military is different than a death on most jobs. Different codes define events that are in some sense the same but in important ways events like death become different because they acquire significant meanings in context. This happens because, as we suggested in the Introduction, certain sovereignties, like that over ones hair, are taken away.

The absence of sovereignty is clearly evident as we seek entrance to airports, particularly in the United States. To many, the barriers to access are accepted as a feature of travel. However, Brigham suggests that we may have reason to rethink technologies like the body scanner, particularly when compared to the alternatives. In looking at scanners as providing access, he suggests the possibility of discarding a prevailing image that has been important to critiques of law. This is the image of "the stranger from the country" standing "before law" which is epitomized by a gate that he cannot pass through. Brigham suggests that the scanner, by providing access to the continued movement, and lately the consumer goods, on the other side of the scanner, the gate becomes less of a barrier and more of a bridge. This is a partial explanation for why many have put up with significant inconvenience since its introduction.

It is clear that humor plays a social function. In the chapter by Lorenz, the function examined is often explicitly contesting established authorities and norms about race. Off the street in a comedy club, ordinary life is examined and the comedy becomes a form of entertainment. It draws on shared practices it may affirm or destabilize. In the most powerful examples, such as the work of socially conscious comedians like Richard Pryor, Chris Rock, or Dave Chappelle, Lorenz shows how the sovereignty of a racial regime is destabilized. Although the ability to laugh about race in the United States is problematic, in the case of this work, the hierarchies around which racial structures are built are not simply scrutinized by the comedian. In the clubs, the scrutiny constitutes the meaning of race.

We called attention to death in the Introduction. It is clearly regulated in special ways that indicate long-standing concern about the end of life. There is nothing here on abortion, the comparable beginning of life struggle that has made streets in front of clinics battlegrounds of the most dynamic and tragic sort. But the movement to avert racial killings discussed by Henao Castro and the black comedy described by Lorenz both highlight the life and death struggles that are the stuff of sovereignty as we have collected it here. And in other scenes of life and death, placing a bounty on frogs turned out not to be such a good idea in Hawaii which is part of a world increasingly sensitive to paying children to kill.

In nation-states, it is not only at the higher reaches, but at a conference table or in a marble temple, that we contest law's authority. In fact, in those places it is often about the details; sovereignty is quite often at "the bottom" or what we call the level of "the street." In the end, this collection has tried to be suggestive. It asks scholars to think of the authority behind law from the ground up rather than the "top" down. In jurisprudence we can't really start at the bottom. Too much has gone on. However, we can suggest the relevance of the street and begin to explore its authorities. These contests, perhaps because they do not always involve uniforms or special chambers, suggest some ordinary considerations that are relevant at all levels. Questions raised, and disputes about, the legitimacy of a handicap parking pass or the authority of an arrest is the stuff of contemporary law. Increasingly, in an era of exploding forms of media, cell phones capable of disseminating images instantaneously, and celebrity culture, the influence from the street on the very structure of power needs greater recognition. We hope to have made a start.

REFERENCES

Connolly, Joe and Bob Mosher. "Leave it to Beaver," Republic Studios (1957–1963).

Hobbes, Thomas. *Leviathan*, 1651.

Holmes, Jr. Oliver Wendell. *The Common Law*. 1881.

Khan, Khizr. "Speech on Army Captain Humayun Khan and in support of Hillary Clinton," Philadelphia: Democratic National Convention, 2016.

Ozzie Nelson. "The Adventures of Ozzie and Harriet," (1953–1966).

Index

About the Contributors

Patrícia Branco is a researcher at Centro de Estudos Sociais (CES), from the University of Coimbra in Portugal, where she is currently developing her postdoctoral research titled *Courts, Communities and Citizens: The (Territorial, Spatial and Symbolic) Effectiveness of Access to Law and Justice in the Present [Portuguese] Reform of the Judicial Organization* (funded by Fundação para a Ciência e a Tecnologia, Ref. SFRH/BPD/102236/2014). From January to June 2015, Patrícia was a fellow at the Käte Hamburger Center for Advanced Study in the Humanities "Recht als Kultur/Law as Culture," from the University of Bonn, Germany, with a project titled *Into, From and Back Again: A Discussion on Courthouse Architecture, the Image of Justice and Literature*. Her current research interests include access to law and justice, in a broad perspective; courthouse architecture, spaces of justice, and the administration of justice; the relations between law and the humanities; and the mutations of family and child law and its connections with gender issues. Among her publications: (2016), "Courthouses as Spaces of Recognition, Functionality and Access to Law and Justice: A Portuguese Reflection," in Oñati Socio-Legal Series, 6; (2015), "Odore di Napoli: What if Jurisprudence Came to us through Smell?," in *Non Liquet: The Westminster Online Working Papers Series* (with Richard Mohr); or (2010), "On Prisons and Theatres: Santo Stefano and San Carlo," in *Law Text Culture* 14.

John Brigham's work has been on epistemologies and law. He argues that we should look at law as a language, the Supreme Court as an institution, and social movements in terms of the laws that constitute them. He has written on what it means to see law and teaches about the ethnographic dimensions of local politics. His course, Ethnography and Policy, focuses on representation with attention to maps, places, and politicians. John Brigham has been involved with the International Roundtable for the Semiotics of Law since its reception and also with the International Institute for the Sociology of Law and the Law and Courts Section of the American Political Science Association. His work includes *Constitutional Language* (1978), *The Cult of the Court* (1987), *The Constitution of Interests* (1996), and *Material Law* (2009).

Jan M. Broekman studied *Social Sciences/Law* in Leiden (Netherlands) and *Philosophy/Psychiatry* in Göttingen (Germany), where he obtained his PhD. He lectured Philosophy and Aesthetics at the University of Amsterdam, and from 1968 to 1996 Contemporary Philosophy as well as Philosophy of Law, Law and Legal Theory at the K.U. Leuven, Belgium—from 1988 to 1991 as Dean of the Leuven Faculty of Law. Since 1996 he was Visiting Professor of Law at the University of Illinois College of Law, Champaign/Urbana, and from 2006 a Distinguished Visiting Professor of Law at the Penn State University Dickinson School of Law, where he established the "Roberta Kevelson Seminar on Law and Semiotics." Broekman has authored more than 30 books and more than 400 scientific articles on Contemporary Philosophy; Semiotics; Law and Legal Theory; Philosophy of Medicine; and Education, Culture and Politics.

Marilyn Brown is Associate Professor of Sociology at UH Hilo. She received her BA in Anthropology from Wellesley College and her PhD in Sociology from UH Manoa. Her research specializations include the following: Criminology, Corrections; Reintegration of Former Prisoners; Gender, Race/Ethnicity and Crime; Corrections and Families; Inequality and Criminal Justice Policy. She is the author of articles on crime and justice appearing in *Theoretical Criminology*, *Crime & Delinquency*, *Critical Criminology*, *Feminist Criminology,* as well as chapters in edited volumes. Dr. Brown has also authored evaluation reports on criminal justice and other programming for a number of Hawaii State agencies. Since coming to UH Hilo in 2003, Dr. Brown has taught courses in Criminology, Juvenile Delinquency; Race, Gender, and Crime; Corrections; Social Institutions; Introduction to Sociology; Sociological Theory; Sociology of Deviance. She has served as previous Director of Women's Studies, Sociology Internship Coordinator, and Chair of the Sociology Department.

Andrés Fabián Henao Castro is Assistant Professor of Political Science at the University of Massachusetts Boston. His research deals with the relationships between ancient and contemporary political theory, particularly in reference to democratic and de-colonial theories and practices, the question of political subjectivity and the distribution of political agency. He is currently working on a book that explores different subject positions and forms of agency imagined in the theoretical reception of Sophocles' tragedy *Antigone*.

His recent publications include the article "Can the Subaltern Smile? *Oedipus* without Oedipus" (*Contemporary Political Theory*) and "Antigone Claimed: 'I Am a Stranger!' Political Theory and the Figure of the Stranger" (*Hypatia: A Journal of Feminist Philosophy*). He is also a member of the international research network *Performance Philosophy* and a columnist for the online journal of political analysis *Palabras al Margen* (Words at the Margins).

Nadirsyah Hosen is a senior lecturer at the Faculty of Law, Monash University, starting from July 2015. He completed his first PhD (law) at the University of Wollongong and a second PhD (Islamic law) at the National University of Singapore. He is the author of *Shari'a and Constitutional Reform in Indonesia* (Singapore: Institute of Southeast Asian Studies 2007) and coauthor of *Modern Perspectives on Islamic Law* (2013 and 2015) and also a coeditor of *Islam in Southeast Asia* (4 vol, 2010). Nadirsyah Hosen and Richard Mohr are coeditors of *Law and Religion in Public Life: The Contemporary Debate* (2011 and 2013).

Allen Linken is an Assistant Professor of Political Science at the University of Alabama. He received his joint JD/MPP from Albany Law School and the University at Albany, respectively, and his PhD from the University of Massachusetts, Amherst. His research interests include the Supreme Court, the United States military, and combining them, the civil-military gap.

Aaron Lorenz is Dean of the School of Social Science and Human Services at Ramapo College in New Jersey. He earned a PhD in Political Science from the University of Massachusetts, Amherst, with a dissertation and book that focused on the constitutive nature of law in music. His current work addresses the relationship between comedy and law, with particular attention on issues of race and class.

Sarah Marusek is Associate Professor of Public Law in the Department of Political Science at the University of Hawai'i at Hilo. Her research interests focus on sites of constitutive law, legal geography, and legal semiotics while engaging legal pluralist frameworks of visual jurisprudence. She teaches courses in jurisprudence, public law, and the US Constitution. In addition to her recently published book *Politics of Parking: Rights, Identity, and Property* (Ashgate, 2012), Sarah has published articles in *Law, Text, Culture*; *Social Semiotics*; *Law, Culture and the Humanities Journal* and the *International Journal for the Semiotics of Law* with book chapters in *Law, Culture, and Visual Studies* (Sherwin and Wagner, (eds.), Springer, 2014) and *Diversity and Tolerance in Socio-Legal Contexts: Explorations in the Semiotics of Law* (Wagner and Bhatia (eds.), Ashgate, 2009).

Richard Mohr is Director of Australian company Social Research Policy and Planning and holds a PhD in sociology from the University of New South Wales. He was coordinator of the Canterbury Area Health Service (southwest Sydney) when the civil war in Lebanon led to mass migration into that area. From 1998 to 2010 he taught in the Law Faculty at the University of Wollongong where he was director of the Legal Intersections Research Centre. His research on courts and court architecture and on legal intersections with urban and ethical issues has been published in journals including the *Australian Feminist Law Journal, Canadian Journal of Law and Society, European Journal of Legal Studies, Indigenous Law Bulletin, Law Text Culture,* and *International Journal for the Semiotics of Law*. Richard Mohr and Nadirsyah Hosen are coeditors of *Law and Religion in Public Life: The Contemporary Debate* (2011 and 2013).

Margaret Mott teaches Politics and Gender Studies at Marlboro College in Vermont and has been writing columns for the local and national media for the last twenty-five years. She is the Program Director of Speech Matters, an intensive semester for undergraduates that develops skills in public speaking, writing commentary, and reframing national debates in collaboration with community partners.

Andrea Pavoni is a postdoc fellow at DINÂMIA'CET—IUL, Centre for Socioeconomic and Territorial Studies, at ISCTE—University Institute of Lisbon. He is assistant professor at the International Summer School on Urban Ethnography at the University of Trento, and coeditor at *Non Liquet* [The Westminster Online Working Papers]. Andrea is mainly interested in exploring the relation between law, space, control, and justice in the contemporary city. His research interests include critical legal geography, urban studies, legal theory, sociology, art, and philosophy. He recently completed his PhD at the University of Westminster with a thesis titled "Exceptional Tunings: Controlling Urban Events." His current project focuses on the mutual relation between urban space and protest, looking at how urban space allow for, modify, or prevent the expression of protests, and how protests in turn affect and modify its social and material form. He recently edited with Andrea Mubi Brighenti the last issue of *Lo Squaderno*, on the "Urban Invisibles."

www.ingramcontent.com/pod-product-compliance
Ingram Content Group UK Ltd.
Pitfield, Milton Keynes, MK11 3LW, UK
UKHW041632031026
15587UKWH00001B/227

9 781498 535038